Issues in Indian Education

Issues in Indian Education

Editor

M.L. Dhawan

ISHA BOOKS
DELHI-110 033

Issues in Indian Education

ISBN: 81-8205-161-4

Published in 2007 in India by
Isha Books,
B-63, Ist Floor, New Gupta Colony,
Near DDA Market, Delhi-110 009
Phone : 9212142040
Email : ishabooks@hotmail.com
Laser Typesetting at: Shree Vaishnavi Creations, Delhi
Printed at Rajdhani Printers, Delhi

PREFACE

The last decade of the century definitely marks a significantly positive note in the history of basic education in India. Though the constitution of the country had made a commitment to providing free and compulsory education to all children upto the age of 14, the task of providing basic education for all received high priority with concrete plans of action mainly after the National Policy on Education was launched in 1986 and revised in 1992. The educational priorities enunciated by the National Policy on Education 1986 have continued through the 90s. This has been reflected in the higher allocation of resources as well as in terms of clearly defined strategies to achieve the goals of education for all. The World Declaration on Education For All (EFA)– 1990 adopted in Jomtien, undoubtedly, gave further fillip to the national commitment for reaching basic education for all children. The Jomtien Declaration together with several positive developments within the country brought to the central stage the need for viewing basic education as a fundamental right of every citizen. India is one of the few countries where during the stabilization phase of structural adjustment, expenditure on education has been stepped up.

Achievements during the last fifty years are not insignificant. An estimated 95 per cent of the rural population living in 826,000 habitations have a primary school within 1 km and about 85 per cent population have an upper primary school within 3 km. More than 150 million children are currently enrolled covering around 90 per cent of the children in the age group of 6-14 years. Recent surveys on literacy rates indicate a phenomenal progress in the 90s. Basic education policies and programmes in the recent years have gone beyond the mere emphasis on numbers to focus on quality concerns in basic education, on the education of girls and disadvantaged sections of the society, the need for people's involvement in basic education programmes and decentralisation of educational management.

Despite such significant achievements and positive goal orientation in the recent years, it is realised that there are serious problems of gender, regional, sectional and caste disparities in Universalisation of Elementary Education (UEE). A significant proportion of students continue to dropout due to socio-economic and cultural factors as also due to lack of adequate infrastructure, shortage of teachers and unsatisfactory quality of education provided. The country still is the home for more than 300 million illiterates. The challenges have been many. Therefore, the review of progress made in the 90s represent this struggle to resolve some of the basic problems and make concrete progress towards the goal of EFA against all odds.

Though the progress made is not insignificant, the country realises that the challenges ahead at the turn of the century are quite daunting, demanding not only continued commitment but also an enhanced attention and resources to meet the challenges in the coming years. The government is fully seized of the fact that nothing less than a whole hearted national effort both in the public and private sectors would be necessary if India is to emerge as a fully literate and economically vibrant nation of the 21st century.

The present book provides authentic information regarding the current trends and issues in Indian education. The topics discussed are Constitutional Provisions of Education in India; Elementary Education; Educational Development in Five Year Plans; Wastage and Stagnation; Kothari Commission;

Yashpal Committee; POA 1992; Education for Employment and Social Development and the future of Indian Education Systems. The subject matter of the book, both as regards the arrangement of chapters as well as the contents is so designed that it can be easily followed by the readers. The publication is useful not only to the students of several Indian universities but also to the teachers, research scholars and educationists.

Editor

Contents

1

CONSTITUTIONAL PROVISIONS OF EDUCATION IN INDIA WITH SPECIAL REFERENCE TO ARTICLE 45 (UEE)

A general overview of the need for literacy and education is outlined to justify literacy being a part of Constitutional Provisions and guarantees. In addition to the simple definition as given in the Census, the broader dimensions of literacy in its relationship with Education and Societal Development are also mentioned. Role of literacy as a part of the Human Rights dialogue and also as an integral part of the Human Development index is also discussed.

Having given unto ourselves a written Constitution, the very preamble of which proclaims Equality of opportunity as an express intent, the concern for literacy as an important parameter is obvious.

Literacy, as defined in Census operations, is the ability to read and write with understanding in any language. A person who can merely read but cannot write is not classified as literate. Any formal education or minimum educational standard is not necessary to be considered literate. Adopting these definitions, the literacy level of the country as a whole was only 29.45 per cent with male literacy at 39.45 per cent and female literacy at 18.69 per cent. As per the latest Census estimates (2001), the

All-India figure has gone up to 65.38 per cent; About three-fourths of our menfolk (75.85 %) are literate whereas over half of our womenfolk (54.16 %) are also literate. As later discussed in this Paper, this should be regarded as no mean achievement, despite the fact that we have not met the Constitutional directives that we have set for ourselves.

ILLITERACY – NATIONAL AND INTERNATIONAL DIMENSIONS

The problems of illiteracy are not confined to India, but are also a malady in developed countries too. Daedalus, the journal of the American Academy of Arts and Sciences, devoted the Spring 1990 issue to study the problem of Literacy in America. The Journal quotes Joseph Murphy, Chancellor, City University of New York who stated: "There are as many as 60 million illiterate and semi-literate adults in America today. Because poverty and illiteracy go hand in hand, the poor are disenfranchised, cut off from the democratic process.

Any account that does not discuss the political interests served by allowing a large proportion of the American people to remain disenfranchised does not touch the heart of the matter. Before the Civil War in the United States it was illegal to teach slaves to read, for reading was acknowledged, as the tool needed to understand the social, historical, behavioral and physical laws that controls the human condition. An apprehension of those forces invests human beings with the capacity to alter the conditions of their lives. It is not too far fetched to draw an analogy between slaves in the nineteenth century and illiterate Americans today." While this may be a strong statement, it reflects the concern on the prevailing levels of illiteracy and its consequent effects.

Illiteracy is one of the major problems faced by the developing world, specially Africa and South-East Asia and has been identified as the major cause of socio-economic and ethnic conflicts that frequently surface in the region. With the limited definition of 'literacy' being adopted for enumeration purposes, there has been concern on the content of a Mass Literacy program.

The focus of mass literacy efforts is in terms of basics – the mechanics of reading and attention to computation in mathematics. It is recognized that these basics are not rooted in the goals of higher-order thinking – conceptualizing, inferring, inventing, testing, hypothesis and thinking critically. It is true that these literacy programs do not have in mind, literacy practice that would promote capacities for independent reasoning, of the kind sought by Third World socially minded pedagogues like Paulo Friere or the leading edge of reformers, business leaders and cognitive psychologists.

A candid analysis of illiteracy's political and cultural consequences throughout the population will necessitate in our seeking to move literacy expectations beyond a rudimentary ability to read, write and calculate. The recognition that 'literacy' has to be situationally relevant has given rise to the concept of 'functional literacy', which has been referred to by the Second Education Commission.

The need to go into the broader aspect is for the purpose of determining the structure of the system. In devising the system, educational and psychological philosophies of Adler, Dewey, Witttgenstein, Chomsky and our own Mahatma Gandhi and other experiences will come into play. Indeed, it is probably in recognition of this limited scope of literacy, that our Constitution makes a reference to education and educational opportunities and not to literacy.

Literacy and Human Rights

Literacy is now part of the Human Rights Dialogue. Now most of the nations of the world have also accepted their obligation to provide at least free elementary education to their citizens. Article 26 of the Universal Declaration of Human Rights declares:

> "Everyone has the right to education. Education shall be free, at least in the elementary and fundamental stages. Elementary education shall be compulsory. Technical and Professional education shall be generally available and higher education shall be equally accessible to all on the basis of merit".

This Right is also repeated in the UN Declaration of the Rights of the Child which seeks to ensure "Right to free and compulsory education at least in the elementary stages and education to promote general culture, abilities, judgment and sense of responsibility to become a useful member of society and opportunity to recreation, and play to attain the same purpose as of education". India has ratified the above, and these have thus the power of domestic laws. From the Human Rights perspective, constitutional guarantees arise automatically.

Literacy and Human Development

Investment potential on human capital has now been recognized. Economists had long assumed that the main component of a country's productive wealth is physical assets. But according to World Bank's assessment for 192 countries, physical capital on average accounts only for 16% of total wealth. More important is natural wealth, which accounts for 20%. And more important still is human capital, which accounts for 64%. Literacy is now part of the Human Development Index. Government of India has also accepted this position, and one of the important components in the National Human Development initiative announced in the Union Budget 1999-2000 is education, forming also a component in the Prime Minister's 'Special Action Plan'.

By improving people's ability to acquire and use information, education deepens their understanding of themselves and the world, enriches their minds by broadening their experiences, and improves the choices they make as consumers, producers and citizens. Education strengthens their ability to meet their wants and those of their family by increasing their productivity and their potential to achieve a higher standard of living. By improving people's confidence and their ability to create and innovate, it multiplies their opportunities for personal and social achievement. Japan's rapid industrialization after the Meiji Restoration was fuelled by its aggressive accumulation of technical skills, which in turn was based on the already high level of literacy and a strong commitment to education, especially the training of engineers.

In the field of Development Economics, literacy holds an important place as a parameter to measure development. It has been recognized that the "Human Development Index" (HDI) developed by UN is a measure of the overall development of the country. One of the three components used in the calculation of HDI is "Literacy" as it is a cumulative measure of several factors that contribute to human development. As per UN Development Report, 2000, India's ranking in HDI is 128, with education index registering a low .55 due to a low adult literacy rate of 55.7 and combined primary, secondary and tertiary gross enrolment of 54.

In their book, "Development Reconsidered", Owens and Shaw have stated: "It is self-evident that literacy is a basic element of a nationwide knowledge system. The most important element of a literacy program is not the program itself, but the incentive to become and remain literate." When people are able to believe that they can improve their lives through their own efforts, when they realize that some newly created opportunity is denied to them by illiteracy, then they will learn how to read, write and count."

Education is thus viewed as an integral part of national development. Development is not only 'economic growth'; rather, it 'comprehended opportunities to all people for better life' with 'man as end of development and instrument'. Education and development are linked in a variety of ways. First, education, as stated earlier, is a human right, the exercise of which is essential for individual development and fulfillment.

The capacity of an individual to contribute to societal development is made possible and enhanced by his or her development as an individual. In this light, education is also a basic need. It is also a means by which other needs, both collective and individual, are realized. Thus, education is the instrument by which the skills and productive capacities are developed and endowed. All these interrelationships of education and development are inseparable from the conception of educational policies. It is in the second order of 'action' that problems arise.

The problems of illiteracy will not solve by itself in the flux of time. Without organized literacy action, illiteracy will continue to stagnate indefinitely along with the associated ills of poverty and underdevelopment. Experience has shown that determined literacy action is the exception and that more often, literacy campaigns are 'turned on' and 'turned off' in line with short-term policy changes. Hence the need for Constitutional guarantees. In the light of the discussions earlier, Literacy and Education have overlapping connotations both as an engine of socio-economic progress as well as for individual growth. An attempt at serious semantic distinction between is not followed here in the discussions.

Aid for Education by State

Concern for literacy arises from the clearly related question as to whether educational expansion has created the conditions for freer individual expression, for a more active participation in the body politic, for what Pericles called "sound judges of policy", and for greater respect for human welfare and dignity. Many feel, as indeed the Constitution makers felt, that education is its own reward- i.e. the more one is educated, the greater is his possibility of developing these qualities. Thus, they believed that the future and hope of mankind lie in educational advancement and a Welfare State has to make suitable provision for the same. Education is valuable by itself for discovering "the treasure within", as has been mentioned by UNESCO.

As stated in the Constitution, the State has to set for itself a Welfare goal. It should, therefore, take upon itself all activities and steps to move towards this goal. Most major classical economists have argued by their extensive earlier writings the need for State provision, under the proposition that the private market would under provide education. E. G. West , in a thought-provoking book on education, argues that a strong case can be made for State intervention in education on two counts, namely, the externality effects of education and the alleged incompetence or ignorance of parents. Advocates of State education in the past have usually rested their case predominantly on the two extra economic considerations of equality of opportunity and social cohesion.

CONSTITUTIONAL PROVISIONS

The provisions contained in the Constitution of India along with a mention of some of the decided cases, which have given a wide amplitude to such provisions. The amendments as affect education are mentioned. There are 16 Articles and other mentions in the Constitution and 4 specific amendments to advance the cause of education.

Education for Social transformation

The Indian Constitution has recognized the significance of education for social transformation. It is a document committed to social justice. The Preamble affirms a determination to secure liberty of thought, expression, belief, faith and worship and equality of status and opportunity and to promote amongst the people a feeling of fraternity, ensuring the dignity of the individual and the unity of the nation.

Literacy forms the cornerstone for making the provision of equality of opportunity a reality. The objective specified in the Preamble contains the basic structure of the Constitution, which cannot be amended, and the preamble may be invoked to determine the ambit of Fundamental Rights and Directive Principles of State Policy. Judicial interpretation has brought alive many an Article of the Constitution, which if read literally may seem to be a colorless Article. Of relevance to literacy, for instance, is the wide interpretation given to the words 'personal; liberty'. In Francis Coralie Mulin v. Administrator, Union Territory of Delhi, Justice Bhagwati observed:

> "The fundamental right to life which is the most precious human right and which forms the arc of all other rights must therefore be interpreted in a broad and expansive spirit so as to invest it with significance and vitality which may endure for years to come and enhance the dignity of the individual and the worth of the human person. We think that the right to life includes right to live, with human dignity and all that goes along with it, namely, the bare necessaries of life such as adequate nutrition, clothing and shelter and facilities for reading, writing and expressing oneself in diverse forms, freely moving about, mixing and co-mingling with fellow human beings."

Articles 246 and 254: Subject-matter of laws made by Parliament and by the Legislatures of the States and inconsistency of laws—Concurrent list and inclusion of education thereunder. The Scheme of distribution of legislative powers under the Indian Constitution - such distribution being a necessary component of a federal political structure - raises interesting issues where co-existence of central and state Laws in a particular area gives rise to litigation. It is only where the legislation is a matter in the concurrent list that it would be relevant to apply the test of repugnancy.

Article 280: Finance Commission—Finance Commission can suggest measures to augment The Consolidated Fund to supplement the resource of the Panchayat in the State as also of the Municipalities.

Article 337: Special provision with respect to educational grants for the benefit of Anglo-Indian community. During the first three financial years after the commencement of this Constitution, the same grants, if any, shall be made by the Union and by each State for the benefit of the Anglo-Indian community in respect of education as were made in the financial year ending on the thirty-first day of March, 1948.

During every succeeding period of three years, the grants may be less by ten percent than those of the immediately preceding period of three years:

— Provided that at the end of ten years from the commencement of this Constitution, such grants, to the extent to which they are a special concession to the Anglo-Indian community, shall cease:

— Provided further that no educational institution shall be entitled to receive any grant under this article unless at least forty per cent of the annual admissions therein are made available to members of communities other than the Anglo-Indian community.

Official language

This whole Part deals with language, an inherent part of Literacy with a specific mention in Art. 350A for facilities for instruction in mother-tongue at primary stage.

There have been specific amendments to the Constitution affecting education, as can be seen in 42nd, 73rd, 74th and 83rd Amendment Acts. These amendments pertain to provisions to enable education being included in the Concurrent List, devolution of powers to local bodies and making elementary education a Fundamental Right formally.

Equality of educational opportunity

Since 'Equality of Opportunity" is a basic feature of the Constitution, being a part of the Preamble itself, judicial interpretation has been sought on the different facets of this principle of equality of educational opportunity. For many, egalitarianism in education is seen as a powerful force for the achievement of a just, more equitable society through its contribution to greater social mobility, the 'breaking of any connection between the distribution of education and distribution of personal income'.

Yet the "equality of education" concept can be given a variety of interpretations, each leading to different policy outcomes. In particular, "equality of education" may concern equality of access to education, equality of educational treatment or equality of ultimate educational performance. Our Courts have wrestled with this problem in the face of affirmative action or what is known as 'positive discrimination' in favour of the deprived sections while at the same time preserving the needs of quality of education and fair play.

The argument in this regard is somewhat on the following lines: "The liberal goal of providing education according to each individual's capacity or aptitude (rather than his socio-economic background) is unhelpful because the criteria used for identifying aptitudes, or 'intelligence' are themselves correlated with the social background. Hence society must adopt special methods to compensate for the deficiencies of the environment in which children grow and which account largely for their unequal educational performance; this would take the form of a national policy of 'positive discrimination' in favour of the underprivileged.

The Constitutional provisions have come in very useful to resolve what are essentially political and ideological objectives and the policy conflict of parental free-choice versus educational equality (should education be available in accordance with parental willingness to pay or in relation to capacity to learn?), to avoid bringing about a marked decline in educational standards.

Litigation and education

The huge volume of litigation and the mass of decided cases interpreting constitutional provisions are thus a sufficient testimony to the usefulness of constitutional provision in this vital field. The pronouncements of the Courts have been on varied subjects, affecting the quality and quantity of educational services not only encompassing service and management equities, but also such academic questions as medium of instruction access and autonomy of institutions. That the Government has sought to bring forward amendments also shows its imperative to continue to use this document to pursue this welfare objective. In fact, the sheer load of litigation may be proving a bane in one sense, negating the very purpose for which such Constitutional provisions are sought. It has also been lamented that follow-up action on Constitutional Amendments had either not taken place, or slow in implementation.

Education and Judiciary

True, economic transformation is the primary function of the Executive and the Legislature. But where Justice is the end product and its content has socio-economic components, the Constitution, which is the nidus of all Power, commands the judges to catalyze and control, monitor and mandate by writs, orders and direction – vide Arts. 32 and 226- so that they may bear true faith and allegiance to the Constitution and say that 'thy will shall be done'. The interventions of the judiciary from time to time upholding the responsibilities of the State in the all-important educational endeavours, have been positive in providing directions.

HISTORICAL BACKGROUND AND REVIEW OF ACHIEVEMENT

A general review of the progress in universalization of literacy including its socio-political and economic dimensions is given. The need for compulsory elementary education and free education at that level and the urgency thereof so as not to carry the burden into the 21st century is emphasized. Though a substantial progress has been achieved in the field of literacy, the basic Constitutional provision of universalization of elementary education, to have been achieved by 1960, is still eluding us; even by 2000, only 90% is targeted to be achieved.

For the purpose of this Consultation Paper, this Review will be confined to two specific aspects, viz.

(1) Literacy, as this has a direct link with the concept of Welfare State enshrined in our Constitution and

(2) Universalization of Elementary Education which has been spelt out as a specific Directive Principle of State Policy, and which provision has been interpreted to be of the nature of a Fundamental Right, and later has been incorporated as such also.

There are several published papers on the subject critically reviewing the progress that we have made in the area of education. As a matter of fact, over the last five decades, a separate sub-discipline in Economics, Economics of Education has developed and there is already published material, which deals at length and in depth the various issues involved. A mass of statistical data is also available in the Census and regular Returns filed by the various State Education Departments and in the various in-depth studies conducted from time to time.

The major advantages of the census data are that they are based on complete enumeration and are, therefore, more reliable than projections and estimates. Further, they provide an opportunity to observe trends over a period of time and draw meaningful conclusions to facilitate planning. As stated earlier, a little above three-fourths of our male population have been found to be literate and a little above half of our female population have also been found to be literate as per this Census report.

Population of India : A little over 1,027,000,000. This figure represents one-sixth of the population of the entire planet.

Growth rate of Population: has fallen by 2.52 per cent over the previous decade

Literacy Rate: At All India level: 65.38 % overall; male literacy : 75.96 % Female literacy : 54.28%. This represents an increase in overall literacy per centage by 13.75% from last Census. The corresponding increases in Male and Female literacy are: 11.83 % and 14.99 %.

Sex Ratio: Has gone up to 933 from the earlier Census figure of 927

The increase of 13.75% in literacy rate in the last one decade, marks a recognition of the combined efforts in the field of elementary education and adult education through the total literacy campaigns.

These figures are interesting in another sense as they represent crossing of another threshold in the Development field. Literacy and economic development may not be directly linked as many studies in the Developing World would indicate. To quote Owens and Shaw: "Literacy has suffered by being treated by the advocates of universal literacy as a kind of panacea for whatever they conceive to be the ailments of an undeveloped country. However, marginal people see no reason to be literate. Literacy does not provide access if people are not organized to participate in development.

For this reason, there appears to be little relationship between literacy and economic growth. When the Age of Development began, the rate of literacy in the Philippines and some Latin countries was considerably higher than in Taiwan and Korea and is still much higher than in Egypt or Comilla county of Bangladesh.

Argentina and Chile combine exceptionally high literacy rates, by Third World standards, with a very low economic growth rates." Having stated this, the point remains that there is, however, a threshold requirement. A distinguished economist, Dr. Malcolm Adiseshiah states: "There is however, a threshold of somewhere around fifty per cent of the population being literate for Development to take place as no country has ever achieved an industrial growth with a literacy rate below fifty per cent...If we want the National Development portrayed in our Draft Plan, we must reach the minimum Adult Education threshold".

Apart from the overall literacy figures, even distribution of these literacy figures, show that all the States excepting for Bihar have achieved this threshold. Even in Bihar, the male literacy figure is above the 50 per cent figure. In a macro sense, this achievement is encouraging.

The other statistic regarding the fall on population growth is also significant and relevant for our purpose as it will mean lesser provision necessary to be made in the Plan budget for new enrolments, lesser in the sense of incremental addition required for school teachers, etc. While quantitative expansion in specific areas at least in the elementary section may still be necessary, its rate will now be less with the control of population increases and more Plan funds can now be diverted to other areas of necessity within the elementary education budget.

The provision in Article 45 is: "The state shall endeavour to provide, within a period of ten years from the commencement of this Constitution, for free and compulsory education for all children until they complete the age of fourteen years".

It is 40 years since the deadline expired, and we are still to achieve it. Admittedly there has been failure in this front, and the revised target is now 2000. In the document Education For All, the Department's own statement on the subject (as expressed through the NIEPA document) is as under: "A review of the progress of basic education shows that goals and targets were fixed in the past on the basis of an inadequate understanding of the significance of education. These targets did not take into account the problem of availability of resources, and the conflicting claims of social and economic planning.

When the Constitution directed the State to endeavour, within a period of ten years, to provide free and compulsory education to all children till 14 years of age (Article 45), it was expressing an ideal to which the whole nation was expected to commit itself. In the event, however, this commitment and the resources, which go with it, were not forthcoming.

The Education Commission indicated targets in a similar time frame and it also made similar assumptions regarding national commitment and the availability of resources. By 1986, the experience of planning more than three and a half decades had amply highlighted the diversity and complexity of the problems the country had been facing in achieving the goal of basic education for all. Notwithstanding this, the Parliament, while approving the National Policy on Education in 1986, chose to approve the following formulation of the target: "It shall be ensured that all children who attain the age of 11 years by 1990 will have had five years of schooling or its equivalent though the non-formal stream.

Likewise, by 1995, all children will be provided free and compulsory education upto 14 years of age." Interestingly, here again the timeframe of roughly a decade was chosen. It became apparent very soon that the targets set for 1900 would not be achieved. It appears that in setting such high targets, the Parliament, like the Constituent Assembly, was reiterating its commitment to the ideal of education for all and was expressing its firm belief that education is a basic right that cannot be denied to anybody. If right from the beginning, it is apparent that the goals are unrealistic and unachievable, they do not lead to the kind of motivation and resource mobilization required. The right approach therefore, is to set realistic targets – realistic not to be defined as easily achievable, but as achievable, with conceivable maximum input of meticulous planning and resources – financial as well as human. We shall therefore proceed to propose realistic targets that we believe can be achieved by the year 200."

THE NATIONAL EFA GOAL STATEMENTS

The goals for Education For All in India Constitute:

1. Expansion of early childhood care and development activities, especially for poor, disadvantaged and disabled children, through a multi-pronged effort involving families, communities and appropriate institutions.
2. Universalization of Elementary Education (UEE), viewed as a complete program of:
   (a) Access to Elementary Education to all children upto 14 years of age.
   (b) Universal participation till they complete their elementary stage through formal or non-formal education programs.
   (c) Universal achievement of at least minimum levels of learning.

Drastic reduction in illiteracy, particularly in the 15 to 35 age group, bringing the literacy level in this age group to at least 80 % in each gender and for each identified disadvantaged group, besides ensuring that the levels of the three R's are relevant to the living and working conditions of the people. Provision of opportunities to maintain, use and upgrade education and, provision of facilities for development of skills to all persons who are functionally literate and those who have received primary education through formal and non-formal channels.

Creation of necessary structures, and the setting in motion of processes which could empower women and make education an instrument of women's equality. Improving the contents and process of education to relate it better to the empowerment, people's culture and with their living and working conditions thereby enhancing their ability to learn and cope with the problems of livelihood and environment.

India has a long tradition of organized education. As a historian has put it, "There is no other country where the love of learning had so early an origin or has exercised so lasting and powerful an influence." However, educational effort in the country has come a long way from this traditional position in its definition, coverage as well as impact. The current educational system in the country operates in an altogether different context from the classical past. The country's commitment to the provision of education for all and its endeavor to achieve this goal in a speedy fashion has to be seen in this complex milieu within which the educational system is currently functioning.

As the veteran educationist Shri J.P.Naik put it: "The Indian Society, especially the Hindu Society has been extremely inegalitarian, and this is the one value on the basis of which the society can be humanized and strengthened. In fact, the issue is so crucial that the Indian society cannot even hope to survive except on the basis of an egalitarian reorganization". Between 1813 and 1921, the British administrators laid the foundations of the modern educational system. The principal positive contribution of the British administrators to equality was to give all citizens open access to educational institutions maintained from or supported by public funds. For instance, the worst difficulties were perhaps encountered when the problem of educating the "untouchable" castes came up.

The first test case arose in 1856 when a boy from an untouchable caste applied for admission to the government school at Dharwar. He was refused admission on the ground that it would result in the withdrawal of all the caste Hindu children from the school and thus in the closure of the school itself. But the decision was sharply criticized by the Governor General of India as well as by the Court of Directors in the East India Company and a clear policy was laid down that no untouchable child should be refused admission to a government school even if it meant the closure of the school.

The British administrators thus established, firmly and unequivocally, the right of every child irrespective of caste, sex or traditional taboos, to seek admission to all schools supported or aided by public funds. The British administrators refused to accept the principle of compulsory elementary education.

The Indian nationalist thought, however, was firmly of the view that the provision of equality of educational opportunity must include a certain minimum general education to be provided to all children on a free and compulsory basis. A demand that four years of compulsory education should be provided to all children was put forward, for the first time before the Indian Education Commission by the Grand Old Man of India, Dadabhai Naoroji in 1881.

Gopal Krishna Gokhale who moved a resolution on the subject in the Central Legislative Assembly in 1910 and again took the proposal vide a bill in 1912, neither of which achieved their objective. At this stage, it is illuminating to read the then announced Indian Educational Policy, 1913.

The Government of India, have decided, with the approval of the Secretary of State, to assist Local Governments, by means of large grants from imperial revenues as funds become available', to extend comprehensive systems of education in the several provinces. Each province has its own educational system, which has grown up under local conditions and become familiar to the people as a part of their general well being.

In view of the diverse social conditions in India there cannot in practice be one set of regulations and one rate of progress for the whole of India. Even within provinces there is scope for greater variety in types if institutions that exists today. The Government of India have no desire to deprive Local Governments of interest and initiative in education. But it is important at intervals to review educational policy in India as a whole.

Principles, bearing on education in its wider aspects and under modern conditions and conceptions, on orientalia and on the special needs of the domiciled community, were discussed at three important conferences of experts and representative non-officials held within the last two years. These principles are the basis of accepted policy. How far they can at any time find local application must be determined with reference to local conditions.

On the question compulsory and free elementary education, the Policy stated: "The propositions that illiteracy must be broken down and that primary education has, in the present circumstances of India, a predominant claim upon the public funds, represent accepted policy no longer open to discussion. For financial and administrative reasons of decisive weight, the Government of India have refused to recognize the principle of compulsory education, but they desire the widest possible extension of primary education on a voluntary basis. As regards free elementary education, the time has not yet arrived when it is practicable to dispense wholly with fees without injustice to the many villages, which are waiting for the provision of schools.

The fees derived from those pupils who can pay them are now devoted to the maintenance and expansion of primary education, and a total remission of fees would involve to a certain extent a more prolonged postponement of the provision of schools in villages without them. In some provinces, elementary education is already free and in the majority of provinces, liberal provision is already made for giving free elementary instruction to those boys whose parents cannot afford to pay fees. Local Governments have been requested to extend the application of the principle of free elementary education amongst the poorer and more backward sections of the population. Further than this it is not possible at present to go."

The public demand for compulsory primary education continued however to grow, and between 1918 and 1931 compulsory education laws were passed for most parts of the country by the newly elected State legislatures in which Indians were in majority. In 1937, Mahatma Gandhi put forward his scheme of Basic Education under which education of seven or eight years duration was to be provided for all children and its content was to be revolutionized by building it round a socially useful productive craft. As a result of all these efforts, the idea that it was the duty of the state to provide free and compulsory education to all children till they reached the age of 14 years was nationally accepted as an important aspect of the overall effort to provide equality of opportunity. Under the wise leadership of Sir John Sargent, the then educational adviser to the Government of India, these ideas were accepted by the British administrators and the Post-war Plan of educational development in India known popularly as the Sargent Plan, put forward proposals to provide free and compulsory basic education to all children in the age group 6-14 over a period of 40 years.

The nationalist opinion did not accept this long period, and a committee under the chairmanship of B.G.Kher proposed that this goal could and should be achieved in a period of 16 years. It was this recommendation that was eventually incorporated in the Constitution as a Directive Principle of State Policy. It was thus not a mere statement of an ideal, but a well-thought out enunciation of a policy, which is yet to be implemented though a substantial component was sought to be achieved by 2000 under the Education for All plan.

Review of achievements – elementary school stage

It is a very healthy administrative practice of the Education Department to publish annually a variety of information on different aspects of education through its Educational Statistics. Even a routine analysis of the variety of information that the government collects in the application for administering the programs, is an eye-opener. While preparing the document Education For All, the Ministry of Human Resource

Development has brought out a compendium of relevant statistics, culled out from the annual statements regularly sent by the State Governments.

A core curriculum is emphasized at the elementary school level. This is a carefully planned curriculum that in content it compares favourably with those adopted in a number of other countries. A common core can help in overcoming discrepancies between the educational opportunities of urban and rural people, and that of men and women, but it cannot eliminate those difficulties unless literacy rates improve, greater participation occurs in school and other changes take place in society. In addition to the regular statistical return system, which is regularly compiled and published under the heading Education in India each academic year, there are also two expert institutions under the aegis of the Ministry of Human Resource Development, viz. National Council of Educational Research and Training (NCERT) and National Institute of Educational Planning and Administration (NIEPA) which carry out regular research and surveys, and in-depth analyses.

NCERT has been conducting regular educational surveys and the report of the Sixth Educational Survey was published in 1995. Highlights of the findings of this survey are:

Sixth All India Education Survey (Conducted by the NCERT): Main Outcomes of the Survey

1. 94 per cent of the Rural Population is served within 1.0 kilometers by Primary Stage
2. 85 per cent of the Rural Population is served within 3.0 kilometers by Upper Primary Stage
3. Of the Total 8,22,486 schools in the country, 5,70,455 and 1.62,805 are Primary and Upper Primary Schools respectively.
4. Of the total 15,39,06,057 pupils enrolled in all the schools, 9,70,29,235 and 5,40,71,058 are children enrolled in Primary grades (Grades I –V) and Upper Primary (Grades VI – VIII) stages respectively.

5. Of the total 41,97,555 teachers, 16,23,379 and 11,29,747 teachers are employed in Primary and Upper Primary Schools.
6. 84 per cent of the primary and 89 per cent of the Upper Primary Schools have pucca and partly public buildings.

Similarly, NIEPA had carried out a research study on the regional dimension of educational development based on Fourth All India Educational Survey data. In the survey, the following attributes of schooling are analyzed:

— Accessibility,

— Availability,

— Quantity,

— Quality,

— Inter-connectivity

— Equity, and

— Utility.

In that study it was found that in spite of the progress in the quantitative expansion of education and the apparent narrowing gaps between different social groups, inequities within the educational system of the country continue to be quite sharp. The variations one observes in the regional distributions have already been highlighted. Inequities get complicated in the case of Scheduled Caste and Scheduled Tribes women in the rural areas of the backward regions. The literacy rate among this group in the 1991 Census was only 16 %. This was followed by SC Rural Male (19.45 %), SC Urban Female (42.25 %). If arranged as an inverse pyramid, the Non-scheduled Urban populations (both Male and Female) are on the top. Presenting the literacy level of different components of the population brings out the nature of this multi-level system of inequities.

Similar study of subsequent surveys and 2001 Census might bring out a better picture, though even after the improved statistics, the pyramidal structure has not undergone any significant change in terms of reduction of inequities in any large measure.

The causes for educational deprivation in India have been analyzed in detail. The Indian Social Institute, in a program of research on schooling, identified three obstacles against universal elementary education. They are:

— Inadequate parental motivation,

— Poverty and

— Low quality of schooling.

Therefore, there does appear to exist (more and more) a case for compulsory education, provided that (1) it is understood to include compulsion on the state to provide adequate schooling facilities; and (2) top-down measures which concentrate on punitive action against parents, are avoided.

The review of the Government's efforts in the direction of universalization of elementary education through school system, shows up both its gains and shortcomings. Gains lay in the direction of quantitative expansion, and shortcomings have been in the direction of quality and equity as between different sections of the populace. But the biggest shortcoming has been as the educationist.

Eradication of illiteracy has been one of the major national concerns of the Government of India since independence. During the first Five Year Plan, the program of Social Education, inclusive of literacy, was introduced as part of the Community Development Program.

Efforts of varied types were made by the States for the spread of literacy. Among these, the Gram Shikshan Mohim initiated in Satara District of Maharashtra in 1959 was one of the successful mass campaigns. It aimed at completing literacy work village-by-village within a short period of 3 to 6 months, through the honorary services of primary teachers and middle-school and high school students, supported by the entire community. It achieved a good deal of success but suffered from the lack of follow-up due to financial constraints and some of its good work was lost as a consequence. In spite of these varied initiatives the program of adult literacy did not make much headway.

The topic was dealt at length by the Kothari Commission which emphasized the importance of spreading literacy as fast as possible. The Commission also observed that "literacy if it is to be worthwhile, must be functional". It suggested the following measures:

— Expansion of universal schooling of five-year duration for the age group 6 - 11.

— Provision of part-time education for those children of age group 11 - 14 who had either missed schooling or dropped out of school prematurely.

— Provision of part-time general and vocational education to the younger adults of age group 15 – 30.

— Use of mass media as a powerful tool of environment building for literacy.

— Setting up of libraries.

— Need for follow up program.

— Active role of universities and voluntary organisation at the State and district levels.

The National Policy on Education in 1968 not only endorsed the recommendations of the Education Commission but also reiterated the significance of universal literacy and developing adult and continuing education as matters of priority. While the formal elementary education program was supplemented by a Non-formal Education system, it was also decided to undertake Adult Literacy programs culminating in the Total Literacy mission approach.

A multi-pronged approach of universalization of elementary education and universal adult literacy has been adopted for achieving total literacy. The National Policy on Education has given an unqualified priority to the following three programs for eradication of illiteracy, particularly among women:-

(a) Universalization of elementary education and universal retention of children upto 14 years of age.

(b) A systematic program of non-formal education in the educationally backward states.

(c) The National Literacy Mission which aims at making 100 million adults literate by 1997.

The major thrust of these programs is on promotion of literacy among women, members belonging to Scheduled Castes and Scheduled Tribes particularly in the rural areas.

The Adult Education Program consists of three components: basic literacy, functionality and civic awareness. The program covers different schemes so that finally it aims at helping learners achieve a 'reasonable degree of self-reliance in literacy and functionality and better appreciation of the scope and value of science. Of course, even before Independence, there were adult education programs. Mahatma Gandhi had education as one of his constructive programs, and as a mass campaign had through his movement, tried to make districts completely literate. Some success was also achieved. For instance Surat District, in erstwhile Bombay Presidency had been totally literate, but again relapsed into illiteracy for lack of follow-up.

There were efforts at spreading by the Baroda Rulers, supplemented by a live library movement. Here again lack of follow-up and sustained efforts caused a relapse into illiteracy among the vulnerable sections. There were voluntary agencies working in the field. Some agencies as the Karnataka Adult Education Council, Gujarat Social Education Committee and Bombay City Social Education Committee has had large programs extending to the whole state or a metropolitan city. Literacy House of Lucknow did commendable work in this field. It came into existence in 1953 when its founder, Mrs. Welthy H. Fisher established it in small verandah at Allahabad, with a view to eradicate illiteracy and promote education in India. It was shifted to Lucknow in 1956.

The University Grants Commission, at its meeting held in 5th May 1971, considered the general pattern of development and assistance towards adult education in the university and agreed that "assistance to universities for program of adult education be made on a sharing basis of 75:25 and that the Commission's assistance to university would not exceed Rs. 3 lakhs for the Fourth Plan period." Departments of Continuing Education took up the work of "University goes to Masses". The slogan "Each One, Teach One" caught the imagination of not only the students, but also a large number of educated individuals, and it looked like these programs will meet a major success. However, like most enthusiastically launched programs, they also fell by the wayside. A Farmers Training and Functional literacy project was launched in 1968-69, coordinating the activities of Ministries of Education, Agriculture and Information & Broadcasting. The Central Advisory Board of Education in its November 1975 meeting asked that the exclusive emphasis on formal system of education should be given up and a large element of non-formal education should be introduced within the system.

In one sense, though the Non-formal education system was launched with its own set of objectives, the main purpose was to tackle the problem of dropouts from the formal system. The dropout from the formal system continues to hover around 50% and have not shown any great variation in the last four decades. It is not difficult to guess the collective identities of the victims, children who fail to survive at school. They are children of landless agricultural labourers and subsistence peasants.

Caste-wise, a substantial proportion of them belongs to the Scheduled Castes that have been granted special rights including reservation in higher education and representative bodies, in the Constitution. The situation of children belonging to many of the Scheduled Tribes is worse, especially in the central Indian belt. Forest-dwelling tribal communities have had to bear the brunt of State initiatives in dam construction, development of tourism with the help of game sanctuaries and mining. Apart from such destabilizing experiences, bias against tribal cultures and languages also makes the school curriculum and the teacher a deterrent for the advancement of tribal education. There are about 40 million rural artisans in India. For them, the current standard school curriculum is trivial, and in a sense irrelevant and demeaning. No wonder, one realizes in a rather simple, unscientific way, these children stop coming to school early. Finally, the child residing in a slum, living in conditions of uncertainly and violence is always a likely case of early withdrawal or elimination.

In keeping with recent trends in the international literacy movement, the emphasis of mass literacy programs in India shifted from 'literacy' to 'adult education' through the intermediate phases of 'functional literacy' and 'non-formal education' during the last fifty years. The Policy Statement of the present program highlights the development of functional competencies and awareness of the adult learners as two of the three equally important components of the National Adult Education Program. The third component is obviously literacy. Our Universities had also been roped into this activity.

The National Adult Education Program (NAEP) was inaugurated on October 2, 1978. In a statement in the Parliament on April 5, 1977, the Union Education Minister declared that "along with universalization of elementary education, highest priority in educational planning would be accorded to adult education." The objective of the NAEP is "to organise adult education programs, with literacy as an indispensable component, for approximately 100 million illiterate persons in the age-group 15-35 with a view to providing them with skills for self-directed learning leading to self-reliant and active role in their own development and in the development of their environment."

In concrete terms, three R's, social awareness and functionality are the three basic components of the NAEP. In spite of careful planning before the launch of this program (it had envisaged a phased program), the Sardar Patel Institute of Social and Economic Research, after a survey carried out in the initial flush of enthusiasm, observed about the progress of the program in a progressive state like Gujarat: "On the whole, while the NAEP in Gujarat was generally found to be addressed to the target groups kept in view under the NAEP and it was found to have some other commendable aspects, all things considered, its achievement in terms of spread of literacy is rather modest, and more so in terms of social awareness and functionality".

The report had gone on to say: "The more crucial aspects like the content of education, pedagogy, etc. can be probed into only if longer time is available, or ideally, on an ongoing basis. It is these aspects which have contributed most to the continuing stagnation of even the spread of literacy in the country. This study is not sufficient to indicate whether breakthrough in these areas is being made, and whether the adult education program is assuming the character of a Mass Movement as would be desirable and is clearly the intent of NAEP".

Then came the National Literacy Mission (NLM). For a short while during the era of the high profile technology missions, some attention was given to issues like immunization, safe drinking water and literacy along with talk of people's participation and social audit of these programs. In 1989, the district-based Total Literacy Campaigns (TLC) emerged as a program strategy for the National Literacy Mission against this background. While it was correctly envisaged that the initial social mobilization for a time-bound campaign provides the inspiration to spark for a mass participation of people, volunteering their time and energy for a cause like literacy, the follow-up program was not worked out clearly.

However, admitting and recognizing the many flaws and failures of the 'campaign approach', even as early as 1994, NLM continued with the same TLC strategy and tried to bolster it with better monitoring, internal evaluation and presently with a revival effort through what is called 'Operation Restoration'. Reviewing the functioning of these programs, Avik Ghosh concludes: "The present focus of NLM on literacy has to shift, and similarly the mission-mode-time-bound thrust of NLM should give way to a more durable and sustained program of adult education that responds to the needs of adults as individuals and also as members of the disadvantaged groups".

The Total Literacy Campaigns, initially at least, helped in fostering a participatory approach in dealing with this issue, though here again, the problem of sustaining the momentum has remained. In the budget for 1999-2000, allocation for the Rural Functional Literacy Project does not find a special mention. The overall allocation to adult education has, however, been increased by about 40%.

Unless it be in the context of revolutionary social transformation, the lack of spectacular success in a program like Adult Education and of sustaining its momentum is understandable. It is after all a far distant cousin in terms of financial outlays to the formal system Further, there is the very real problem of pedagogy.

For instance, as Prof. Jalaluddin says: "While 1652 mother tongues have been identified in the recent censuses in India, only 15 major literary languages have been accorded political status under the Eighth Schedule of the Indian Constitution. Then there is the problem of script. In the context of a nationwide adult literacy and education program, the question of the acquisition of more than one writing system or even script by linguistic minorities becomes an important area of language planning. The term biliteracy is used in this context in India." Further in countries like India which have a long tradition of transmission of ideas and wisdom orally, such individual and societal transformations through a mass literacy campaign, are rather a form of renewal in nature than being additive or extensive".

There is also the problem continued sustenance of the campaign approach. There are some hopeful signs of ICT-supported services being used to bridge the gulf. Some collaborative partnership of the Government of India and non-governmental agencies in partnership with International Organizations and private sector has been mooted and the results of such collaborative efforts may perhaps show a way.

And yet, the importance of this component cannot be gainsaid. "In our country, numerous persons enter adulthood without proper education and consequently their self-confidence is shaky. In a fast-changing environment of economic and cultural change, they will continue to be edged out unless their capacities are actively consolidated and improved so as to encounter the world outside on equal terms". This program can be in the nature of a Sunset program; but till then, i.e. literacy becomes self-sustaining fact with self-arising demand for its very usefulness and need for a fuller life, no Government should be allowed to ignore this aspect.

It is perhaps wise to reminisce on the "Education For All" document which says: "It will be against the spirit of the Constitution to allow elementary education to suffer from inadequacy of resources. As far as funding elementary education and literacy programs is concerned, it should be viewed in the framework of the Constitution. It is not just the Department of Education, but all the government departments, which should be made to allocate substantial resources for elementary education, as no sector can develop significantly with illiterate masses. In fact, the whole nation should feel responsible for the development of education in the country."

In the system of central planning we are used to in this country, only the resources required from the government or public sector agencies are taken into account. However, for an activity like education, there are considerable costs borne by the children and parents. These costs are not included in the financial implications presented, except for the provision of incentives like books and uniforms to the weaker sections.

The Constitution has directed that education for children in primary and upper primary levels of education should be free. This has been so far taken in practice, to mean that schools should not charge any fees. The cost incurred by parents for education of their children has been ignored and has not been considered as a violation of the directive of free education. In view of the paucity of resources, it may be pragmatic to continue this approach and let the parents bear costs of this nature, while underscoring that ideally these costs should be borne by public funds.

We may also have to move from the concept of exclusive responsibility of the government for education to shared responsibility between the government and the community. This would not be difficult, keeping in view the tradition in India of community support to education from ancient times. This will be also consistent with the general approach of decentralization, community involvement and people's participation. For safeguarding democracy and strengthening the foundations of the integrated nation, it is necessary not to compromise with the requirements of these basic needs in education. It should be noted that without adequate resources, financial, physical and human, our target of Education For All will remain unachieved even by the turn of the century. If we have to enter the twenty-first century without the burden of the unfulfilled goals originally proposed by the Constitution makers of India, substantial resources should be allocated to elementary and adult education programs.

FUTURE

The need to go into a learning mode as also conditions for creating capabilities in the education system to meet the needs of knowledge growth, communication expansion, reinforcement of cultural roots is indicated. Changing needs of Educational Technology and entry of computers and Integration of Information and Communication Technology demand new structures, which the system should be able to assimilate. Renewal of education also calls for provision for regular reviews, which reckons also changing scenarios and developments in emerging technologies.

In a UNESCO publication, "Education in Asia and the Pacific", Raja Roy Singh has rightly written:

> "The dynamics of education and its role in each society in development and transformation make it essential that education continuously renews itself in order to prepare for a future rather than for obsolescence. This renewal process derives from a variety of sources which include: the growth of human knowledge, which is the basic component of education; the heritage of collective experience and values which education transmits to the new generations; the means and methods of communication by which knowledge and values are transmitted and the new values and aspirations which the human spirit adds to the collective experience and wisdom of the past or by which the heritage of the past is reinterpreted and reassessed."

The books Learning to Be and The Learning Society are pointers to the future directions that educational process will have to take. Now learning process is replacing the teaching process. Nobody teaches any one, but men learn from each other. In other words, all are learners. The aim of education is not to fit people into a system but to help them develop their human powers.

Three distinct global developments that may affect future of education are:

1. *Knowledge Growth:* The speed with which the growth of knowledge is now taking place, its range and sweep, are epitomized in the expansion of knowledge in science and technology. It is estimated that in the period 600 BC to AD 1700, the body of scientific knowledge doubled every 1000 years; from the beginning of industrialization until the early twentieth century, the doubling period accelerated to about 200 years; and now in many scientific fields, knowledge is doubling every 15 years or so. Moreover, the lag between a discovery in a fundamental science and its technological application has narrowed remarkably. This enormous growth in the volume and application of knowledge impacts on every aspect of modern life. Parallel to the rapid growth of knowledge is the increasing velocity with which knowledge is being circulated.

   New configurations in the fields of knowledge are emerging and are tending to efface to some extent at least, the old established demarcation lines between the natural sciences and the social and human sciences. Cross over points are emerging between the major fields of human activity. Another direction of advance is the aggregation of different components of traditional disciplines into new integrated fields. The most practical conclusion that we draw on education planning is, therefore, that the options open to learners in regard to fields of study should not be closed too early.

2. *Education and Communication:* In perhaps no other fields has there been such a profound revolution as in communications and informatics. The communication technologies have multiplied and became more and more powerful. The development in computer technology will soon affect every individual. Telecommunications and data processing have already increased dramatically the volume of information readily available as well as its accessibility. Integration of information and communication technologies

is a new challenge before the educational administrators. This calls for:

— a need for research and development in the information and communication technology;

— creation of scientific and technological capacity to crucially use these technologies which represent a power of unlimited possibilities;

— discrimination and selectivity arising from information overload. There is also an increasing danger of the deliberate manipulation of information such that the models of reality that people learn from the media are either incomplete or distorted. In curriculum development, that which is omitted may be as important as that which is included.

Education and culture

The other source of educational renewal is the cultural heritage reflected in the whole range of expressions, which give meaning and worth to the society's being. The need for a reaffirmation of cultural identity is more urgent today because of the tendency towards uniformity and homogeneity generated by economic and material forces and the mass media. Next only to the family, the school is the most important institution for the transmission of cultural values. Role of education, an indispensable role, is to be a medium in which the various new influences are assimilated in the cultural stream. Education has a vital role in promoting the processes by which scientific and technological knowledge is assimilated in the fabric of national life without detriment to the people's values. There is a 'cultural' dimension in every subject taught in the schools. This needs to be brought out in the methods of instruction.

The tools and techniques available for pedagogy and androgogy are also undergoing a major change. Educational Technology is the new addition to the armamentarium of pedagogy in the future. The phrase 'Educational Technology' was defined by the National Council of Educational Technology (UK) as the development, application, evaluation of systems, techniques and aids to improve the process of human learning. It has a wider connotation than simply the use of electromechanical and other aids in teaching. It places as much stress on educational ideas as on educational inventions. It can only be of value if it is really integrated into the entire system. There are two approaches – hardware and software - in educational technology.

The hardware approach is based on the application of engineering principles for developing electromechanical equipment like motion pictures, tape recorders, teaching machines, computers, videotape, closed circuit television, etc. The second approach, i.e. software approach uses the principle of psychology for behavior modification purposes. There are two trends or directions of educational technology: towards mass instructional technology and towards technology designed for individual instruction. Mass transmission technology capable of making educational messages is available to millions of children and adults. Television is the most obvious example of mass instructional technology. Teaching machines are examples of individual instructional technology

Distance learning

Distance learning, an aspect of use of Educational Technology, can thus transform traditional learning. Learning at one's own pace and at his convenience will get stressed. Attending formal classroom instruction puts severe stress both on the learner and the Society. The former has to schedule his activities in the structured requirements of a formal classroom, which for a person already working may be difficult. The latter has to grapple with difficult-to-find resources to provide for the escalating costs of education. Distance education overcomes these hurdles. Use of satellites is rapidly changing the concept of conventional education. Students need no longer be limited by lack of access, shortage of teachers or interference from work.

Computers

Entry of computers in the Educational Field can be stated to have caused a paradigm shift in the field of technology so much so that we cannot afford to be left out of computer literacy in any future plans for education. With computers, the technological revolution can be stated to have come into the classroom. Technology is an enabling tool. It facilitates the process of writing so that students and teachers alike can interact with the text in useful ways that are difficult with paper and pencil. Experience at MS Swaminathan Research Foundation as well as in many villages in Pondicherry and Madhya Pradesh have demonstrated that a high level of formal education is not necessary to gain operational computer literacy, and as a functional education tool, it is valuable.

Computers across the Curriculum

The term 'Computer literacy' covers aspects both of learning about the computers and of learning with, from and through the computers. It involves consideration of the application of the computers in the educational settings and the society at large. The Computer is a general-purpose tool and can be effectively used in a large number of activities in the teaching-learning process. Some of the common programs are:

1. Computer Assisted Instruction (CAI): In this mode, the Computer acts as a teacher teaching new skills or concepts or providing practice for learners.
2. Computer Based Learning (CBL) or Computer Assisted Learning (CAL) which could be assisted for a variety of purposes such as Simulations and Modeling, Instructional Games, Information Handling, Demonstrations, etc.
3. Computer Managed Learning (CML) where the Computer serves as a tool to help in the management of student learning.

The changing methods of storing information now mean that computer literacy becomes a fundamental component of literacy itself. Commonly included in the objectives of computer literacy are:

(a) An awareness of Information Technology and how it affects day-to-day living.

(b) An understanding about the importance of information to aid decision-making processes.

(c) An understanding of Man: Machine interaction so that the tool can be used effectively.

Integration of Information and Communication Technologies

Integration of Information and Communication Technologies (ICT) with school needs serious consideration. Teachers, educators, curriculum developers, evaluators and others will have to redefine their roles to tackle ICT rich environment and harness its full potential for the benefit of learners. Information media are bringing about dramatic changes and are facilitating the communication of information between instructor and learner. These media have also produced a basic easing of spatio-temporal limitations and creation of new learning spaces based on information networks. These may call for structural changes. Our politico-administrative structures should be interpreted flexibly enough not to obstruct these winds of change.

Renewal and periodic reforms

(a) International experience

A reference has been made in the beginning of this section for the need for renewal process. Updating is very essential in educational processes. In this field, both individuals and nations have been known to slide down unless a conscious effort is taken to keep 'awareness' at the best pitch. Knowledge expands and values undergo a change taking subsequent experience into account. As the noted American analyst David Halberstam says in 'The Next Century': "National security was no longer an index of weaponry (essentially a missile and tank count), if it ever really was, but a broad array of factors reflecting the general state of national well being. It included the ability of a country to house its people, to feed them, to educate them, to provide them with opportunities in keeping with their desires and education, and to instill in them trust and optimism that their lives were going to be valued and fruitful." According to him, though the 20th century was an American century, the next century was no more theirs. It was possible to make 20th century an American century because of its concern for 'humane' values and democratization. Ensuring cultural and ethical values while at the same time adopting 3 R's is a challenge that has to be adequately tackled.

Concerned with maintaining its economic and social initiatives without losing sight of the various cultural accumulations and traditions, the Japanese Government decided to adopt the following five concrete measures for educational reform: (I) the development of life-long structures; (ii) the diversification and reform of institutions of higher education; (iii) the enrichment and reform of elementary and secondary education; (iv) reforms for coping with internationalization, (v) reforms for coping with the information age and (vi) the reform of educational administration and finance. Similar studies for reforms have been undertaken in other countries too. And if Japan has been cited as an example, it is to point out the need for the reforms even in the best of circumstances.

(b) National experience

For the future, in our case, of particular reference is the need to focus on the core and permanent aspects of education so that Constitutional guarantees can ensure that the most important aspects are not lost sight of. Our Indian experience has also been spelt out in many a fora. J.P.Naik identified the causes for our failure in the field of primary education: (a) We have made no attempt to introduce those radical structural changes in the formal system of elementary education. (b)Exclusive reliance on full-time formal education has an inherent bias in favour of classes and a built-in unsuitability for the education of the masses. (c) There is a general view that standards in education have continually and alarmingly deteriorated in the last few years, which may be only partially true. (d) There should be an early end to the dual system which we now run at all stages under which the classes have access to a small group of high quality elite institutions while the masses are compelled to study in public institutions of poor quality.

Thus the causes for apparent failure of universalisation of primary education are many; the overall picture is a mixture of light and shade. Standards have definitely improved in certain sectors. The number of good institutions and of first-rate students have considerably increased at all stages.

There has been a steady improvement in average qualifications and remuneration of teachers and some improvements in curricula and teaching material. But there has also been an immense increase in such negative factors as the rapid increase in sub-standard institutions, deterioration in facilities and conditions of work and service in large number of schools and colleges, of the breakdown of the examination system through large-scale practice of unfair means. The list can be enlarged to cover different aspects. To maintain social cohesion, is an aim of education as also the purpose of our Constitution. Hence also the need for vigil on this front.

PROMOTING LITERACY

A possible Model for achieving the goals of universisalization of literacy and primary education in the country is suggested, where the main theme is decentralization and development of a Systems Model to facilitate mobility and life-long learning and education.

It has already been mentioned that the constitutional goal of universalization of elementary education directed in Article 45 has long since expired. In the approach paper to the Tenth Plan, the non-achievement in this field has been accepted, and the revised target year to achieve universal access to primary education has been pushed to 2007. Similarly, the targets for progress in literacy has now been fixed at 72% by 2007 and 80% by 2012.

In view of the progress already achieved, these targets are not unrealistic. Nevertheless there is need for readiness to accept modifications and changes and even new structures to achieve the goal, instead of merely relying on the existing scheme of things, alone. Fresh initiatives will be necessary. As far back as 1966, the Second Education Commission observed: "It is no longer desirable to undertake educational reforms in piecemeal fashion, without a concept of the totality of the goals and modes of the educational process. To find out how to reshape its component parts, one must have a vision of the future. This search for practical alternatives are parts of a genuine strategy of innovation seems to us to be one of the primary tasks of any educational undertaking."

In one sense, it is true that the education system has undergone many types of changes and experiments. Many a new thought and idea has been tried out and implemented at some point of time and in some part of the country. The various Departments of Education of the Universities all over the country have been deliberating over the various facets of the problem and the treatises submitted for the M.Ed. and Ph.D courses are a veritable storehouse of ideas. Then, there are the various Centres of Advanced Studies which can distill the various ideas and have also been rendering advisory services. The number of enquiry commissions, whether it be the Royal Commissions, or Commissions appointed thereafter headed by Indians of eminence, are not insignificant. As instances of the latter, the reports of the Radhakrishnan Commission or the Kothari Commission have been truly incisive and have been given due consideration and even acceptance.

Purpose of Education

True enough, education is a 'vast, shapeless and vexatious subject'. In a country of continental proportions, with its different communities and people with different socio-economic backgrounds, and literally living in different centuries in terms of thought, the aims of education can be at variance with the thoughts of experts in the field. And even among the latter, there are different perceptions.

There is a need for a core curriculum to bring nearly all pupils above a certain threshold of learning, for thereafter all subsequent learning is made easier. But then, there is also the concern for democratization of primary education. As a UNESCO publication puts it: "A primary school that fails to achieve certain minimum and useful objectives, that fails to meet the people's needs, that fails to interest either the children or their parents, will inevitably end up by losing in one way or the other".

In efforts to bring in certain integration, even well-planned curriculum contents have to be toned down. In Gujarat, for instance, after the introduction of the new education policy after the acceptance of the Kothari Commission Report, because of the end-of-term certificate or diploma, the final examination content had to be toned down and alternative subjects had to be offered. Instead of New Mathematics, Commercial Arithmetic and instead of New Science, Everyday needs of health and hygiene, were allowed. In that very State a battle royal was waged on the introduction of English at the V Standard or VIII Standard. The battle was both political and legal. Then there is the different perception of what the 'average' rural lad or lass needs. We have thus in both Gujarat and Maharashtra, parallel streams of the normal school system and the basic and post-basic schools. At the secondary the plethora of examination bodies in addition to the different State Secondary Examination Boards is part of the same malady of what is perceived as the purpose of education. Even the medium of instruction whether it should be mother tongue only at the primary education level has been a matter of many an academic and legal disputes.

In such an environment, innovative experiments could be inhibited because of the competing and variant expectations. At the same time, what it portends is the fact that in our country, there could perhaps be no one solution. In a multilingual and multicultural environment where the people also live in varying socio-economic background and in different centuries even in the realm of thinking patterns, one pattern is certainly not the answer. The problems of universalisation of education are also even otherwise real.

In the special issue of the International Yearbook of Education on "Primary Education on the threshold of the twenty-first century", Ramamoorthi identified the following as the main problems, difficulties and obstacles to the universalisation of primary education in most of the developing countries:

1. A lack of financial resources coupled with the escalating cost of education.
2. A high rate of population growth in relation to the available limited resources
3. Deteriorating and inadequate physical facilities for education, such as an inadequate number of school buildings, essential scholastic and other educational materials
4. An inadequate supply of trained teachers,
5. Inhibitory cultural attitudes in these countries' communities, particularly bias against the education of girls and the physically and mentally handicapped. It should be pointed out that economic constraints tend to entrench these inhibitory attitudes.

6. High drop-out rates in primary schools
7. Unattractive terms of service for teachers.

Thanks to sustained efforts taken by Government of India both in the field of education and Family Welfare, the problems are no more insurmountable, as can be seen from the positive trends in the Census and Educational Survey reports. While the problems of resources will continue to plague us, the problem of community involvement has to be more constructively thought out. Centralized governments and administrations will have to move towards a pronounced form of decentralization of primary education.

There have been innovations and changes made in the system. Instances are many where the State Government have handed over Government Schools to private education trusts for management along with required funds. In Maharashtra and Gujarat, many a Sarvajanik Sikshan Society has come up to take up such responsibility. Similarly there have been technical schools and participating schools also. Why these efforts did not yield expected results is a matter of study. However, the fact that an experiment failed at one point of time or at a particular surrounding, may not be a bar to try it again at another point of time or place. While it is true that what is right in theory may always be right in practice, it is definitely true that what is wrong in theory can never be right in practice. Within that parameter, experimentation will have to go on and decentralization is a key to this process of experimentation.

FUNCTIONAL LITERACY THROUGH MODERN INFORMATION TECHNOLOGY

Specially in the area of Adult Education, the concept of functional literacy has been discussed earlier. Conventional methods of education involving mastering a script, learning words and sentences, etc., that have no direct relationship to everyday life such learners, have to give place a learning that is directly relevant to them. The Education Division of the Tata

Consultancy Services claims to have evolved a system where the learners are exposed to a set of words and pictures that have a direct relevance to them. A set of about 500 words or so form the vocabulary, and by repeated exposure of these words and pictures, the learners become familiar with them and learn to recognize them. This knowledge enables them to even read newspapers and magazines and activates an interest in the learner to know more. If necessary, they can then join a formal education program. Video projections and large computer screens aid such learning process.

Can the present model with its structured hierarchy of time-dependant learning levels, single point entry, isolation from society and the marketplace, outdated learning content, irrelevant evaluation techniques and class-biased survival be replaced or at least be supplemented by a Systems Model? The latter model will need the following action steps:

1. Launching the non-formal education sub-system for the two priority groups- school drop-outs in the age group 6-14 years, and working adult illiterates in the age group 15-40 years, involving devising functional curricula, producing learning materials, mobilizing teaching resources from trained teachers as well as progressive farmers, engineers, musicians, dramatists and sportsmen, and using existing buildings, laboratories and workshops for running the concentrated courses.

2. Reorganizing the existing formal education sub-system into multiple-entry and exit points at its different levels, so that students could enter, leave and reenter the school and university system at any one of several points to answer the call of work in the home, farm, factory or office, continue their education through organized non-formal programs and reenter the school or university at appropriate points when they so desire in order to acquire further learning skills. The launching of the non-formal education system and the reorganization of the formal system will help the system serve the majority now excluded.

3. Establishing the relationship between the two sub-systems involving crossover points and the feed-in and feed-out provisions and the nexus between their educational content, methods and technologies of teaching and learning.
4. Vocationalizing the second level through a system of diversified learning experiences in higher secondary schools and technical schools so that such work-based education is freely available to all up to the age of 15 or 16 years in school and out of school and becomes the constructive skill forming a terminal point for 80 per cent of the full-time students entering the school stream.

NGOs and Corporate Institutions should be encouraged to take interest in such programs. Most of the NGOs are, however, dependent only on government funding for their activities, and funding them for this activity will be only an indirect government support. With large business houses expressing interest in Welfare measures, at least in the geographical regions in which they operate, they can be encouraged to contribute to such causes. Local Institutions like Panchayats and Gram Sabhas should also be encouaged to take interest in these activities by impressing on them the fact that an educational community is innovative, peace-loving and involved in community affairs. Such experimentation will have to continue and hence the need for flexibility, periodic review and autonomy and the host of other institutional safeguards spelt out in the concluding sections.

ISSUES FOR CONSIDERATION

Some issues arising from the foregoing discussions, which should find a way as constitutional or legal provisions into our educational structures, are discussed. The need for consensus, application of sunset laws to avoid obsolescence, special considerations and structures because of the altruistic nature of the pursuit etc are some of the directions indicated.

Universalization of Education: Need for Consensus

Fortunately for us, there is a general consensus about universalization of elementary education as our credo. This issue has to be beyond politics – in fact, the whole basis for access to educational opportunities at all levels has to be a non-party matter and discussion of its aspects should be beyond party politics an cut across party lines. All major political parties have put it high on their agenda. It is also a positive factor that successive governments have expressed their priority for education. This has now been made an important component of National Human Development Initiative (NHDI) and also the Prime Minister's Special Action Plan. In a situation when the need for strong political commitment is being increasingly felt, these proclaimed intentions of the government are certainly welcome, and help to keep the momentum alive.

When education has had a strong and consistent political commitment in the State, the tangible achievements it can mark, is indeed remarkable. As far back as 1819, the ruler of Travancore in south Kerala called for the State to meet the cost of education. Facilities were provided for everyone to have access to education either free or at a small nominal cost. The State continued to make progress and Universal Literacy was achieved in 1991. The State continues to top the literacy chart even in the Census 2001. The case is cited to indicate the importance of enlightened leadership with progressive views to achieve goals.

Educational Opportunity as a Fundamental Right

Education is a value in itself and is the bedrock on which any edifice of equality of opportunity can be erected. It opens the road to progress and literacy is a measure of human development. It is easier to plan for sound economic development and a stable political system in an educated society. There is, therefore, every reason to canvass for Right to Education being incorporated as a Fundamental Right.

Under the Constitution as originally enacted, education was primarily a State subject. The relevant entry in the State List read "Education including universities subject to the provisions of entire 63,64,65 and 66 of List I and 25 of List III" Thus education was exclusively a responsibility of the States, the Central Government being concerned directly with certain areas like coordination, determination of standards in technical and higher education etc. In 1976, by a constitutional amendment education became the joint responsibility of the Central and State Government. The Constitution (Forty-second Amendment) Act, omitted Entry 11 from the State List and amplified Entry 25 in the Concurrent List. Entry 25 of the Concurrent List. Entry 25 of the Concurrent List which, as so amplified, no reads:

> "25. Education, including technical education, medical education and universities, subject to the provisions of entries 63,64,65 and 66 of List I; vocational and technical training of labour."

The implication of this amendment is that education has become a Concurrent Subject which enables the Central Government to legislate in such fields as, for example, school education.

Apart form this concurrent sphere, the Constitution places certain educational matters within the exclusive jurisdiction of the Union. These are: maintenance of Central Universities and institutions of national importance, declared as such by Parliament by law; all Union agencies and institutions for professional, vocational or technical training or for promotion of special studies or research; and the coordination and determination of standards in institutions of higher education or research and scientific and technical institutions.

Article 28 provides that no religious instruction shall be provided in any educational institution wholly maintained out of State funds. Article 29 further provides that no citizen shall be denied admission into any educational institution maintained by the State or receiving aid out of State funds, on grounds only of religion, race, caste, language or any of them. According to article 30 , all minorities, whether based on religion or language, shall have the right to establish and administer educational institutions of their choice. In addition, the State shall not, in granting aid to educational institutions discriminate against any educational institution on the ground that it is under the management of a minority, whether based on religion or language.

Besides, some of the Directive Principles, set out in Part IV of the Constitution, also have a bearing on national educational policy. For instance, article 45 enjoins that the 'State' shall endeavour to provide for free and compulsory education for all children until they complete the age of fourteen years. Article 46 requires the 'State' to promote with special care the educational interests of the weaker sections of the people, which include, in particular, the Scheduled Castes and Scheduled Tribes.

Article 350A places a special responsibility on the Government to safeguard the interests of the children belonging to linguistic minority groups and to see that they have adequate facilities to receive at least primary education through their own mother tongue. Article 351 further places a special responsibility on the Government of India for promoting the spread of Hindi language and for its development so that it may serve as a medium of expression for all the elements of the composite culture of India.

Yet another provision in the Constitution which has an indirect but significant bearing upon the role of the Government of India in education is entry 20 of List III, which is concerned with "Economic and Social Planning". Education Planning being an essential element of economic and social planning, the Government of India and the State Governments have to work together in preparing and implementing the national plans for the reconstruction of education. The Government of India are also responsible under the Constitution for the administration of the Union Territories and have for this purpose executive and legislative authority for all subject including education.

EVOLUTION POLICY

It will be seen that the Constitution of independent India made new demands on the education system of the country. Broadly speaking, the first and the foremost educational demand was that of universal elementary education. Another important demand was to provide equal opportunity to all the people emanating from India's decision to become a democratic republic.

Thus a major task before the country was to reorient the system of education so as to adjust it to the changing needs and aspirations of the people. Consequently the post-independence period was marked by the examination of our education system by several commissions and committees. The most notable among them were three: (i) the University Education Commission appointed 'to report on Indian University Education and suggest improvements and changes'- to suit present and future requirements of the country, (ii) the Secondary Education Commission was set up to examine the prevailing system of secondary education in the country and suggest measures for its reorganisation and improvement, and (iii) the Education Commission of 1964-66.

1. The University Education Commission

— wanted Indian higher education to be built on the foundations of Indian history and philosophy and so commended the right balance between the life material and the life spiritual in its content;

— emphasised the need for quality teachers and new methods such last utorial system;

— made recommendations in respect of examinations reforms;

— advocated the mother tongue as medium of instruction;

— emphasised the need for oral and religious education;

— expressed concern over the deteriorating standards and recommended raising of the college age, implying and eleven year schooling followed by a three year degree course;

— pleaded for better admission procedures and recruitment of teachers based on merit.

2. The Secondary Education Commission

— defined the scope of secondary education and recommended to make it a terminal stage, as well as a preparation for higher education;

— recommended the addition of a practical bias to the study of theorctical courses;

— argued for the mother tongue as the medium of instruction in the entire school stage;

— recommended dynamic methods of teaching;

— advocate for the introduction of moral and religious education with a view to character building;

— emphasised the need for guidance services in education;

— suggested measures to reform system of examination.

The question of evolving a national policy on education in its various aspects had come up before the Parliament time and again and the Members had evinced keen interest in the subject. Moving a resolution in Lok Sabha on May 1, 1964 on 'National Policy on Education', a private member Shri Siddheshwar Prasad charged that it deserved. He said that education policy of the Government lacked clarity, a definite philosophy and uniformity. He desired a Committee comprising members of Parliament be set up to go into the question of a national policy on education in all its aspect. The idea for formulating a national policy on education was also supported by other members.

Intervening in the debate, the then Minister of Education agreed that there should be a national and coordinated policy on education. He announced that the Government had decided to appoint a National Commission comprising outstanding educationists to go into all the aspects of education in the country. As such, in his view, a Committee of members of Parliament would serve no purpose. He requested the member to withdraw the resolution which was, by leave of the House, withdrawn.

2

ELEMENTARY EDUCATION

Universalisation of Elementary Education (UEE) has been accepted as a national goal in India since Independence. The founding fathers of our Constitution recognised UEE as a crucial input for nation building. The Directive Principles of State Policy envisage that the state shall endeavor to provide free and compulsory education for children up to 14 years of age within a period of 10 years. The National Education Policies so far have reiterated the constitutional directive. The National Policy on Education 1986 resolves to provide free and compulsory education of satisfactory quality to all children up to 14 years of age before the commencement of the twenty first century.

The colonial regime prior to our Independence in 1947 established a system of education that had limited access and denied mass education. It gave greater emphasis on conformism to socio-political and economic systems obtaining in the country in those times. Macaulay explicitly stated that the objective of the education system was to create a new breed of Indians as similar to Europeans as possible. It was on account of this that the Indian National Movement developed a strong critique of the British System that only imparted 'learning skills' and not 'life skills' and that did not respect Indian traditions. The national movement also expressed the global sentiment of education for all and Gopal Krishna Gokhale's Compulsory Education Bill reflected the spirit of India's freedom movement.

The imperatives of the colonial education policy promoted alternatives, notable being Mahatma Gandhi's "education for life" and Rabindra Nath Tagore's approach of education for self-development, reflected through Shantiniketan. Dr. Zakir Hussain's thrust on 'Nayee Taleem' was also based on Gandhiji's philosophy of education for life. Gandhiji's emphasis on "Swawalamban" sprang from his belief that the State was not the best agency to promote education. He believed that education is a process of empowerment. It integrates physical, mental and emotional development. He stressed that education must promote respect for manual labour rather than abhorrence for it.

The fervour for freedom and patriotism to achieve "swawalamban", made our leaders search for an alternative approach to elementary education. Article 41 and 45 of the Constitution enunciating the Directive Principles of State Policy on education provided the basis for the new approach. 14 States and 4 Union Territories enacted Legislation for free and compulsory primary education. All States have exempted children from tuition fee up to upper primary classes. However, compulsion has not been enforced due to socio-economic and political considerations.

EXPANSION AND GROWTH OF ELEMENTARY EDUCATION

The thrust of the Central and State Governments in universalising elementary education so far has been on three aspects namely, universal access, universal retention and universal achievement. Concerted efforts made in these areas have resulted in significant expansion of elementary education in the country. The number of primary schools has increased from 2.10 lakh in 1950-51 to 5.90 lakh and number of upper primary schools from 13,000 to 1.71 lakh respectively in 1995-96. During this period, Gross Enrolment Ratio (GER) at primary levels has increased from 43% in 1950-51 to 104.% in 1995-96. 95% of the rural population in the country have a primary school within 1 kilometre and 85% an upper primary school within a distance of 3 kilometres. With 15 Crore children enrolled and 3o lakh teachers, we have one of the largest elementary education systems in the world. The proportion of girls in classes I-VIII as also women teachers has increased steadily.

Results of efforts towards UEE

No. of Institutions (in lakhs)

	1950-51	*1995-96*
Primary Schools: Classes I-V	2.10	5.90
Upper Primary Schools: Classes VI-VIII	0.13	1.71
Total	2.23	7.61
No. of Teachers (in lakhs)		
Primary Schools: Classes I-V	5.38	17.40
Upper Primary Schools: Classes VI-VIII	0.36	11.65
Total	6.24	29.05

Gross Enrolment

	1950-51	*1995-96*
Primary Stage		
Total Enrolment (in million)	19.2	109.73
Gross Enrolment Ratio percentage	43.1	104.30
Upper Primary Stage		
Total Enrolment (in million)	3.1	41.01
Gross Enrolment Ratio percentage	12.0	67.20

Quality Improvement

The quality of elementary education has been one of the major concerns right from 1950s. The National Policy on Education, 1986 brought to the forefront the need for quality improvement in terms of learning achievement of children. As a result, greater efforts have been made to impart competency based learning, particularly from 1990 when the Minimum Levels of Learning (MLLs) were introduced. A clear shift from teacher dominated teaching to a child centred approach has been observed in most states. Integrated Textbooks which include workbooks are replacing traditional books. A large number of teaching, learning and reading materials have been developed, with active participation of teachers and NGOs. Efforts are continuing to promote competency based learning both at primary and upper primary levels by re-orienting and training teachers. Results so far have been encouraging.

Policy and Planning

The period after Independence saw a linear expansion of the elementary education system through allocation of additional resources. It was in 1964 that the Central Government recognised the need to take a holistic view of education and appointed the Education Commission. The Commission was entrusted with the task of evolving a national system of education. It recommended a radical transformation in the prevailing education system and highlighted the need for the "common school approach" to promote equity and social justice. The first National Policy on Education, 1968 recommended free and compulsory elementary education and equalisation of educational opportunities especially for girls and children belonging to SCs and STs. The National Policy on Education 1986 and its Programme of Action, was enunciated on the basis of a detailed review of the country's educational performance. The policy resolves to achieve UEE by 2000 AD.

The plan allocations for elementary education have increased steadily, though still not adequate to fulfil the constitutional commitments. Fifty years of freedom have seen higher levels of spending by the Central and State Governments to provide quality of education for all. Better school infrastructure, more and better-paid school teachers, timely availability of subsidised or free text books in regional languages, provision of scholarships, uniforms and mid day meals have all received attention of state governments who are the main providers of elementary education. The Central Government increased its allocations for elementary education after 1976 when education became a concurrent subject. These allocations were aimed at providing additional funds to resource poor states on the basis of the principle of equalisation and for quality improvement.

The period following the adoption of National Policy on Education (NPE), 1986 saw the introduction of a number of centrally sponsored schemes to cater to the specific needs of the elementary education sector. These included Operation Blackboard to improve school environment, enhance retention and learning achievement of children by providing minimum essential facilities in all primary schools; restructuring and strengthening of Teacher Education to upgrade pedagogical skills of teachers through establishment of dedicated teacher training institutes at District level (DIETS); Non-formal Education Programme to provide alternative education facilities for girls, working children and children in far flung areas; Minimum Levels of Learning to improve learning achievements of children; and the National Programme -of Nutritional Support to Primary Education, commonly known as Mid-day Meal Scheme, to provide nutritional support to children in primary classes.

Plan expenditure on elementary education has increased to nearly 50% of Central expenditure on Education. States continue to discharge the main responsibility for management, expansion and maintenance of schools. Since there is considerable variation in their fiscal capacity to do so, there is need for targeted interventions to improve primary education in such states.

External Assistance

Following the World Conference for Education for All (EFA) in Jomtien (Thailand) in March 1990 there is a greater commitment and willingness on the part of multilateral and bilateral aid agencies to invest in primary education in developing countries. A major internationally assisted programme namely District Primary Education Programme (DPEP) was launched in 1992 with assistance from World Bank and European Union.

The programme adopts a holistic approach to promote primary education through decentralized planning and integrated programming at district level. The programme has been extended to 149 districts in 14 States in 1997. The Lok Jumbish and Shiksha Karmi Projects are two other successful internationally assisted projects. Lok Jumbish, meaning a people's movement for UEE, has a holistic understanding about the problem of UEE and is implemented by establishing an interface between the local community, the teaching profession, the educational administration and the learners. The Shiksha Karmi Project envisages a paradigm shift in delivery of primary education. Inspired by the concept of barefoot teachers, the project has effectively responded to the problem of teacher absenteeism in the remote and inaccessible areas of Rajasthan.

Internationally assisted projects for basic education have focussed attention on decentralisation, people's participation, construction of school buildings, development of innovative teaching learning materials, participative teacher training, enhancement of institutional capacities and improvement in learning levels. The overall strategy and approach of these projects gives priority to low literacy areas, girls and disadvantaged sections of society.

Decentralisation and Community Mobilisation

The process of decentralisation has been an encouraging feature of our efforts to universalise elementary education. NPE, 1986 visualises direct community involvement in the form of Village Education Committees (VECs) for management of elementary education. The POA, 1992 emphasised micro-planning as a process of designing a family-wise and child-wise plan of education by which every child regularly attends a school or a NFE centre, continues his or her education at a place suitable to him/her and completes at least eight years of schooling or its equivalent at the NFE centre.

The Seventy-third and Seventy-fourth Constitutional Amendments have hastened the process of community management of elementary schools. These amendments have created a congenial ambience for the Panchayat Raj Institutions (PRIs) to play a more dynamic role. These institutions now provide a greater voice to women, scheduled castes and scheduled tribes. Increasingly PRIs and VECs are becoming involved in social mobilisation, planning and supervision for UEE. The introduction of micro-planning and school mapping have brought the school closer to the community while sensitising people to issues and problems in their local schools.

Recent trends in community participation indicate a greater thrust on empowerment of communities. Mobilising the communities to take responsibility to ensure quality education for every child is the core strategy of several innovative initiatives in elementary education including DPEP, LJP, SKP and BEP. Genuine community involvement is the key factor for the success of LJP and SKP in Rajasthan. LJP has had a positive effect on the empowerment of locally elected people, especially women at village level who are often active members of the LJ core teams and Mahila Samoohs.

The VECs, carefully formed and trained through environmental building activities in the LJ, are actively involved in school matters. SKP has constituted VECs in 2000 villages to promote community involvement in primary education and encourage village level planning. DPEP is making useful investments in orientation and training of VEC members. An important role of the VEC is to mobilise resources for maintenance, repair and construction of school buildings. The VECs also help in determining the school calendar and school timings in consultation with the local community.

Roel of NGOs

NGOs are emerging as important partners in efforts of the Central and State Governments towards UEE. They have been instrumental in mobilising social support for UEE, development of socially relevant curriculum, contextual teaching learning materials, innovative teacher training, pedagogic renewal, review and evaluation of educational experiments, action research for UEE, and designing of alternative education programmes. The participation of NGOs together with community support has helped to improve the physical conditions and environment of elementary schools as well as promotion of education for girls and children belonging to SCs and STs and working children. As of now, nearly 750 NGOs are supplementing the Governmental efforts towards UEE by rendering cooperation and resource support to Non-formal Education with assistance from the Government.

Over the years, the Centre and the States have made considerable investments in promoting elementary education. The Fifth All India Educational Survey reflects that 94.06 per cent of the rural population was served with primary schools/ sections within a walking distance of one kilometre and 85.39 per cent of them was served with middle school/section within a distance of three kilometres.

Despite this level of expansion of education, vast ground is yet to be covered for fulfilling the constitutional mandate of UEE. Drop-out rates are significant: retention of children in schools is low : wastage is considerable (in 1987-88 drop-out rates were 46.97 in classes I to V and 62.29 in classes I to VIII). There are striking disparities in access to elementary education - disparities as between regions, rural and urban areas, boys and girls, the affluent and the deprived and the minorities and the others. The clientele to be serviced in the age-group of 5-14 is of the order of eighteen crores, constituting about twenty-seven per cent of the population, according to 1981 Census.

Operation Blackboard

The scheme of Operation Blackboard was started in 1987-88 to bring about substantial improvement in facilities in primary schools with the aim of improving retention. It has three interdependent components, namely, provision of (i) a building comprising atleast two reasonably large all-weather rooms with a deep verandah and separate toilet facilities for boys and girls (ii) atleast two teachers in every school, as far as possible one of them a woman, and (iii) essential teaching-learning material including blackboards, maps, charts, toys and equipment for work experience. Funds for construction of school buildings are provided mainly from rural development schemes. Funds for the other two components are provided by the Department of Education. The scheme envisaged coverage of primary schools in all the blocks/municipal areas in the country in a phased manner.

In order to operationalise the revised policy of the government regarding school facilities the following three subschemes are proposed under Operation Blackboard during the Eighth Plan :

i) Continuation of the ongoing Operation Blackboard to cover the remaining schools identities in the seventh Plan.

ii) Expansion of the scheme of Operation Blackboard to provide three teachers and three class rooms to Primary schools where enrolment exceeds 80.

iii) Extension of the scope of Operation Blackboard to upper primary schools.

Minimum Levels of Learning (MLL)

The strategy to improve learning acquisition in schools focuses attention on what is happening in the classroom, and seeks to bring the principles of equity and quality to bear upon it. The strategy aims at laying down learning outcomes expected from basic education at a realistic, relevant and functional level, and prescribing the adoption of measures that will ensure that all children who complete a stage of schooling achieve these outcomes. These outcomes define the MLL.

The following are the different steps for introduction of MLL in schools:

(i) an assesment of the existing level of learning achievement;

(ii) a definition of the MLL for the area and the time- frame within which it will be achieved;

(iii) reorientation of teaching practices to competency based teaching; (iv) an introduction of contiguous, comprehensive evaluation of students learning; (v) review of textbooks and revision, if required;

(vi) provision of inputs as necessary including provision of physical facilities, teacher training, supervision and evaluation, etc., to improve learning acquisition of MLL.

The aim of the MLL strategy is also to provide to the system a measure for performance and efficiency analysis. The endeavour will be to monitor learning achievement to direct greater resources where levels of learning are lower and to consicously accelerate the pace of development in the needy areas, thereby reducing the disparities and equalising standards. Ultimately this will lead to improvement of the quality and the performance of the system.

During 1991-92, the Ministry provided financial assistance to 18 projects under the scheme 'experimental and innovative projects' for implementation of MLL programme. These projects covered 2000 schools, 3,00,000 students and 8,000 Teachers. A sum of Rs.69 lakh was given to them for conducting their activities. These projects have also continued their activities during 1992-93. A small team of resource persons has been constituted to provide necessary guidance to the project directors. This team will also assist in providing intensive orientation to teachers and state personnel. In addition, action has been initiated to prepare and distribute test items to complete the Item Bank for all the three subjects.

SCHEME OF OPERATIONALISING MICRO-PLANNING

Micro- Planning, a process of designing a family-wise and child-wise plan of action for education has been conceived as a major strategy for achieving the Universalisation of Elementary education (UEE).

The main objective of the scheme of Micro-Planning is to ensure that every child regularly attends school or NFE centre and completes at least five years of schooling or its equivalent at the non-formal education centre and also achieves essential minimum levels of learning. The three essential aspects of UEE namely access, participation and achievement are the main tasks of micro-planning. The important components of the scheme include : participatory planning with community involvement, decentralization of administrative functions, improvement of school facilities, adoption of MLL strategy and convergence of services in the area.

The activities proposed to be undertaken are environment building, survey to ascertain educational needs, formation of Village Education Committee (VEC) for involvement of community, enrolment drive training/workshop for VEC members, teachers/volunteers, opening of new schools/NFE centres and appointment of additional teachers/shikshakarmis based on assessed educational needs, and monitoring and evaluation.

The scheme will be implemented through District Shaksharta Samitis (District Literacy Societies), DIETs, SCERTs and Non- Government Organisations (NGOs).

Non-Formal Education (NFE) System

Non-formal education has become an accepted alternative channel of education for children who cannot attend full-time schools due to various socio-economic constraints. To reach this large segment of marginalised children, we in India have been running, since 1979-80, a programme of NFE for children in the 6-14 age group, who have remained outside the formal system. These include drop-outs from formal schools, children from habitations without schools, working children, children who have to remain at home to do domestic chores, and girls who are unable to attend formal schools for a variety of reasons.

The enlarged and modified version of the NFE programme now in operation visualises NFE as a child-centred, environment-oriented and flexible system to meet the diverse educational needs of the geographically and socio-economically deprived sections of society. Non-formal education is designed to overcome the shortcomings of the formal school and make education a joyful activity.

Decentralised community participation through village education committees (VECs) in planning, running and overseeing the programme has been considered crucial for its success. Although the focus of the programme is on the educationally backward states, it also covers urban slums and hilly tribal and desert areas in other states as well.

Today, the programme is being implemented in 20 states and union territories through the state governments and voluntary organisations. While there are more than 226,000 NFE centres in the state sector, there are about 29,000 run by voluntary agencies. About 44 per cent of all the NFE centres are exclusively for girls, who are the main victims of socio-cultural and socio-economic factors.

The estimated enrolment capacity is about 6.3 million children. Under the NFE programme, efforts are now being made to further improve quality, allow greater flexibility to implementing agencies and relocate NFE centres on the basis of microplanning/area survey. The NFE programme is being linked to ground realities, allowing for continuous experimentation. Development and scaling-up of effective NFE models that can help the learners to learn at their own pace is a major thrust area.

The need to lay down minimum levels of learning (MLL) emerged from the basic concern that irrespective of caste, creed, location or sex, all children must be given access to education of a comparable standard. The MLL strategy is an attempt to combine quality with equity. It lays down learning outcomes in the form of competencies or levels of learning for each stage of elementary education. The strategy also prescribes adoption of measures that will ensure achievement of these levels by children both in formal schools and in NFE centres.

The focus of the MLL strategy is development of competency-based teaching and learning. Preliminary assessment of the existing levels of learning achievements has revealed that they are quite low across several districts. Minimum levels of learning in respect of three subjects, namely language, mathematics and environmental studies, have already been laid down for the primary stage. It has been stressed that the emphasis should be on concept formation rather than on content.

The burdens of non-comprehension and overload of content are forcing children to resort to rote memorisation. The issues of content versus concept, understanding versus rote memorisation, unachievable content load versus achievable set of competencies, have been integrated into the new MLL approach. Minimum levels of learning have been specified in terms of competencies expected to be mastered by every child by the end of a particular class. The programme has been initiated throughout the country with the help of voluntary agencies, research institutions and others concerned. Minimum levels of learning for the upper primary stage are now being finalised.

The role of non-formal part-time education in providing education to working children, and children in habitations without schools has been recognised since the Education Commission of 1964-66. During 1979-80, the scheme of Non-formal Education (NFE) was introduced as an alternative strategy to impart education to children, who for various reasons cannot attend formal schools.

The NPE envisaged a large and systematic programme of NFE to achieve UEE. The scheme was revised in its content and emphasis in 1987-88. Although its focus is on the ten educationally backward States, namely, Andhra Pradesh,

Arunachal Pradesh, Assam, Bihar, Jammu and Kashmir, Madhya Pradesh, Orissa, Rajasthan, Uttar Pradesh and West Bengal, it has been extended to cover urban slums, hilly, tribal and desert areas and areas with concentration of working children in the other States as well.

Under the scheme, central financial assistance is given to the States/ Union Territories in the ratio of 50:50 and 90:10 Centre-State sharing basis for running general (co-educational) and exclusively for girls centres respectively. Assistance to the extent of 100 per cent is provided to voluntary agencies for running NFE centres for experimental and innovative projects and District Resource Units.

The revised NFE scheme has been visualised as a child—centred and environment oriented system to meet the educational needs of the comparatively deprived geographical areas and socioeconomic sections of society. Other features of the scheme are its organisational flexibility, relevance of curriculum, diversity in learning activities to relate them to the learner's needs and de- centralised management. The programme is being implemented on a project basis, generally co-extensive with the community development block, each project having about 100 NFE Centres.

NCERT has been involved in the development of teaching- learning material of a standard quality in conformity with MLL designed to suit learners needs. NCERT has been sanctioned a project for the development of training modules. Under this project, NCERT has trained key persons in each State nominated by the State Government, who in turn are responsible for training the NFE supervisors and instructors. In this way multi-level training personnel has been made available to provide technical and administrative support to NFE field functionaries.

Six research institutes have been engaged to conduct the external evaluation of the scheme in 8 States, viz., Andhra Pradesh, Bihar, Gujarat, Madhya Pradesh, Orissa, Rajasthan, Uttar Pradesh and West Bengal. The institutes are likely to submit their reports during the current financial year 1992-93. A project "Computerised Planning for Education" (COPE) is being implemented to develop a Management Information System (MIS) for Non-formal Education. The project covers the entire State of Madhya Pradesh.

CULTURAL DIMENSION OF EDUCATION

Four and a half decades ago, we in India had taken a pledge through our Constitution that within a period of ten years from 1950, free and compulsory elementary education would be provided to all children up to 14 years of age. Since 1950, determined efforts were made towards the achievement of this goal. Over the years, there have been very impressive increases in the number and spread of institutions as well as enrolment.

Today, India has about 574,000 primary schools (classes I-V) and 156,000 upper primary schools (classes VI-VIII), the number of teachers in them being 1.705 million and 1.082 million respectively. The enrolment at the primary and upper primary stages is 109 million and 40 million respectively. The Indian elementary education system is thus one of the biggest such systems in the world, providing accessibility within 1 km to over 825,000 habitations covering 94 per cent of the country's population. During the past one decade the enrolment rate has grown close to 100 per cent at the primary stage.

However, universalisation of elementary education (UEE) in its totality is still an elusive goal and much ground is yet to be covered. Drop-out rates continue to be high (36.3 per cent in classes I-V and 53 per cent in classes VI-VIII), retention of children in schools is poor, achievement levels are low, and wastage is considerable. Despite increased participation of girls, disparity still exists, more particularly among scheduled castes (SCs) and scheduled tribes (STs).

In the National Policy on Education (NPE) 1986, with revised modifications in 1992, we resolved to achieve the goal of UEE by the turn of the century, emphasising three aspects:

universal access and enrolment, universal retention up to 14 years of age, and a substantial improvement in the quality of education. The resolve is spelt out unequivocally and emphatically in the programme of action (POA) 1992, which gave unqualified priority to UEE. One is therefore pinning great hopes on the new innovations and alternative strategies which are being applied to ensure that the shortcomings and inadequacies, which did not allow us to realise this goal so far, are overcome, and the new resolve will not have to be extended further.

The Education for All (EFA) Summit of the nine high-population countries held in New Delhi in December 1993, which was an offshoot of the World Conference on Education for All held in Jomtien, Thailand, in March 1990, culminated in a policy declaration and framework of strategies for its implementation. The policy declaration called for providing basic education facilities for every child and consolidating efforts towards basic education for children, youth and adults.

In the context of an integrated approach of basic education for all people, literacy and adult education programmes are to be improved and extended, eliminating disparities of access and improving the quality and relevance of basic education. It can be said that the Indian NPE 1986 and its POA 1992, while resolving to ensure free and compulsory education of satisfactory quality to all children up to 14 years of age by the year 2000, adumbrated the policy statement made at the EFA Summit.

Alternative Strategies and New Innovations

Some of the major initiatives and strategies are:

— Disaggregated target setting and decentralised microplanning, which will provide the framework of universal access and community participation.

— Strengthening alternative channels of schooling such as the non-formal education (NFE) system for those who cannot avail of conventional full-time schooling.

- Introduction of minimum levels of learning (MLLs) at primary and upper primary stages to improve learner's achievement.
- Improvement of school facilities by revamping the scheme of Operation Blackboard (OB) and connecting it to the MLL strategy.
- Establishing linkages between programmes of early childhood care and education (ECCE), primary education, literacy and UEE.
- Addressing the more difficult aspects of access, particularly to girls, disadvantaged groups and out-of-school children.
- Restructuring of teacher training in view of the changed strategies and programmes.
- Availing of external financial support for basic education.
- Launching the National Elementary Education Mission (NEEM).

Disaggregated Target Getting and Decentralised Microplanning

In India, states like Kerala, which have achieved universal literacy as well as UEE in terms of school participation with social indicators as good as those of the best among the Third World countries. On the other, we have States like Bihar and Madhya Pradesh, with indicators as bad as those of the Sub-Saharan countries.

One of the new strategies to achieve UEE is adoption of disaggregated target setting and decentralised planning. Our long experience with the pursuit of UEE has established that UEE is contextual. The contextuality varies widely across the country. Even in a State like Kerala, where participation is near universal, much requires to be done in respect of quality and achievement.

In such states, the pursuit of UEE would be mainly in the areas of quality, facilities and achievement, while in other states participation and demand aspects would need more attention. Therefore, the attempt would be to prepare district-specific and population-specific plans for UEE within the broad strategy frame of microplanning through people's participation. Microplanning has been defined as a family-wise and child-wise design of action to ensure that every child regularly attends a school or an NFE centre and completes 8 years of schooling at a pace suitable to him or her and attains an essential level of learning.

Guidelines for operationalising microplanning have been prepared and distributed to the state governments. The concepts of microplanning and local level capacity building have been given currency and efforts launched to decentralise educational planning and management. Microplanning exercises have already been undertaken in several states to ensure that all children receive primary education of satisfactory quality either through formal schools or through part-time NFE centres.

To operationalise the strategy for UEE through disaggregated target setting and decentralised planning, a new scheme titled District Primary Education Programme (DPEP) has been evolved. The concept of DPEP is a beachhead for effecting improvements and full-scale development of the entire elementary education sector. The overall goal of the programme is the reconstruction of primary education as a whole in the districts instead of piecemeal implementation of the various schemes. The fundamental principle of DPEP is capacity building at all levels to evolve further strategies which are replicable and sustainable. The specific objectives of the programme are:

— to reduce differences in enrolment, drop-out and learning achievement among gender and social groups to less than 5 per cent

— to reduce the overall primary drop-out rate to less than 10 per cent

- to raise average achievement levels by at least 25 per cent over measured baseline levels and ensure achievements of basic literacy and numeracy competencies and a minimum of 40 per cent achievement levels in other competencies by all primary school children,
- to provide, according to national norms, access for all children to primary education classes (I-V), i.e., primary schooling wherever possible or its equivalent non-formal education.

The programme would strengthen the capacity of national, state and district institutions and organisations for the planning, management and evaluation of primary education. NEEM has recently been set up to oversee, among other things, the implementation of this programme throughout the country.

PROGRAMMES OF EARLY CHILDHOOD CARE AND EDUCATION (ECCE), PRIMARY EDUCATION, LITERACY AND UEE

Early childhood care and education (ECCE) is viewed as a crucial input in the strategy of human resource development, as a feeder and support programme for primary education, and as a support service for working women of the disadvantaged sections of society. Since the age-span covered by ECCE is from conception to 6 years, emphasis has been given to a child-centred approach and play-way and activity-based learning in place of formal methods of teaching including introduction of the 3 Rs. Keeping in mind the role of ECCE as a support service in UEE, it is deliberately directed to the most underprivileged groups, those who are still outside the mainstream of formal education.

The aim of ECCE is that every child should be assured access to the fulfilment of all basic needs. It involves the total development of the child in every aspect including the physical, psychomotor, cognitive, language, emotional, social and moral. The present ECCE programmes include:

- — the integrated child development service (ICDS)
- — the scheme of assistance to voluntary organisations for running early child education (ECE) centres
- — *balwadis* and day-care centres run by voluntary agencies with government assistance
- — pre-primary schools run by state governments, municipal corporations and other agencies
- — maternal and child health services through primary health centres, sub-centres and other agencies

The ICDS is today the biggest programme of early childhood development, serving about 15 million children and 3 million mothers. Appropriate linkages are being established between ECCE programmes, primary schools, NFE centres and other related schemes of UEE.

As with all educational indicators, gender disparities are conspicuous in regard to enrolment and retention. Over the past 25 years, enrolment of girls at the primary stage has grown from 5 million to 47 million and at the upper primary stage, from 0.5 million to 16 million. But disparities persist. Today girls account for only 46 per cent of the enrolment at the primary stage and 38 per cent at the upper primary stage. The drop-out rates of girls at the primary and upper primary stages are higher than those of boys. Regional disparities are also conspicuous. The very low female literacy (20 to 29 per cent) in some of the major north Indian states causes grave concern. The rural girls are doubly disadvantaged by non-availability of educational facilities and by their domestic chores.

Concerted efforts are now on to reach out to the girl child in rural and remote areas and urban slums by designing special NFE programmes with a view to getting them back into the formal stream. The NFE programmes are being dovetailed into the total literacy campaigns (TLC) to reach out to the girls in the 10-20 age group. Programmes for continuing education are being designed to ensure that neo-literates and school-going girls have access to reading materials.

An important constraining factor for female education is the lack of women teachers in rural areas. Therefore, special efforts are being made to recruit women teachers and to augment teacher training facilities for women so that adequate numbers of qualified women teachers are available. Co-ordinated efforts are also on to provide the necessary support services to enhance their participation and performance.

We in India are unambiguous about removal of disparities and attainment of equality of education opportunities for SCs, STs and other backward sections including girls. A number of strategies aimed at accelerating their rate of enrolment and retention have been detailed and are being implemented. Because of the affirmative policies of the government, the enrolment of these categories has increased considerably at the primary stage. The participation of SCs and STs at the primary level is more or less in proportion to their share in the population. Drop-outs, though declining, continue to be significantly large [primary stage (classes I-V), SC 49 per cent, ST 64 per cent; upper primary stage (classes VI-VIII), SC 68 per cent, ST 79 per cent]. Gender disparities are conspicuous among SCs and STs.

To ensure universal access and enrolment of SC children in rural areas, priority is given to the needs of SC habitations and hamlets in opening primary and upper primary schools. For SC children access and enrolment are assured primarily in the formal schools. Where they are not able to attend these, provision is made for non-formal and distance education centres. Every ST habitation is being provided with a primary school or other suitable institution. In tribal areas, the educational plan is being implemented in an integrated manner. Pre-school education, non-formal education, elementary education and adult education are being organically linked and integrated to ensure achievement of total literacy of the entire population.

Adequate incentives are given to the children of SC, ST and other backward sections in the form of scholarships, uniforms, textbooks, stationery and midday meals. All schools, NFE centres, and pre-school centres in SC/ST habitations are being equipped with necessary infrastructural facilities in accordance with the norms laid down for Operation Blackboard and for achieving MLL. Operation Blackboard has already covered almost all schools in tribal areas. Indigent SC/ST families are given incentives to send their children, particularly girls, to school.

RESTRUCTURING OF TEACHER TRAINING

Teacher performance is the most crucial input in the field of education. In the ultimate analysis, the national policies on education have to be interpreted and implemented by teachers as much through their personal example as through teaching-learning processes. With a view to improving the quality and competence of teachers, a centrally sponsored scheme of Restructuring and Reorganisation of Teacher Education (RRTE) was launched in 1987.

During the period 1987-90, nearly 1.8 million teachers were trained under the programme of mass orientation of school teachers (PMOST). Most of them were primary and upper primary teachers. The main objective of the programme was to orient teachers in the main priorities and directions envisaged in the NPE 1986 and to improve their professional competence.

Among the other main components of the RRTE, as far as elementary education is concerned, are:

- setting up of District Institutes of Education and Training (DIETs) in all districts to provide good quality pre-service and in-service training to elementary school teachers and adult education/non-formal education personnel and to provide resource support to these systems
- organising Special Orientation Programmes for Primary Teachers (SOPT) with a view to providing training to

teachers in the use of OB materials and orienting them towards MLL strategy with a focus on teaching of language, mathematics and environmental studies

More than 300 DIETs have already become operational and have started conducting training programmes. The SOPT launched in 1993-94 is now going on in almost all states and more than 115,000 teachers have already been trained. A National Council for Teacher Education (NCTE) was set up in 1993 with statutory status for the effective implementation of all teacher education and training programmes and to achieve planned and co-ordinated development of the entire teacher education system throughout the country. The regulation and proper maintenance of norms and standards in the teacher education system is the responsibility of the NCTE.

BASIC EDUCATION

As a matter of policy and principle, India had not been seeking financial support from external agencies to implement its programmes of basic education. This situation changed in 1991-92, when a conscious and strategic decision was taken to avail of external assistance to achieve the goal of Education for All (EFA).

Today a number of agencies including the World Bank, Unesco, Unicef, Swedish International Development Agency (SIDA), International Development Association (IDA), and the British Overseas Development Agency (ODA) are sharing our concerns in this area. A new phase has, therefore, emerged — a phase of partnership between the inherent potential of the country and financial and other support from external agencies.

Launching the National Elementary Education Mission (NEEM)

With the objective of mobilising all the resources — human, financial and institutional — necessary for achieving the goal of UEE by the year 2000, a National Elementary Education

Mission (NEEM) was set up in August 1995 with the District Primary Education Programme (DPEP) as its core. This Mission will monitor and implement all the meticulously formulated strategies based on microplanning, and will ensure that free and compulsory education of satisfactory quality is provided to all children up to 14 years of age by the turn of the century.

Tamil Nadu has achieved 100% enrolment at the Primary level but the problem of retaining the children in the system has been a disturbing factor. Our Government took several incentive schemes.

1. Nutritious Meal Scheme.
2. Free Uniform for pupils of I to VIII Std.
3. Free Text books.
4. Free Chappals.
5. Free Bus Passes.
6. Free supply of slates.

These measures have helped to bring down the drop out rate from 54.9% to 19.3% at the Primary School level. To enrol and retain girls, the Tamil Nadu Government has taken a positive decision to appoint only Women teachers exclusively in primary schools up to Class V. Yet another step in this regard is the establishment of Mother Teacher Councils in all Schools to support the School system and enhance its function. It is the desire of the Tamil Nadu Government that all habitations with a population of 500 and above do have schools of their own and that all the existing 459 single Teacher Schools are converted into two teacher schools. The Operation Black Board Scheme has been fully implemented.

The Government of Tamil Nadu has also drawn up a scheme for assistance from World Bank/UNICEF to strengthen Primary Education quantitatively/qualitatively. Karnataka has traditionally accorded high priority to education. Of particular significance and satisfaction is the fact that within the sector the State accords special consideration to primary education. Over the last two decades, the School Education system in the State has expanded enormously. The, number of children in classes 1-7 has increased from 28.35 lakhs to 74.78 lakhs. The net enrolment rate of the State is estimated to be around 77% for the age group 6-10 and 48% for the age group 11-13.

While these are no doubt impressive gains made in the field of education, the issues relating to retention of quality and equity continues to engage the State Government. The drop out rates are even today unacceptably high. Recognising that enrolment in schools should not be taken as automatic and a one-time effort, the State Government has taken special measures to boost up enrolment and to enhance retention. To elaborate, a special enrolment drive was undertaken in the State during July, 1993. As many as 4.73 lakh children were either enrolled afresh or brought back to the school, system during the intensive door to door drive with the slogan 'Retain kids in School'. We intend to conduct such enrolment drives every year with the help of the community and village education committees.

In order to ensure high retention and also to provide better quality schools in the rural areas, the State Government has also introduced an entirely recast and innovative 'Akshaya Scheme'. The scheme endeavours to provide incentives to children to attend schools and also to make the school environment more attractive so as to ensure that the child enjoys going to school.

Thus, as a part of the programme every child in classes 1 to 4 is given incentive to attend school regularly through distribution of free food, textbooks and uniforms. In keeping with the programme of Action, 1992, brought out by the Union Government, the scheme also make available resources for all-round development of the child. Akshaya makes provision for musical instruments, development of school play-fields and creation of school libraries. To inculcate a siprit of adventure and enable cultural exposure. to school children, Akshaya also Provides for excursions to places of cultural and educational interest. A sum of Rs. 67 crores has been provided by the State Government for the Scheme during the current year.

The State Government is fully committed to the ambitious but essential goal of Universal Elementary Education by the year 2000 AD. It has already resolved that by the end of VIII five year plan one teacher and one class-room for every class would be provided by the Government. Accordingly, a new programme of constructing 12,000 class-rooms annually during the remaining period of 8th five, year plan has been taken up. Similarly it has been decided that 20,000 teachers would be recruited by the end of the 8th five year plan and steps have already been taken to recruit 5,000 teachers during the current year.

With the objective of improving the quality of rural schools, model schools have been established in each, assembly constituency. These schools are to be provided with all essential infrastructural facilities. These facilities, it is intended, would be extended to, other schools gradually. The State Government is also considering the possibility of inculcating cherished values of our society in these schools through specially developed curriculum in moral science.

The State Government is also laying emphasis on the all-round development of the school children. Physical education is being made integral part of the higher primary schools and it has been decided that schools having more than 4 teachers would have one teacher for physical education.

Special care is being taken by us to encourage schooling of girl students and students from backward sections of the society and scheduled caste and scheduled tribes. Thus, girl students are given free uniform and text books up to class 7 and are students belong to scheduled caste and tribes. The State Social Welfare Department has introduced a special scheme of incentives for girl students. For girls from rural areas attending 80% classes or more the State Government provides Rs. 25/- per month for 10 months for students in class 5 to 7 and Rs. 50/- for students in classes 8-10.

Special efforts have been made in the recent past to expedite the recruitment of teachers. In future recruitments to primary schools, it has been proposed, 50% posts would be reserved for women. 15% weightage is also proposed to be given to rural candidates. Also, apart from the 4% overall reservation already available to the physically handicapped, the State Government has also taken a decision to fill up posts of. music teachers in schools with qualified blind candidates only.

As far as the specific agenda items of today's meetings are concerned, we would like to mention that the State Government has already initiated action for the preparation of its programme of Action. Regarding the CABE Committee report on Decentralised Management, Karnataka already has a well established Zilla Parishad set-up and is fully committed to Decentralised Management of Education. The State has Village Education Committees at the Panchayat level.

District plans are formulated at the district level. Each State should be allowed to determine its own pace towards the decentralisa- tion. Also, a close interaction between different state governments would be very useful particularly for the States who are venturing into this area for the first time.

As for as the Yashpal Committee report is concerned no one can perhaps disagree with the view that out school children are over- burdened. There is considerable merit in the recommendations made by the Committee. However, personally of the view that the actual conditions of our schools vary so much from region to region and area to area that there cannot be one prescription for all schools in all the States. Therefore, there is need to take a look at some of the recommendations of the committee keeping in view schools and their actual conditions in the rural areas before introducing the innovations that have been suggested.

About the proposed National Commission with the statutory powers to evaluate textbooks, there is, think, need for greater clarity and explication of the proposal. That textbook should be free of communal and sectarian biases as also gender bias and that they should no be exploited for political purposes is a un-expectionable idea. The textbooks are not manipulated and that interests of students and academic excellence are the only criteria for textbook preparation is to be more carefully examined.

The CABE Committee on teachers' representation in Legislative Councils has made some far reaching recommendations. The recommendations have no doubt been made after due consideration and after taking into account the utility of having had teachers' representation in Legislative Council in the past. Hon'ble Minister for Human Resource Development for having convened this meeting of the Central Advisory Board of Education (CABE) with a view to focusing upon some of the vital aspects concerning education. It is indeed heartening to note that under the stewardship of Sri Arjun Singh, the CABE has been functioning very actively, through its various Committees. The different subjects coming up for discussion today are a reflection of the shared concern for making education effective and relevant to present-day Society.

In Andhra Pradesh, an educationally backward state, the decadal growth rate of literacy between 1981-91 is happily higher than the national average. Similarly, the state is witnessing a positive trend in education of girls. Andhra Pradesh will contribute handsomely towards the national efforts in achieving the goal "Education for All by 2000 A.D." It is in this context that the State Government are preparing the Programme of Action which is at an advanced stage.

The march towards "Education For All by 2000 A.D." and more particularly "Universalisation of Elementary Education" cannot be successful unless we evolve appropriate technologies in Education. In this context, Non-Formal Education plays a very important role.

Universal access in Andhra Pradesh is assured not only through formal and non-formal systems but also the Open School system which has been introduced in 4 districts and which has made impressive strides. Then the Government of India introducing the scheme of Orientation of Primary Teachers. The scheme may also be extended to cover every teacher atleast once in years. Any effort in this direction would not be a waste. In this regard, would strongly recommend setting up of SUB DIETs atleast in States like Andhra Pradesh where DIETS have been established in all the districts.

The magnitude of the task of School Education both in terms of scope as well as number is so large, that it calls, for proper planning and monitoring. The need for a projectised approach in education cannot be, over emphasised. Andhra Pradesh is among the select States to be covered by the District Primary Education Programme (DPEP). The Union Minister that Andhra Pradesh will successfully implement the programme.

The Residential School system in Andhra Pradesh has been the forerunner of similar efforts olike Navodaya schools. Nevertheless, the cost is so heavy that we have to think in terms of providing equally good but perhaps less costly secondary education. The second aspect is to provide prevocational education below the plus 2 stage.

The CABE Committee on the Decentralised Management of Education as well as the National Advisory Committee on reducing the academic burden (Yashpal Committee) for having completed such delicate tasks so successfully. Both these issues are of such far reaching importance that they should be subjected to more detailed discussion before this august body takes any firm decisions. The CABE Committee on Decentralisation of Management that Education cannot be complete without the community involvement and that appropriate mechanisms will have to be evolved to involve the Panchayati Raj Institutions. The 73rd Amendment Bill which is now on the statute book is itself an enabling legislation and gives wide scope to each State to evolve its own mechanisms within the basic framework, depend- ing upon each State's specificity.

The Education process, there is also a certain apprehension among every section of society that education will be adversely affected unless the linkages between Panchayati Raj institutions and the education infrastructure is properly handled. Therefore there is need for a delicate handling of the entire subject. Therefore, arrangements for education will also have to be dovetailed with arrangements procedural as well as infrastructural, in the other fields.

The process of text-book development is itself undergoing considerable evolution. Till this is stablised and till the capacities are developed at the sub-state level, it may be premature to attempt such initiatives. Audio-Visual Education can go a longway in reducing the learning burden through formal text-books. In this regard, acknowledge Government of India's assistance in provision of colour Television sets to schools.

Text-books form a vital input in both formal and non-formal education. Andhra Pradesh has a long tradition of text-books being written and produced under Government supervision by academic experts. The National struggle for freedom, Constitutional rights and duties of citizens, principles of secularism and democracy are all reflected in text-books alongwith a degree of academic excellence, appropriate for each level.

An expression of national concern through a forum like this should be sufficient to deter any attempts at such wilful distortion. As a supplementary effort we could consider constitution of a Standing Committee of CABE to continuously monitor the text-books so that any harmful deviation could invite the collective opprobrium.

EXPENDITURE ON ELEMENTARY EDUCATION

Redesign of curriculum and methodologies and a machinery

for effective implementation are mentioned as illustrations of such key result areas which need priority. Gandhiji's perception of the goal of education as being the establishment of a nonviolent and non- exploiting social and economic order. It is opined, rightly so, that Gandhiji's perception is extremely relevant, even more so now, and that the purpose of education in a modern democratic society should be attainment of the goal set out by Gandhiji in the long run.

The life-long process should help the learner to be and to become, and to acquire the discernment to unlearn when the situation demands and not to be a prisoner of outmoded dogmas and shibboleths. Seen in this perceptive the schools as well as the higher institutions of learning only Provide the "beginning education" - a right perspective which recalls to mind the old saying that education Is what remains when one forgets what all one learns at school.

The beginning education provides the foundation knowledge - a mix of manual and cognitive skills, of attitudes and values - which can help the learner to begin a life-long exploration of the self, of the community and of the world at large. Education Is a process of empowerment - power to explore - and of liberation - freedom from dogma, superstition and prejudice. From this perspective education can also emerge as an instrument of social change, of promoting the right values that should guide citizens in a modern, secular democracy.

Education must find a part of the solution to the problems facing the body politic and should foster national goals such as national unity and secularism, scientific temper and modernisation, work culture and work ethics. The acculturing role of education should be given importance as acculturation is basic and essential to education.

Four specific goals and roles of education are specifically delineated

— provide a sound knowledge base on which one can build later on

— provide opportunities to acquire skills of a diverse nature.

— provide a climate for nurture of values so as to develop character, conviction and commitment as well as the ability to understand the context and meaning for actions and decisions

— Interventionist roles and catalytic roles of education for promoting national cohesion and unity.

All these goals are in a sense eternal verities and have informed the educational philosophy of eminent thnkers of India. They also inform the policy perspective of NPE 1986. Apart from this combative role, value education has a profound positive content, based on our heritage, national goals universal perceptions. It whould lay primary emphasis on this aspect."

The importance of developing more appropriate curriculum, through new designs and planning the transaction methodologies. According to the Committee the curriculum, while full of content. tends to be selective presentation of facts; the selectivity may conceal bias and may foster wrong values. The curriculum, sometimes tends to gloss over reality out of fear that this will arouse communal passion. Thus to illustrate, the unfair treatment of SCs and STs and minorities is often glossed over, similarly, the history taught neglects the contribution of masses and work culture, an urgent national need, is ignored. The biased inclusions and exclusions follow a hidden curriculum fostering stereotypes and myths.

The perceptions of the Committee are unexceptionable and NPE 1986 inform also. Thus para 8.4 of NPE states that "the growing concern over the erosion of essential values and an increasing cynicism in society has brought to focus the need for readjustments in the curriculum in order to make education a forceful tool for the cultivation of social and moral values."

Organisational Structure

The Department of Education has been one of the four

constituent units of the Ministry of Human Resource Development. The Ministry was reorganised in October 1999, placing the Departments of Culture and Youth Affairs & Sports under a separate Ministry. In order to give thrust to the activities relating to elementary education and literacy, the erstwhile Department of Education has also been reorganised, creating a separate Department of Elementary Education and Literacy. The remaining activities of the Department of Education are to be handled in the redesignated Department of Secondary Education and Higher Education . In the matters relating to these two Departments, the Minister for Human Resource Development is assisted by a Minister of State. Each Department is headed by a Secretary to the Government of India. Presently, Secretary, Department of Secondary and Higher Education is also incharge of the Department of Elementary Education and Literacy. He is assisted by a Special Secretary and an Additional Secretary.

The Department is organised into bureaux, divisions, branches, desks, sections and units. Each bureau is under the charge of a Joint Secretary or Joint Educational Advisor, an officer of equivalent rank.

Subordinate Offices/Autonomous Organisations

The Department has four subordinate offices and several autonomous organisations including Central Universities, Institutes of Technology and other institutions of higher learning and research. The subordinate offices are:

— The Directorate of Adult Education (DAE), New Delhi;

— The Central Hindi Directorate (CHD), New Delhi;

— The Commission for Scientific and Technical Terminology (CSTT), New Delhi; and

— The Central Institute of Indian Languages (CIIL), Mysore.

The important autonomous organisations are:-

— The University Grants Commission (UGC), New Delhi, a national level organisation responsible for coordination and maintenance of standards in the area of higher education;

— The All India Council for Technical Education (AICTE), New Delhi, responsible for coordination and maintenance of standards in the area of technical education;

— The National Council for Teacher Education (NCTE), New Delhi, responsible for maintenance of standards and for development of teacher education;

— The National Council of Educational Research and Training (NCERT), New Delhi, a national level resource institution in the school education sector; and

— The National Institute of Educational Planning and Administration (NIEPA), New Delhi, a national level resource institution, specialising in educational planning and administration.

The names of organisations/institutions in various sectors of education under the Ministry are given in the Annexure.

Functions of the Department

Education is a concurrent subject. Concurrency implies a meaningful partnership between the Union Government and the States. The National Policy on Education (NPE), 1986, clearly define the roles of the Union Government and the States.

The Union Government has a responsibility to reinforce the national and integrative character of education, to maintain quality and standards, to study and monitor the educational requirements of the country in regard to manpower for development, to cater to the needs of research and advanced study, to look after the international aspects of education, culture, and human resource development and in general to promote excellence at all levels of the educational system.

The Department has been closely interacting with the States and Union Territories to fulfil the role assigned by the

NPE. The Department has also been striving to achieve the objective of development of human potential in the education sector through a countrywide network of field organisations, academic institutions, etc.

Progressive Use of Hindi

An official language implementation committee has been set-up under the chairmanship of the Joint Secretary (language) for implementation of the official language policy of the Union Government. The committee considers the problems faced in the acceleration of the use of Hindi in the Department and suggests measures to solve the same. The committee also reviews the progress made in the use of Hindi in sub-ordinate offices and autonomous bodies under this Department.

All notifications, resolutions, general orders, circulars, advertisements, etc., are issued bilingually. All name-plates, notices, rubber stamps, seals, letter heads, etc., are prepared both in Hindi and English languages. The communications received in Hindi are replied to in Hindi. The performance budget and annual administrative report of the Department are prepared both in Hindi and English. As more than 80 per cent of the staff possesses working knowledge of Hindi, the Department has been notified under rule 10(4) by the Department of Official Languages. This Department has notified 32 offices, under its control, under rule 10(4). A number of sections in the Department where more than 80 per cent of the staff possesses working knowledge of Hindi, have been specified under rule 8(4) to use Hindi in their official work. Staff members who do not have working knowledge of Hindi are being deputed for training in Hindi. Similarly, the employees who require and do not possess knowledge of Hindi typing and stenography are being imparted training.

All efforts are being made in the Department of Education to promote the use of Hindi in official work. The Department of Secondary Education & Higher Education, Department of

Elementary Education and Literacy, its subordinate offices and autonomous bodies are celebrating the year, from 14 September, 1999 to 14 September, 2000, as official language golden jubilee year. In the month of September 1999 a Hindi Pakhwara was held and a number of competitions were organised during the period.

The winners placed at first, second and third positions were given awards in these competitions. In addition, a number of employees were given consolation prizes. An appeal was issued from the offices of the Minister and the Secretary in the Department of Education urging all officers and staff to accelerate the use of Hindi in their official work. As in the last year, the first sub-committee in the Committee of Parliament on Official Languages conducted inspections of a number of offices in the Department to acquaint itself with the progress made in the use of Hindi. The required follow-up action was also taken.

FUTURE CHALLENGES

The country has undoubtedly been successful in evolving a national structure for elementary education in the last fifty years. Primary education is now provided in the mother tongue or regional language in all the States and UTs. There has been substantial increase in access to elementary education, with reduced class, caste and sectional disparities. First generation learners, girls and the under privileged sections of society have been provided with unique opportunities for vertical mobility. Literacy standards have substantially improved across all the States and UTs. National Literacy rate has increased from 15.% in 1951 to 52.% in 1991. An impressive academic support system has been built up at national and state level through NCERT, NIEPA, NCTE, SCERTs, CIEMATs, DIETs, BRCs, and CRCs to provide technical support and guidance to the elementary education system.

Despite substantial achievements, the task of UEE is far from complete. Schools and enrolments have certainly increased but so have the number of out of school children. The country today has one of the largest illiterate populations in the world. Caste, gender, class and regional disparities in UEE though reduced, are still glaring and persistent. While the demand for quality education is showing perceptible increase because of improved awareness and social mobilisation through organised efforts such as TLCs and PLCs, supply is generally inadequate.

The educational administration in most states and UTs is yet to effectively tackle endemic problems concerning shortage of teachers, teacher absenteeism, inadequate and improperly designed school buildings, lack of teaching learning equipment, need based teacher training, and a curriculum related to real life requirements. Teachers' esteem in a society that worshipped Gurus is low. They are called upon to do variety of non-teaching jobs, leaving little time for teacher-pupil interaction. Teacher education, considered crucial to improve quality of education, has not made the vital difference in the classroom.

A traditional style of administration and the tendency for centralisation is impeding genuine people's participation and effective partnership with NGOs. Lack of transparency and rigid procedures have not facilitated confidence building measures necessary for empowerment of women and the poor

Imperative in these shortfalls is the need to consolidate the gains, design specifically targeted programmes to reach the unreached, improve quality of education making it contextually relevant and related to real life, and make UEE a social movement. Research in educational planning, management and training should be given greater attention in our endeavour to improve learning achievement of children in schools.

The recent measures initiated by the Government, namely DPEP, Mid-day Meal Programme and the proposal for NEEM, the National Programme Media advocacy and Publicity for UEE and the Joint GOI-UN System Education Programme are expected to address some of these challenges more effectively. The proposed National Elementary Education Mission should evolve strategies for reaching the unreached and achieving the goal of UEE within a given time-frame in a systematic, sustained and integrated manner by involving all segments of civil society in this national endeavour.

The resolve of the Government to make elementary education a fundamental right of all children of 6-14 years is expected to spur the government and non-government sectors to take necessary measures to achieve UEE. It is a demonstration of political will and administrative resolve to achieve UEE and eradicate illiteracy. Efforts of the Government to mobilise resources for education to the extent of 6% of GDP will also help in hastening the process of universalising elementary education.

Undeniably, we face a gigantic challenge to achieve UEE. Provision of free and compulsory education to all children until they complete the age of 14 years is a Directive Principle of the Constitution of India. Since 1950 determined efforts have been made towards the achievement of this goal. Over the years there has been a very impressive increase in the number and spread of institutions as well as enrolment.

The National Policy on Education (NPE), 1986, and its Programme of Action (POA) gave unqualified priority to UEE and introduced many innovations.

First, the emphasis was shifted from enrolment per so to enrolment as well as retention. Secondly, the NPE, 1986 sought to adopt an array of meticulously formulated strategies based on micro-planning, to ensure children's retention at school. Thirdly, the NPE, 1986 recognised that unattractive school environment, unsatisfactory condition of buildings and Insufficiency of instructional material function as demotivating factors for children and their parents.

The Policy, therefore, palled for a drive for a substantial improvement of primary schools and provision of support services. To this end, the scheme of Operation Blackboard was conceived. Fourthly, the NPE, 1986 commanded the adoption, at the primary stage, of a child-centred and activity-based process of learning. Fifthly, the NPE, 1986 and its POA postulated a large programme of restructuring of teacher education.

The NPE, 1986 also sought to address the most difficult aspect of access, viz., access to education of millions of girls and working children. A large and systematic programme of Non-Formal Education (NFE) was introduced as an integral component of the strategy to achieve UEE.

A positive externality of the Total Literacy campaigns, has been that in many districts covered by the campaign there has been an upsurge in the demand for primary education. This has confirmed the need to pay more attention to the "demand side" in strategies for achieving UEE and highlighted the need for a disaggregated approach to the problem of UEE.

Significant developments have taken place in the area of learner achievement. The NPE, 1986 provided for laying down Minimum Levels of Learning (MLL). MLL have been laid down for the primary stage with the intention of reducing the curriculum load and making it more relevant and functional for those children who have no support for learning at home or outside the school. It is now acknowledged that UEE cannot be accepted as having been achieved unless children passing out of school acquire MLL; achievement has come to be assigned equal importance alongwith access and retention.

Another important development was the World Conference on Education for All (EFA) held in March 1990, in Jomtien, Thailand. In order to harness increased donor interest in the basic education, as a result of the Conference, it was decided to formulate comprehensive basic education projects in educationally backward States. EFA Projects have been taken up in Bihar and Rajasthan with external assistance.

The NPE, 1986 was reviewed during 1990-92 and certain modifications necessitated by the developments since its adoption were effected. The Revised Policy Formulations (RPF) brought about following modifications :

i) Achieving essential levels of learning has been specifically incorporated as one of the thrust areas.

ii) Scope of Operation Blackboard (OB) was enlarged to provide three reasonably large rooms and three teachers in every primary school; it was also decided to extend OB to the upper primary stage.

iii) It was specifically laid down that at least 50 per cent of the teachers recruited in future should be women.

iv) Taking a realistic view of the enormous task of achieving UEE in its entirety (access, retention as well as achievement), the RPF envisage that free and compulsory education of satisfactory quality should be provided to all children upto 14 years of age before the commencement of the twenty-first century.

v) Taking note of the effectiveness of the Mission mode in social sectors, particularly literacy, the RPF envisage launching of a national mission to ensure the achievement of UEE by the year 2000.

In the Eighth Plan the strategy for UEE envisages adoption of disaggregated target setting and decentralised planning. The attempt would be to prepare district-specific, population-specific plans for UEE within the broad strategy frame of Microplanning through people's participation and introduction of Minimum Levels of Learning (MLL) in schools to improve learner achievement. Microplanning will provide the framework for universal access and universal participation while MLL would be the strategy frame for universal achievement. The Department of Education is formulating an IDA assisted project for funding district primary education projects on these lines with preference being given to educationally backward districts and districts where Total Literacy Campaigns have generated a demand.

3

DEVELOPMENT IN FIVE YEAR PLANS

Education is the most important single factor in achieving rapid economic development and technological progress and in creating a social order founded on the values of freedom, social justice and equal opportunity. Programmes of education lie at the base of the effort to forge the bonds of common citizenship, to harness the energies of the people, and to develop the natural and human resources of every part of the country. Developments of the past decade have created a momentum for economic growth; yet, there are large deficiencies in the sphere of education, which must be removed speedily if progress is to be sustained and enduring. It is one of the major aims of the Third Plan to expand and intensify the educational effort and to bring every home within its fold, so that from now on, in all branches of national life, education becomes the focal point of planned development.

In the field of general education, as distinguished from technical education, the main emphasis in the Third Plan will be on the provision of facilities for the education of all children in the age group 6—11, extension and improvement of the teaching of science at the secondary and university stages, development of vocational and technical education at all levels, expansion and improvement of facilities for the training of teachers for each stage of education, and increase in scholarships, freeships and other assistance. There will be special concentration on the education of girls, and the existing disparities in levels of development in education between boys and girls will be substantially reduced.

All elementary schools will be oriented to the basic pattern. Reorganisation of university education along the lines of the three year degree course will be completed, and facilities for post-graduate studies and research work will be further expanded and improved. At all stages of education, the aim must be to develop both skill and knowledge and a creative outlook, a feeling of national unity which stands above region, cast and language, and an understanding of common interests and obligations.

Over the decade 1951-61, the number of students increased from 23.5 million to 43.5 million. The increase in the number of pupils in the age-group 6—11 was 79 per cent, in the age-group 11—14, 102 per cent, and in the age-group 14—17, 139 per cent. The proportion of children in these groups attending schools rose respectively from 43 to 61 per cent, 13 to 23 per cent and 5 to 12 per cent. In the course of the Third Plan, the total number of pupils at school is expected to increase by 20.4 million, 15.3 million in the age-group 6—11, 3.5 million in the age-group 11—14 and 1.6 million in the age-group 14—-17.

During the first two Plans, the number of schools increased by 73 per cent from 230,555 to 398,200, increase in the number of primary schools being 63 per cent, in middle schools 191 per cent, and in high schools 128 per cent. Progress in basic education at the elementary level is reflected in the increase in the proportion of junior basic schools and senior basic schools from 16 per cent to 29 per cent and from 3 per cent to 30 per cent respectively. Reorganisation of secondary education has mainly taken the form of conversion of high schools into higher secondary schools, establishment of multipurpose schools providing for a variety of courses, and expansion of teaching facilities both for general science and science as an elective subject.

The All-India Educational Survey, which was undertaken during 1957-59, revealed important gaps in the distribution of educational institutions. Thus, for the country as a whole in 1957, about 29 per cent of rural habitations and about 17 per cent of the rural population were not served by any school. In some States these proportions were very much higher.

Progress in establishing new schools during the first two Plans was relatively greater in respect of middle and high schools than in the case of primary schools. With the provision of educational facilities for the entire population in the age-group 6—11, this trend will be corrected to a considerable extent in the course of the Third Plan. The Plan envisages increase in the number of primary schools by 73,000, of middle schools by 18,100 and of high schools by 5,200. The total number of schools in the country will go up by about 24 per cent to about 494,500.

The proportion of trained teachers has increased during the period 1951—61 from 59 to 65 per cent in primary schools, from 53 to 65 per cent in middle schools, and from 54 to 68 per cent in high schools. These figures suggest that progress in providing trained teachers has not been on an adequate scale. As a result of the more intensive programmes proposed for the Third Plan, the proportion of trained teachers in each category is expected to rise to about 75 per cent. It is considered that the targets in respect of trained teachers at present formulated by States should be regarded as provisional and every effort made to improve upon them.

There has been a large increase in the number of students in universities and colleges, the total enrolment for arts, science and commerce courses being 360,000 in 1950-51, 634,000 in 1955-56 and about 900,000 in 1960-61. During the Second Plan, for the country as a whole, the proportion of students taking science courses increased from 33 per cent to about 36 per cent. In some States progress was specially marked, but there are others where there are still considerable lags.

The Third Plan envisages that of the increase of 400,000 students at the university stage, about 60 per cent should be in respect of science classes, bringing the proportion of students taking science courses to over 42 per cent. Developments in university education in relation to arts, science and commerce during the first two Plans and the proposals for the Third Plan.

The total outlay on education, including engineering and technological education, was Rs. 153 crores in the First Plan and Rs. 256 crores in the Second Plan. Programmes included in the Third Plan entail a total outlay of Rs. 560 crores. For programmes, other than those relating to engineering and technological education set out in the following Chapter, outlay during the First Plan was Rs. 133 crores, and during the Second Plan Rs. 208 crores, while programmes for the Third Plan involve a total expenditure of Rs. 418 crores including a provision of Rs. 10 crores for cultural programmes.

In addition to provisions under the head 'Education, resources to the extent of Rs. 37 crores are expected to be available under the community development programme and of about Rs. 42 crores under the programme for the welfare of backward classes thus bringing the total provision for general education in the Third Plan to Rs. 497 crores, as against Rs. 250 crores during the Second Plan.

Provisions in each Plan for education, as in other fields, are in addition to resources provided for 'maintaining' institutions established upto the end of the preceding Plan, as well as to contributions from non-government sources. It is estimated that over the Third Plan period 'maintenance' of educational institutions will involve a total expenditure of about Rs. 700 crores as against Rs. 375 crores in the Second Plan.

The contribution from non-government sources is difficult to estimate precisely. Over the past decade this contribution has increased from about Rs. 50 crores to about Rs. 90 crores per year. In the course of the Third Plan, on account of the transfer of responsibility for elementary education to panchayats and panchayat samitis and greater effort on the part of corporations and municipalities this contribution is likely to increase to about Rs. 120—130 crores per annum.

EDUCATIONAL DEVELOPMENT UNDER FIVE YEAR PLANS

Pre-school Education

The need for expanding facilities for preschool education is being increasingly stressed. In the past progress in this direction has depended mainly on the work of voluntary organisations and the establishment of a number of balwadis. The number of children enrolled in pre-school classes rose from 28,000 in 1950-51 to 75,000 in 1955-56, and is now estimated at about 300,000. There are at present about 5,000 balwadis; of these about 2,500 are assisted by the Central and State Social Welfare Boards. The existing balwadis need to be improved and provided with trained child welfare workers (bal sevikas).

The Third Plan provides for setting up of six training centres for bal sevikas. In the programme for education Rs. 3 crores have been allotted for child welfare and allied schemes at the Centre and about Rs. 1 crore in the States in addition to resources available under the community development and social welfare programmes.

Schemes for child welfare now being formulated by the Ministry of Education include improvement of existing balwadis opening of new balwadis, expansion of the training programme for bal sevikas and a number of pilot projects for child welfare in which education, health and welfare services will be organised in an integrated manner. Schemes for children, specially the setting up of balwadis will continue to be an imp^rtant part of the programmes undertaken for women and children in community development blocks and in welfare extension projects.

Elementary Education

The Constitution envisaged the provision of free, universal and compulsory education for children upto the age of 14 years. In view of the magnitude of the task, it was agreed early in the Second Plan that as a first step facilities should be created for the education of all children in the age-group 6—11. This is one of the central aims of the Third Plan, to be followed by extension of education for the entire age-group 11-14 during the Fourth and Fifth Plans. The principal problems in providing facilities for the entire age-group 6—11 in the course of the Third Plan period arise from the following factors :

— difficulties of bringing girls to school in sufficient numbers;

— extreme backwardness of certain areas and certain sections of the population in the matter of education ; and

— wastage' due to parents taking away children from school as soon as they are able to add to the family income so that more than one-half of the children do not reach class IV, thus failing to gain permanent literacy.

A very large gap still exists between the proportion 01 boys and girls attending school. In 1960-61, about 80.5 per cent of the boys were in school as against about 40.4 per cent of the girls. Among States in which the proportion of girls tails much below the average tor the country as a whole, are Rajasthan (15 per cent), Uttar Pradesh (20 per cent), Jammu and Kashmir (21 per cent), Madhya Pradesh (19 per cent), Bihar (27 per cent), Orissa (24 per cent) and Punjab (36 per cent).

The National Council for Women's Education carefully considered the special measures needed for promoting the education of girls at the primary, middle and secondary stages and made a series of recommendations. These include the provision of quarters for women teachers, special allowances to women teachers working in rural areas, condensed educational courses for adult women so as to enlarge the supply of women teachers, stipends for women teacher trainees, attendance prizes and scholarships, appointment of school-mothers in co-educational institutions and provision of the necessary amenities. To some extent proposals on these lines have been embodied in the plans of States. It is suggested that the various provisions which have been made in these plans should be reviewed afresh at an early date and, from the second year of the Plan additional steps should be taken to expand specially those facilities which aim at enlarging the supply of women teachers and attracting them to service in the rural areas.

The problem of providing educational facilities in backward areas is in part one of ensuring that the institutions are so located that almost every child can go to a school within easy walking distance from his home. The findings of the Educational Survey, referred to earlier, will assist States in planning and locating of new schools from this aspect. Scattered habitations, such as hilly tracts, present certain obvious difficulties in these, it will be necessary to provide additional facilities, even though these will be relatively more expensive.

Apart from the poverty of parents, the circumstances which lead to wastage are lack of properly qualified and trained teachers, defective curricula and insufficient appreciation of the value of education by parents. Closely allied to 'wastage' is 'stagnation' which occurs in the case of children who continue in the same class for more than a year. Introduction of compulsion, appointment of trained and qualified teachers, improvement in the methods of teaching, greater understanding on the part of parents of the desirability of letting their children remain at school, and the planning of school holidays, so that they coincide with the harvesting and sowing seasons, are among the steps to be taken to reduce the incidence of 'stagnation' and wastage'.

The programme for extending education to all children in the age-group 6—11 is of such crucial importance that financial considerations as such should not be allowed to come in the way of its successful execution in any State. There may, however, be other limitations which may be more difficult to overcame in a short period; for instance, the measure in which some of the poorer or more backward sections of the population or the more backward areas respond to the drive for education, the time needed to persuade all parents to send their daughters to school, the extent of participation and eagerness on the part of the local community, the ability on the part of education authorities to obtain a sufficient number of teachers, both men and women, who will indentify themselves with the communities in which they work and, finally, the practical steps taken to provide reasonabe conditions and prospects to the vast body of teachers working in primary schools.

Taking all these factors into account it is at present estimated that by the end of the Third Plan about 90 per cent of the boys and about 62 per cent of the girls will be at school, the overall percentage for the age-group 6—11 being 76. The Third Plan, about 15.3 million additional children will come into schools, of whom 8.6 million are likely to be girls. Differences in levels of development between States will be narrowed to some extent, but they will still be quite considerable.

Middle school education (11—14 years):— During the decade 1951—61, the number of children in the age-group 11—14 doubled, while the number of girls increased nearly threefold. Nevertheless, at the end of the period, as compared to 34 per cent of the boys only about 11 per cent of the girls were at school. The Third Plan envisages almost a doubling of the number of girls at school as against the total increase for the age-group of about 54 per cent. The disparity between boys and girls will, however, be still a marked feature, for, against 40 per cent of the boys at schools from this age-group the proportion of girls is likely to be less than 17 per cent.

The main problems which arise in the expansion of facilities for children in the age-group 6—11 are found in a more accentuated form in the next age-group 11—14, specially in rural areas. The difficulties of providing schooling facilities for backward areas and for scattered populations are even greater in the case of middle school education than in that of primary education.

In the more backward areas and among the more backward sections of the population, rapid development of middle school education can take place only after the necessary foundations at the primary level have been laid. Accordingly, in the Third Plan, for these areas, it will be necessary to concentrate on the expansion of primary education for these groups. The question of providing facilities on a part-time basis for training in suitable vocations or by way of continuation classes is at present being studied. It should be possible to organise such courses to an increasing extent at middle schools, basic schools, junior technical schools and other centres. The possibility of organising vocational training on a full-time basis for children in the age-group 11—14 should also be examined.

For expanding facilities for the education of girls, the various recommendations of the National Council for Women's Education should be considered further on the lines suggested earlier for primary education. For practical and administrative reasons, the programme of education for the age-group 6—14 visualised in the Constitution has been divided into two stages, 6—11 and 11—14. If the entire age-group 6—14 is considered together, it will be seen from the table below that over the past ten years the number of children at school has gone up from 22.3 million to 40.6 million, the proportion of the total population in the age-group rising from about 32 to 49 per cent. In the case of boys the proportion has risen from 46 to 65 per cent, and in the case of girls from 18 to 31 per cent.

The Third Plan postulates an increase in the number of children in the age-group 6—14 about equal to that achieved during the preceding decade. For girls the proportion in the age-group should go up to about 46 per cent and for boys to about 73 per cent, the overall proportion increasing to nearly 60 per cent. These figures provide a measure of the task that remains to be carried out during the Fourth and Fifth Plans.

Reorganisation of school education along basic lines has been a key programme since the First Plan. During the Third Plan it is proposed to convert about 57,760 schools into basic schools, to orient the remaining schools to the basic pattern, to remodel all training institutions along basic lines, to establish basic schools in urban areas, and to link up basic education with the development activities of each local community.

Progress towards fully developed basic schools will inevitably be spread over a long-period, since the number of elementary schools involved is large and the majority of the existing teachers have yet to be trained in the techniques of basic education. By way of preparation for conversion into basic schools, a programme for orienting all existing schools to the basic pattern was initiated during the Second Plan. This aims at the adoption of a common syllabus in all basic and non-basic schools and the introduction of simple drafts and activities like social service, community living, and cultural and recreational programmes, which do not involve much expenditure or require teachers fully trained in basic education. With a view to completing the process of orientation during the earlier phase of the Third Plan, it is proposed that schools should be given simple equipment needed for the purpose and teachers who have not been trained in basic education should be given short orientation courses.

Trained Teachers in Schools

Perhaps the most important measure 101" the expansion of basic education is the provision of larger facilities for the training of teachers for basic schools and the reorganisation of existing training centres along basic lines. At the end of the Second Plan, elementary school teachers were being trained in 1307 institutions, of which about 70 per cent were already organised on the basic pattern. By the end of the Third Plan, the number of training institutions will increase to 1424 and all of them will impart training on basic lines, the number of pupil-teachers on rolls being about 200,000 as compared to 135,000 in 1960-

61. For teachers who have not been trained in basic education, short-term courses of training in the simpler aspects of basic education are to be provided.

In most States the period of training for elementary school teachers is proposed to be extended to two years with a view to ensuring a greater measure of thoroughness both in regard to courses and methods. In a number of training schools extension departments will be established for improving the quality of teaching in schools in the neighbourhood. Towards the end of the Second Plan, 276 new training institutions were set up in preparation for the introduction of universal primary education during the Third Plan. The State schemes provide for equipment, buildings and other facilities for these and other institutions. A factor limiting the expansion of basic education is that it has been largely confined to rural areas. A number of experimental basic schools are, therefore, proposed to be set up in urban areas, so that the problems of basic schools in urban areas can be clearly identified and solutions found for them in cooperation with training colleges.

Community Effort

Provisions made in the plans of States need to be supplemented by local community effort in programmes such as organisation of enrolment drives, persuading parents to send girls to schools, construction of school buildings, and provision of additional equipment and furniture to schools and of mid-day meals and free clothing for the poorer children. In several States encouraging results have been achieved in the mobilisation of local resources, and it is expected that local support will be forthcoming in even greater measure as Panchayati Raj institutions are established in different States.

Several States have provided in their plans for mid-day meals for children attending schools, notably, Madras, Kerala, Andhra Pradesh, Mysore and Orissa. In Madras, which has the largest programme in this field, one million children are expected to benefit in addition to about a million already being served by the programme. About 40 per cent of the expenditure is being met by the local community. The movement for mid-day meals provides a special opportunity for each urban or rural community not only to participate in the educational effort, but also to improve nutrition and health in the schools and to assist the poorer students. Although the programme is at present what limited on account of financial considerations, it is suggested that State Governments should endeavour to provide for it, at any rate, wherever local communities come forward to take their due share in it.

Secondary Education

Development of the economy and the large increase in the number of secondary schools and in the number of students of the age-group 14—17 enrolled in them have altered the character of the demands which secondary education is called upon to meet. New social groups are seeking education and are coming within its influence. Expansion has brought into secondary schools a larger range of abilities and aptitudes. Secondary schools have to be so reorganised that they provide diversified educational service to pupils according to their needs. In the middle and lower grades of many branches of economic life, in administration, rural development, commerce, industry and the professions, the requirements of trained manpower have to be met after the necessary training, by products of secondary schools.

The programme for the reorganisation and improvement of secondary education, which was taken up following the report of the Secondary Education' Commission, has proceeded along several lines and is designed both to enlarge the content of secondary education and to make it a self-contained unit within the educational process. The measures envisaged are the conversion of high schools into higher secondary schools, development of multipurpose schools with provision of a number of elective subjects along with and in addition to the academic course, expansion and improvement of facilities for the teaching of science, provision of educational and vocational guidance, improvement of the examination and evaluation system, enlargement of facilities for vocational education, increased facilities for the education of girls and the backward classes and encouragement to merit through scholarships. Reconstruction along these lines involves a major revision of the secondary school curriculum and the introduction of new techniques and procedures. Subjects such as general science and social studies and the variola elective courses are relatively new concepts in the secondary school curriculum and call for a new orientation on the part of the secondary school teacher. In turn, this has necessitated a countrywide programme of in-service teacher education organised by State Education Departments as well as special extension services.

Secondary school teachers have to be thoroughly prepared for handling the new subjects efficiently. The teacher education programme at the pre-service level has also to be reorganised in line with the changes that have taken place at the secondary level. The standard of science education has to be raised to a level which will effectively support the future scientific advance of the nation. Shortcomings which have been observed in the working of the multipurpose schools have to be remedied and the scheme placed on a stable footing.

Educational and vocational guidance programmes have to be extended to reach as many schools and pupils as possible. Several other measures have also to be taken to strengthen the entire programme of the secondary school reorganisation, such as improvement in craft teaching, organisation of school libraries, the better use of audio-visual techniques, etc. Special emphasis is, therefore, to be given in the Third Plan to the consolidation and improvement of quality in all aspects of secondary education reorganisation.

Enrolment:—In the first two Plans the number of secondary schools increased from 7288 in 1950-51 to nearly 16,600 at the end of 1960-61. The number of children enrolled in classes IX to XI increased from about 1.2 million to 2.9 million. Although the number of girls in these classes increased from 200.000 to 520,000 during this period, girls constituted less than one-fifth of the total number attending secondary schools.

Higher secondary schools:—One of the principal recommendations of the Secondary Education Commission was that high schools should be upgraded to higher secondary schools so as to make the curriculum more broad-based than in the past and to provide better standard of education by providing an additional year in school. This would make secondary education a terminal point for a large- proportion of students who have to enter life directly at the end of the secondary school. During the first two Plans 3121 higher secondary schools were established in different States. This number is expected to rise to 6390 by the end of the Third Plan.

Science education:—The Second Plan gave high priority to the expansion and improvement of science education at the secondary stage. The Secondary Education Commission had recommended that every secondary school pupil should study general science as a compulsory subject, so that he gains a basic quantum of scientific knowledge as part of his general education. In addition, provision was to be made for science as an elective subject for those students who wished to pursue higher studies. By the end of the Second Plan a programme of general or elementary science has been introduced in almost all secondary schools, while science of an elective standard has been provided in about 4625 schools. However, a considerable proportion of schools lacks the basic minimum requirements in respect or laboratories and equipment and also suitable text-books and handbooks.

Teachers have to be prepared in the integrated approach which is required in the teaching of general science. It is also necessary to encourage students in creative and original activity in science. This was sought to be done during the Second Plan by establishing science dubs in selected secondary schools and training colleges. About 450 such science clubs were established during this period.

In the Third Plan, in addition to proving general science in all the secondary schools as a compulsory subject, more than 9,500 out of 21,800 secondary schools will also have science of an elective standard. The completion of this programme is expected to provide a more satisfactory foundation than at present for the further expansion of science education at the university stage during the Third and subsequent Plan periods. A number of supporting measures are also proposed to be taken to improve and strengthen the teaching of science.

The existing science syllabi in force in different States will be reviewed and modified where necessary, with a view to integrating them with the science syllabi at the earlier and later stages of education. A programme of preparation of teachers' hand-books, students' manuals, science text-books and supplementary reading material in science will also be undertaken.

The present shortage of science teachers will be made up to as large an extent as possible by increasing facilities of science education at the university stage and by providing various types of in-service training in content and methodology for the existing science teachers. The training of laboratory assistants in the techniques of handling laboratory apparatus v/ill also be taken up during this period. In addition, steps will be taken to standardise designs of science apparatus and to get them manufactured in the country itself. In order to coordinate, guide and direct the entire programme of science teaching as well as the training of key personnel, a central organisation for science education is proposed to be set up in the Third Plan. A scheme of science talent search is to be introduced with a view to identifying promising talent at the secondary stage and providing opportunities for its development.

Multipurpose schools:—One of the main defects in the secondary education system was its unilateral character, only one type of academic course being provided for all students irrespective of their individual aptitudes and abilities. The Secondary Education Commission, therefore, recommended the setting up of multipurpose schools, which would offer a number of practical courses along with the academic stream, so as to present the pupil with a variety of courses, out of which he could make his choice according to his special interests.

During the first two Plans 2115 multipurpose schools were established. These offer one or more practical courses in Technology, Agriculture, Commerce, Home Science and Fine Arts in addition to humanities and science. Although the concept of the multipurpose school has been readily accepted and the scheme has expanded rapidly, certain difficulties have been encountered, such as the lack of teachers trained to teach the practical subjects, insufficient teaching material, specially text-books and handbooks, limited range of elective courses and inadequacy of educational and vocational guidance facilities.

During the Third Plan, therefore, it is proposed to concentrate on the consolidation of the scheme by strengthening the institutions already established, the programme of expansion being limited to about 331 new schools. An integrated teacher training programme for the multipurpose schools is to be undertaken, and for this purpose four regional training colleges will be established which will prepare teachers for the multipurpose schools through in-service and pre-service training programmes both in the practical and the scientific' subjects. Steps will also be taken to stimulate greater experimental work in multipurpose schools for providing courses of study suited to different levels of ability, including special programmes of education for gifted students.

Educational and vocational guidance:— The successful organisation of secondary education requires the provision of a well-planned programme of educational and vocational guidance which will help parents and pup ls in selecting the most suitable educational courses and most satisfying vocational pursuits. The lack of such an organised programme of guidance has been one of the handicaps in the working of the multipurpose schools in the past.

During the Second Plan, in addition to setting up of a Central Bureau of Educational and Vocational Guidance, State Bureaux of Educational and Vocational Guidance were established in 12 States. These bureaux have been carrying out a programme of training of career masters and counsellors, test construction and guidance services to schools. The guidance movement, however, has not yet made a significant impact on secondary schools. It is, therefore, proposed in the Third Plan to strengthen the State Bureaux in such a manner as to help them to carry the guidance programme farther into the field and also to ensure a minimum programme of career information service in as many secondary schools as possible,

Teaching of crafts:—The reorganised curriculum of secondary schools includes crafts as one of the core subjects. The problem of securing craft teachers in sufficient numbers and improving the teaching of crafts is one of great importance both for secondary education and for vocational education. A special study of the problem is, therefore, being undertaken by the Ministry of Education, and the findings of the study will be utilised to formulate a programme for draft and vocational education.

School libraries:—Another aspect of secondary education which needs particular attention is the organisation of school libraries. Steps were taken in the First and the Second Plans for the improvement of school libraries but much remains to be done in the way of ensuring better utilisation of library facilities and improving the reading habits of pupils. Use of library resources has to be an integral part of class teaching. During the Third Plan it is proposed to set up a few model school libraries in the demonstration schools attached to selected training colleges to serve both as models for the organisation and running of libraries as well as training centres for teacher librarians. A study is already under way of the existing organisation of the secondary school libraries and the directions in which improvement should be undertaken.

Post-basic schools:—In some States post-basic schools were started by way of continuation at the secondary stage of senior basic schools. There are at present about 66 such schools. The relationship between post-basic schools and higher secondary schools has been recently considered by a committee, and it is proposed that these schools should be assisted to improve their standards of curriculum, instruction, equipment, laboratory and staff, so as to place them at par with the higher secondary and multipurpose schools. Until these steps have been taken, the school final examination of the post-basic schools may be regarded as equivalent to certificates awarded to students of higher secondary schools for employment and other purposes.

Training of teachers:—The number of training colleges has risen from 53 in 1950-51 to 236 in 1960-61. In the Third Plan the number of training colleges is expected to increase to 312. The existing training colleges will also be strengthened and expanded to increase the supply of trained teachers. White these measures take care of the numerical supply of trained graduate teachers, steps will also have to be taken to reorganise and strengthen the training college programme in order to align it with the current needs of the secondary school. Special emphasis in this matter will be given to pre-service training of teachers in science and social studies, introduction of new techniques of evaluation, provision of a variety of special, subjects, such as guidance and audio visual education and the organisation of research.

To provide in-service training facilities for secondary school teachers, extension centres were established during the Second Plan at 54 selected training colleges. These centres have been carrying out a comprehensive programme of in-service training, covering seminars, workshops and conferences, audio-visual, library and guidance services and publications. Each centre provides extension service to a number of schools in the area allotted to it , and intensive training for a group of selected schools (about 20) in the immediate neighbourhood.

The extension service programme has been found to be a valuable medium for continuous in-service training and as a means of keeping the training colleges and the secondary schools in close touch with each other. It is proposed to extend the scheme to a larger number of training colleges during The Third Plan with the ultimate object of making extension service an integral part of the work of every training college.

University Education

With the expanding base at the elementary and secondary education, the demand for higher education has greatly increased over the past decade. The number of universities has increased from 27 in 1950-51 to 32 in 1955-56 and to 46 in 1960-61, and about a dozen more universities are likely to be added during the Third Plan. The number of colleges rose from 772 in 1955-56 to 1050 in 1960-61. During the Third Plan about 70 to 80 colleges will be added every year. The rapid expansion in the numbers of universities and colleges in recent years has led to a number of problems. These have been reviewed in the report of the University Grants Commission for 1959-60.

The Commission has stressed that if deterioration is to be avoided, increase in the number of students should be accompanied by corresponding expansion of physical and other teaching facilities. In the Third Plan larger facilities are being provided for diverting students to vocational and technological education. However, the problem is one of large dimensions and, even after taking into account these facilities the number of those seeking admissions to the courses of higher education in arts, science and commercê will be large and suitable criteria for selection have to be adopted. In addition to the provision in the Plan for expansion of facilities for higher education, proposals for evening colleges, correspondence courses and the award of external degrees are at present under consideration.

Science education: The programme for expanding facilities for science education during the Third Plan has been described earlier. This will involve larger provision of scientific equipment as well as appointment of more science teachers. It is proposed to prepare standard lists for scientific equipment for the guidance of educational authorities. Schemes will also be initiated for the manufacture and supply of such equipment at low cost. A large number of scholarships will be provided to the meritorious science students. A continuing review of standards of teaching and examination in science and technology, at all levels, will also be carried out and preparation and publication of standard text-books for use in the education programmes will be undertaken.

Post-graduate studies and research:— Post-graduate studies and research in science and humanities will be further expanded in the Third Plan. Assistance was made available to universities during the Second Plan for additional accommodation, laboratory equipment and library facilities. Measures taken by the University Grants Commission during the Second Plan related to the development of new departments in universities in specialised fields of scientific study such as geophysics, astronomy, astrophysics, applied geology, oceanography, applied physics and animal genetics.

In humanities, departments of Buddhistic and African studies and institutes or department were developed for studies in Hindi, linguistics and social sciences, and for archaeology, musicology, music. etc. The University Grants Commission also initiated a scheme during the Second Plan for awarding postgraduate and research scholarships and fellowships Programmes initiated during the Second Plan will be continued and further developed during the Third Plan.

The University Grants Commission will assist universities and post-graduate departments of colleges in the development of post-graduate studies and research, special emphasis being placed on science education. The number of students expected to undertake postgraduate studies in science courses is expected to increase by about 7000 for post-gradual studies and 1000 for research. In all- there will be an increase of about 70 per cent in the enrolment of science students at the post-degree level. The number of additional arts students will be 7000 and 2000 respectively

Women's education:—Shortages of educated women available for taking up various occupations point to the need for increasing the proportion of women students in colleges and universities. The proportion of women students 'to the total enrolment in Indian universities was about 13 per cent in 1955-56 and about 17 per cent in 1960-61, and is expected to be about 21 per cent in 1965-66. During the Second Plan, the University Grants Commission provided liberal assistance for women's colleges and women's hostels. This will be continued in the Third Plan. Further, in order to encourage women students, special scholarships will continue to be provided. A proposal for setting up an institute for training women in organisation, administration and management is at present under examination.

Rural institutes:—Eleven Rural Institutes were established in the Second Plan with the object of providing higher education after the secondary stage to the rural students in their own setting for developing rural leadership, and for stimulating active participation of the rural population in welfare and community development programmes. The Institutes were intended to train rural youth for specialised jobs in fields like rural development, cooperation, social welfare, social education and small-scale industries. Diploma courses in rural services, rural civil engineering, agriculture and health services were offered in the rural institutes. The enrolment of the Institutes by the end of the Second Plan was over 2300 and the annual output in various courses was over 500.

This scheme is still in an experimental stage and will be continued in the Third Plan, so that flie Institutes can develop their activities fully. The working of a few rural institutes was assessed by special committees and measures for improvement have been taken in the light of their recommendations. In the Third Plan, it will be necessary to examine the full potentialities of these Institutes and their contribution towards meeting the manpower requirements for rural development so as to equip them fully to the development needs of rural communities.

Three-year degree course:—With a view to bringing about qualitative improvement in higher education, in most of the universities, the three-year degree course in arts, science and commerce following the higher secondary school examination or a year's course at the pre-university stage after the present matriculation or equivalent examination, has been already introduced.

The three-year degree course also includes other reforms such as improvement in the teacher-pupil ratio, introduction of tutorial system, general education, improvement of libraries, laboratories and instructional buildings. Periodical conferences, seminars, summer schools and refresher courses will continue to be organised as in the Second Plan for teachers in d"Serent subjects. Teachers will also obtain special grants for visiting centres of research for short periods. Among additional amenities for students are the provision of hostels, hobby workshops, non-resident students' centres, health centres, counselling and student aid funds.

Girls' Education

Some aspects of the problem of girls' education at different stages have been touched upon earlier in the discussion of elementary, secondary and university education. There are a few broader aspects of the subject which need further consideration. Over the past decade, while the additional number of boys enrolled in schools was 13.2 million, in the case of girls the additional enrolment was only 6.8 million. The census of 1961 has shown that, as against a literacy rate of 34 per cent for men, only about 13 per cent of the women are literate.

Consequently, by far the most important objective in the field of education during the Third Plan must be to expand facilities for the education of girls at various stages. According to the programmes which have been formulated, taking age-group 6—14, the proportion of girls at school should increase to 46 per cent, compared to 73 per cent for boys. Out of about 20.4 million additional children to be enrolled in schools during the Third Plan in the various age-groups, about 10.3 million are expected to be girls, their proportion in the lowest age-group being 56 per cent. At the end of the Third Plan, the disparity between boys and girls, although somewhat reduced, will still be considerable. Even to achieve the estimates mentioned above, a massive effort will be needed throughout the country and, more especially, in those States where the education of girls has seriously lagged behind.

It is estimated that of the resources available under the Plan for the development of education about Rs. 175 crores will be devoted to the education of girls, of which about Rs. 114 crores are for education at the primary and middle school stages. As stated earlier some provision has also been made for special schemes intended to support the general programme for girls' education. It is suggested that in implementing the various, provisions made for girls' education in their plans, States should keep in view detailed recommendations contained in the Report of the National Committee on Women's Education.

As has been pointed out, special emphasis must be laid on creating suitable conditions for encouraging parents to send their daughters to schools, educating public opinion, increasing the number of women from rural areas who will take up the vocation of teaching and inducing women from urban areas to accept posts of teachers in rural schools. It is proposed to evaluate carefully from year to year the progress made in implementing the programme for girls' education and to take such further measures as may be needed for realising the targets set for the Third Plan.

In the field of girls' education, it is specially necessary to study closely such successful methods as may be evolved in different parts of the country and to make such experience available generally. In drawing up annual plans also, care should be taken to see that the programme for girls' education is not held back for lack of financial resources and that the social and organisational limitations which impede progress at present are eliminated as early as possible.

Scholarships

Expenditure on scholarship programmes rose from about Rs. 3.5 crores in 1950-51 to over Rs. 8 crores in 1955-56 and to about Rs. 11 crores in 1957-58. It is expected to increase to about Rs. 18 crores by 1960-61. The number of scholarship-holders rose from 3.6 lakhs in 1950-51 to 8.8 lakhs in 1956-57. Of the latter about 7.8 lakhs were in schools and, about 1 lakh in colleges and universities. In addition to this, by 1956-57 free studentships and other financial concessions were available to about 50 lakhs of students—1.5 lakhs in colleges and universities and 48.5 lakhs in schools. The proportion of students in colleges and universities receiving scholarships and stipends was 9 per cent in 1950-51, and is at present estimated to be about 16 per cent. These scholarships will be continued in the Third Plan.

An important scheme for scholarships is that relating to post-matriculation scholarships for scheduled tribes, scheduled castes and other backward classes which was taken up several years ago and now benefits over 50,000 students at an annual cost of Rs. 2.7 crores. At the pre-matriculation stage, 4 to 5 million children belonging to these groups received scholarships and other concessions in 1960-61, and the expenditure incurred under this head during the Second Plan was Rs. 12 crores.

In the Third Plan, provisions for new scholarships in different fields are as follows :

— education programme pre-university stage 4-9

— university stage 6-0

— programme for the welfare of backward classes pre-university stage 11-0

— university stage 6-0

— technical and vocational education engineering and technology 8-0

— craftsmen 2-0

— total 37-0

Besides the provisions mentioned above, there are research scholarships and fellowships provided by the University Grants Commission and scholarships schemes in fields such as agriculture, health, scientific research, etc. State plans provide for extension of the existing schemes for scholarships. Among schemes undertaken by the Ministry of Education reference may be made to national scholaral agencies. Under the programme for the welfare of backward classes, it is expected that the number of scholarship-holders in the school stage will increase to about 7 million. In the field of technical education, it is expected that as against about 6000 students now receiving scholarships or other assistance, the number will rise to about 32,000 or 18 per cent of the total enrolment.

In view of the importance attached to scholarships in the Third Plan, it is suggested that State Governments and the Central Ministries concerned should review their existing schemes with the object of ensuring that, subject to continued good performance, the rules under which scholarships are given do in fact enable promising students in need of assistance to complete their education and that ordinarily help is not discontinued at intermediate stages. For such students there should be adequate provision not only at the post-matriculation stage, but also in the secondary classes.

In the case of students drawn from the economically backward sections, the aim should be to ensure adequate provisions for the numbers forthcoming and also for assisting an increasing proportion to reach the higher stages in education. There are some categories of personnel required in large numbers tor which, in the ordinary course, there would be inadequate supply of candidates, for instance, science teachers, women teachers, nurses, etc. Such categories should be carefully identified in each State and an attempt made to select promising students at the post-matriculation stage and assist them with scholarships and stipends through the entire period of training. They should be given the prospect of assured employment and should, in return, be under obligation to serve for prescribed periods.

Teachers' Salary Scales And Conditions of Service

The problem of raising the salary scales of teachers received special attention towards the end of the First Plan. During the Second Plan considerable progress was made and expenditure of about Rs. 30 crores is estimated to have been incurred on increasing the salaries of school teachers. As a result, the basic salaries of elementary teachers and, to some extent, of secondary teachers, were improved in almost all the States. In addition, expenditure was incurred on raising the salary scales of university teachers. In the Third Plan provision has been made by some of the States for improving the salaries and allowances of teachers.

Attempts will continue to be made during the Third Plan to improve the social and economic status of teachers. The institution in 1958 of national awards for outstanding work in the field of teaching is a useful innovation. The number of these awards is to be increased in the Third Plan. The Plan also provides for merit scholarships for the children of elementary and secondary school teachers.

EDUCATIONAL RESEARCH AND TRAINING

Any system of education requires for its growth a vigorous programme of research in educational objectives, methods and techniques. It is especially important in India today where the whole system is being modified to suit the changing needs of a rapidly developing society. During the first two Plans, a number of research institutions were set up. The National Institute of Basic Education has conducted a series of investigations into various problems connected with basic education and has organised short-term training courses and seminars for key personnel in the States and published a number of valuable studies on various problems.

The National' Fundamental Education Centre has studied problems of social education and trained a number of batches of District Social Education Organisers. The National Institute of Audiovisual Education carries out research in various media of mass communication—both ancient and modem—and has organised a number of seminars for key personnel working in this field.

The Central Bureau of Educational and Vocational Guidance has built up a number of objective tests for conducting examinations in different subjects and for assessing the special abilities and aptitudes of students with a view to guiding them in then- choice of courses and careers.

The Bureau organises seminars and short-term courses for guidance personnel in the States. In addition to the development of vocational and educational guidance, these measures will facilitate the introduction of mental health services in schools and colleges, including counselling for personal and emotional problems of students. The Ministry of Education has assisted in the setting up of similar units also in the States. The Central Bureau of Text-book Research studies text-books adopted in various States from the point of view of their content as well as the procedures followed in their selection. Criteria for evaluating textbooks have also been worked out, and workshops for training writers in the preparation of text-books are also arranged.

Training colleges were assisted during the Second Plan in carrying out investigations into problems of secondary education. The Directorate of Extension Programmes for Secondary Education has studied various problems pertaining to secondary education such as examination reform, syllabi for new subjects for reorganised secondary schools, problems of science' education, diversification of courses and others.

During the Third Plan research activities described above will be continued and expanded. With a view to developing at the national level a centre of training and research, it is proposed to establish National Institute of Educational Research and Training in which will be merged me existing Central Institute of Education and other Central Institutes and agencies referred to above. It is proposed that the National Institute of Educational Research and Training should be an autonomous organisation and that its functions should cover different areas of educational research, including elementary, secondary, social and audio-visual education, as also the training of key personnel in these and other fields. The programme of extension services through the training institutions will be coordinated and guided by the National Institute.

Extension departments will be started in 120 elementary teacher training institutions, which will take up research in selected areas and provide in-service training for elementary school teachers.

TEXT-BOOKS

The problem of text-books has been assuming greater urgency in recent years. The main aspects to be considered in a text-book are its content, method of presentation, printing, get-up and price. The procedure for selection of text-books is another important question. To over-come difficulties experienced in respect of text-books. State Governments have started, on an experimental basis, 'nationalisation' of textbooks.

The experiment is too brief to warrant definite conclusions being drawn from it. Steps will have to be taken to select, train and encourage writers and illustrators, to increase the supply of paper and to provide suitable printing machinery. The Centre and the States will need to coordinate their efforts in large scale production of text-books with a view to reducing costs as well as keeping certain national objectives uniformly in view. To bring down the price of foreign books, on which inevitably considerable reliance has to be placed at the university stage, arrangements for getting them printed in India are under examination. The interest of Indian writers must, of course, be fully safeguarded. The problem of translation of standard text-books into various languages and the writing of original books in these languages have become important in view of their greater use in the universities.

Examination Reform

The existing examination system has become inadequate for the needs of secondary education which has expanded in the scope and variety of its objectives. It has dome in for considerable criticism in recent years. The Secondary Education Commission laid special emphasis on the need for improvement of the examination system. A programme of examination reform was, therefore, taken up towards the end of the Second Plan when an Evaluation Unit was set up in the Directorate of Extension Programmes for Secondary Education. The programme envisages the reform of examination techniques in gradual stages and is designed for the following purposes :

— identifying and defining the specific educational objectives underlying the study of various school subjects ;

— aligning the techniques' of external examinations to these objectives, so that the examination questions and other tests may measure the attainments with reference to them;

— making corresponding changes in internal examinations ;

— giving increasing weightage to internal assessment; and

— introducing improvements in teaching techniques and curricula in the light of the educational objectives indicated for each subject.

The programme so far accomplished has helped to introduce a large body of teachers to the new concepts and techniques through seminars and workshops and to make training colleges, secondary school boards and others familiar with the problems of the examination reform. Considerable preparatory work has also been in progress. Work along the lines mentioned above will be intensified during the Third Plan. It is also proposed to set up State evaluation units which will work in coordination with the Central unit in implementing the programme. The University Grants Commission has assisted the establishment of examination research units in three universities. Further research work will also be organised and evaluation personnel trained in larger numbers. Research and evaluation units will be set up in some of the universities.

Development of Hindi and Sanskrit:— For the development of Hindi, during the first two Plans schemes were initiated for the evolution of Hindi terminology, production of dictionaries and original literature, translation of books of university level into Hindi and regional languages, and publication of popular books in Hindi through private publishers. Financial assistance was given to voluntary institutions engaged in the propagation of Hindi. Books' were distributed as 'free gifts' to school libraries and other educational institutions in the non-Hindi speaking areas. Grants were given to certain States for the expansion of facilities for the training of Hindi teachers and for setting up Hindi teachers' training colleges. Funds were also provided for the appointment of Hindi teachers in secondary schools in non-Hindi speaking States as well as for revising their pay scales. The programmes and schemes started during the First and Second Plans will be continued and expanded in the Third Five Year Plan.

In order to consider the question of the state of Sanskrit education in the country in all its aspects and recommend measures for its development, the Ministry of Education appointed the Sanskrit Commission, which made its recommendations in 1957. Implementation of these recommendations commenced during the Second Plan. The Central Sanskrit Board was set up in 1959 with a view to advising the Government of India on matters relating to propagation and development of Sanskrit and some steps have been taken in consultation with it. Programmes for the Third Plan will include production of literature, research scholarships, development of Gurukulas, modernising Sanskrit pathashalas, preparation of dictionaries and establishment of Central Sanskrit Institute for training teachers. Some States have also provided for programmes along these lines.

Education of the handicapped:—During the Second Plan several schemes for the education and training of the handicapped were initiated. These will' be continued in the Third Plan. The National Centre for the Blind will be strengthened and a national Braille library started. A training centre for the adult deaf and a school for the mentally deficient children will also be established. The scheme of scholarships under which assistance is given for higher education and also for technical and professional education to the handicapped students will be further expanded. Emphasis will be laid on the development of services for the handicapped through voluntary agencies and on the provision of special employment exchanges for the physically handicapped.

PHYSICAL EDUCATION, SPORTS AND YOUTH WELFARE ACTIVITIES

Among the significant developments in this field during the

Second Plan reference may be made to the establishment of the National College of Physical Education at Gwalior (which was the first degree college of its kind in the country), the setting up of Bal Bhavans to cater to the recreational needs of children, the launching of a national physical efficiency drive on the basis of carefully graded physical tests and the organisation of youth groups in rural areas as part of the community development programme. Towards the end of the Second Plan the National Institute of Sports was set up for training high grade coaches in different games and sports. In the sphere of youth activities, grants were given for the construction of stadiam, swimming pools, open-air theatres, etc. Steps were also taken for the promotion of the activities of the National Cadet Corps, Auxiliary Cadet Corps, Bharat Scouts and Guides and the National Discipline Scheme. During the Third Plan period all these programmes will be continued. The National Institute of Sports will be developed so as to provide for all the major games. With the help of coaches trained at the Institute, a national coaching scheme providing for widespread coaching facilities will be introduced so that the standard of sports can be steadily raised. The national physical efficiency drive will be further intensified so that it has greater impact. A National Children's Museum is also proposed to be established as a complement to the Bal Bhavan.

SOCIAL EDUCATION AND ADULT LITERACY

As was stated in the First Plan, social education implies 'an all-comprehensive programme of community uplift through community action'. Social education, thus, comprises literacy, health, recreation and home life of adults, training in citizenship and guidance in improving economic efficiency. In the last analysis, in the setting of democracy, the success of planned development, which encompasses the needs of millions of people, depends on the spread of social education and a progressive outlook and the growth of a sense of shared citizenship. Yet, the educational aims of agriculture, community development, health and other welfare programmes are among the most difficult to realise. Over the past decade, in several directions there has been a measure of progress, as in the development of community centres, reading rooms in villages, organisation of youth groups and mahila mandals, and the revitalisation of village panchayats and the cooperative movement.

One aspect of social education, and in some ways the most important, has, however, caused concern. Between 1951 and 1961, literacy has increased only from about 17 to about 24 per cent. The introduction of Panchayati Raj at the district and block levels and the important role assigned to village panchayats render it imperative that in as short a period as possible a substantial proportion of the adult population should become capable of reading and writing. This is essential in their own interest as in that of the community as a whole. As sufficient progress has not been achieved so far in this direction, the problem is now being studied a fresh with a view to working out means for the rapid expansion of adult literacy.

Programmes of the Ministry of Education provide for the further development of the National Fundamental Education Centre as a part of the National Institute of Education, production of literature for neoliterates, assistance for voluntary organisations in the field of social education and expansion of library facilities. The educational plans of States provide for libraries and continuation classes and, to a limited extent, for adult schools and other schemes for promoting adult literacy. The main provisions for social education are made under the community development programme through the schematic budget. Altogether, in the Third Plan, about Rs. 25 crores are expected at present to be available for social education.

Any large-scale and effective programme for adult literacy must be based on the closest possible cooperation at every level of personnel engaged in education and in community development. It will call for a pooling of the available resources in men and money, mobilisation of voluntary workers and organisations and development of adult education and literacy work at the block and village levels, and in every city and town, so that it takes the character more and more of a popular movement.

Social education and adult literacy have to be developed as extension activities undertaken by educational institutions, specially village schools, in collaboration with panchayats and cooperatives and voluntary organisations. The broad aim should be that wherever a group of persons sufficient to- constitute a class desires to attain literacy, the requisite facilities by way of teachers and teaching materials should be made readily available.

Every educational institution should be involved in this effort, and individual teachers participating in it should be given suitable honoraria. At the same time, the village panchayat and other agencies should make their due contribution towards the effort. While Social Education Organisers, Block Education Officers and individual educational institutions should work closely together to place the facilities needed at the service of local communities, it will be primarily for Pancliayat Samitis, village panchayats and voluntary organisations to create and maintain popular enthusiasm and develop adult education and literacy on a continuing basis in a manner related organically to their own needs and conditions. At every step the local leadership, the teachers and the voluntary workers should be drawn into the movement for the expansion of literacy both among men and among women. Proposals for a large-scale programme of adult literacy on these lines are being drawn up by the Ministry of Education in consultation with the Ministry of Community Development and Cooperation, and it is hoped that appreciable progress will be realised during the Third Plan.

Libraries: An adequate system of libraries is an essential part of any well-organised system of education. The Library Committee which reported in 1959, set up by the Government of India indicated the large gaps between the present position and the demands of an adequate system of libraries. These can, however, only be filled through a long term and properly phased programme. During the Third Plan, steps will be taken to set up or develop all the four National Libraries at Delhi, Calcutta, Bombay and Madras. There are provisions also for strengthening libraries at the State headquarters and tor increasing the number of libraries at the district and taluka levels. Besides these, educational institutions have libraries of their own. These will be improved and strengthened during the Third Plan. An Institute of Library Science was set up during the Second Plan to train key library personnel. This will be further developed during the Third Plan. Other universities also have facilities for research in library science and facilities for training library personnel.

CULTURAL PROGRAMMES

India's exceptional heritage in art, literature, dance, drama and music has to be further developed in response to the urges of a new generation. Archaeological monuments and ancient art are to be preserved and re-interpreted for communicating India's underlying cultural unity. Among important steps already taken are the establishment of the Lalit Kala Akademy (academy of fine arts), the Sahitya Akademy (academy of letters) and the Sangeet Natak Akademy (academy of dance, drama and music), the National Museum and the National Gallery of Modern Art. The other schemes carried out in the Second Plan were the reorganisation and development of museums and libraries and preparation of gazetteers which will be developed through the Third Plan Work of revision of District and Indian Gazetteers initiated during the Second Plan will be carried further. A scheme for the publishing of ancient manuscripts, cataloguing and preserving them and building up a microfilm library of rare manuscripts and for the acquisition of such manuscripts forms part of the Plan.

Along with Hindi and Sanskrit, it is of the utmost

importance to develop modem Indian languages. It is proposed to undertake the preparation of bi-lingual dictionaries, award prizes for translatons, arrange for the preparation of encyclopaedias in the various regional languages, and of English-Indian language dictionaries, and publish old manuscripts and rare books as well as catalogues and bibliographies. The Plan also provides for the linguistic survey of India.

Contemporary Indian literature has been surveyed recently by the Sahitya Akademy. The National Book Trust is taking steps to encourage the production of good literature and to make such books available at moderate prices for libraries, educational institutions, and the public in general. The National Book Trust also aims at translation of well known books from foreign, languages and of standard books from one Indian language into another.

In the development of India's cultural unity, considerable importance must be attached to the propagation of Indian languages and their literatures in different parts of the country. This aspect has been emphasised by the Central Advisory Board of Education which has recommended the study at the secondary stage by every student of an Indian language other than his own mother-tongue. Facilities for the study of Indian languages are being provided at some universities. In the context of the Third Plan they need to be established on a much wider basis.

Reorganisation and development of museums will be undertaken on the lines recommended by the Expert Museum Survey Committee, 1955, and on the advice of the Central Advisory Board on Museums which has been established for this purpose. A project for the acquisition of art collections for the National Gallery of Modem Art is included in the Plan, and committees have been set up to advise the Government. The Salar Jung Museum at Hyderabad has been taken over by the Central Government and will be developed as a National

Museum for the South India.

The Department of Archaeology has schemes like assessment of Monuments, copying of ancient paintings and survey of antiquities which will be continued in the Third Plan along with the strengthening of the Excavations Branch. A National Trust will be established to look after places of historical interest and national beauty which do not fall within the purview of the Department of Archaeology.

The Third Plan provides for research in the field of Anthropology and Ethnography. Trained personnel required for the various schemes will be made available and creative talent encouraged through scholarships for students and young workers in different cultural fields. Along with these, a few overseas scholarships have also been included.

Cultural relations with other countries will continue to be encouraged during the Third Plan. Among schemes subserving this objective are the development of the Indian Council for Cultural Relations, construction of the International Students' Home in the Delhi, University and re-productions of paintings, sculptures and Indian Art for the use of cultural organisations in foreign countries. The scheme for establishing Buddha Jayanti monument in Delhi which started in the Second Plan will be completed in the Third Plan. Existing institutions of higher learning and research will be further developed.

Among other programmes are the setting up of a National Theatre and also a large open-air theatre in Delhi. In the Second Plan an expenditure of Rs. 4 crores was incurred on various cultural programmes, Rs. 2.6 crores at the Centre and Rs. 1.4 crores in the States. The Third Plan allocation is Rs. 10 crores—Rs. 6 crores at the Centre and Rs. 4 crores in the States.

National Integration

The success of economic planning in India will largely depend upon our capacity to hold together as a nation in the midst of diversity of language, region, caste and religion. Unity in a democracy must be based on the consciousness of a common cultural heritage and commonly accepted future goals and on a constant effort to realise them. India has a rich and composite culture to which every section of the community has contributed and of which it has every reason to be proud. The essentials of this culture are broad-mindedness and mutual tolerance, balance between the material and the spiritual, and the cooperative way of life in which various individuals in a group are bound together by commonly accepted rights and obligations. India's future goals are embodied in the Constitution and her development plans are among the principal means for realising them'.

Educational institutions have a vital role to play in bringing about national integration and social cohesion among the younger generation. The school programme should be designed to awaken in the pupils an awareness of national oneness and for this purpose, includes community living based on cooperative self-help and democratic principles, the study of India's history and culture in the curriculum at various stages of education and suitable textbooks to inculcate moral and social values among students.

The school programme has to be supplemented by other activities such as programmes for bringing students together on a common platform and enabling them to gain first-hand knowledge of the diversified culture of the country through educational tours, the development of modem Indian and classical languages and making their rich store-house of literature available to larger numbers in different parts of the country through translations and the revival and development of India's composite cultural heritage through fine arts, dance, drama, music and literature.

Various steps taken to create more widespread understanding of the Plan among students are intended to strengthen the forces of integration and national unity in a positive and constructive manner. One State Government has recently approved a scheme of 100 scholarships a year to be given to graduate and post-graduate students from different States which provision for residential facilities. Proposals on these lines can be of great value in promoting national integration.

MONITORABLE TARGETS FOR THE TENTH PLAN AND BEYOND

— Reduction of poverty ratio by 5 percentage points by 2007 and by 15 percentage points by 2012;

— Providing gainful and high-quality employment at least to the addition to the labour force over the Tenth Plan period;

— All children in school by 2003; all children to complete 5 years of schooling by 2007;

— Reduction in gender gaps in literacy and wage rates by at least 50 per cent by 2007;

— Reduction in the decadal rate of population growth between 2001 and 2011 to 16.2 per cent;

— Increase in Literacy Rates to 75 per cent within the Tenth Plan period (2002-3 to 2006-7);

— Reduction of Infant mortality rate (IMR) to 45 per 1000 live births by 2007 and to 28 by 2012;

— Reduction of Maternal Mortality Ratio (MMR) to 2 per 1000 live births by 2007 and to 1 by 2012;

— Increase in forest and tree cover to 25 per cent by 2007 and 33 per cent by 2012;

— All villages to have sustained access to potable drinking water within the Plan period;

— Cleaning of all major polluted rivers by 2007 and other notified stretches by 2012.

HIV/AIDS targets within the Tenth Plan period:

— 80% coverage of high risk groups through targeted interventions;

— 90% coverage of schools and colleges through education programmes;

— 80% awareness among the general population in rural areas;

— reducing transmission through blood to less than 1%;

— establishing of at least one voluntary testing and counselling centre in every district;

— scaling up of prevention of mother-to-child transmission activities up to the district level;

— achieving zero level increase of HIV /AIDS prevalue by 2007)

Malaria targets within the Tenth Plan period:

— ABER (Annual Blood Examination Rate) over 10 per cent

— API (Annual Parasite Incidence) 1.3 or less 25% reduction in morbidity and mortality due to malaria by 2007 and 50% by 2010. --

BASIC SERVICES

Over the years, India's Five Year Plans have continued to emphasise poverty eradication and attainment of economic equality and social justice as key objectives. The Eighth Five Year Plan identified human development as an overarching goal of development. The Plan incorporated strategies to create jobs, contain population growth, eradicate illiteracy, universalise elementary education, and provide safe drinking water and primary health care facilities to all. A commitment to achieve the goal of human development has been reiterated in the Ninth Five Year Plan.

Recognising a close nexus between poverty and powerlessness, and given UNDP's global mandate of poverty eradication, UNDP India in close consultation with the Government decided to support interventions which promote access to basic services in the areas of health, education and prevention of HIV/AIDS. UNDP interventions focus on empowerment of communities as a basic prerequisite for human development, and are being implemented in convergence with ongoing UNDP-supported initiatives in other areas.

Health

The lack of access to quality health care has been identified as a leading cause of human deprivation in India. Yet, the overall annual expenditure on health care in India in recent years is estimated at about 4.5 per cent of the GDP, a high figure by any standards. The importance and preference given to curative care over promotive and rehabilitative primary health care is seen as a cause behind the paradoxical situation of high health expenditures and poor health outcomes.

Expensive disease-oriented programmes tend to enhance dependency and weaken community capacities to cope with the issue of prevention. Experience has shown that wherever people have been empowered and provided appropriate information, resources and encouragement, the efforts have yielded better results at a much lower cost. UNDP interventions with the Government in the health sector are directed towards facilitating a fresh consideration of these issues from a social perspective. The effort is to make visible the links between health and poverty, and to demonstrate a range of equity-based interventions that would have a direct, even critical bearing on public health.

Primary Education

Impressive gains have been made in education, yet the goal of universalisation of primary education is still elusive. While 95 per cent of villages have a primary school within walking distance, some 69 million children between the ages of 6-14 years are out of school. UNDP's focus is on enhancing the capacities of communities and teachers to support improvement of the quality of primary education.

Children out of School

UNDP's approach to the problem of out-of-school children, proposes that all such children be included into the schooling system irrespective of whether they work in agriculture, in industry or at home. In the Indian context, many commentators and development agencies have sought to distinguish between children who work at home, in agriculture or in assisting petty family business from those who work outside the home for a wage. For UNDP there is no such distinction because in both cases, the children's Constitutional right to education is denied. Moreover, since it is primarily girl children who work at home assisting their mothers in the household tasks of looking after younger siblings, cooking, cleaning, washing etc., such a distinction would discriminate against female children.

4

WASTAGE AND STAGNATION

Education has been facing some special problems like wastage, stagnation and dropouts at different levels. The reasons for these problems have been studied by many researchers in the past. It is worth having a glance at the studies on these problems conducted in the recent past. Of the nine studies analysed, four dealt with the problem of wastage in school education in Assam, four examined the problem of wastage at school level in Bihar, Rajasthan and Uttar Pradesh, and one study attempted to trace the incidence of dropout and maladjustment among students in relation to creativity and social structure of the school.

Wastage and stagnation were higher in rural areas than in urban and suburban areas, and it was higher at the primary stage than other stages. The training of teachers had no impact on reducing wastage and stagnation. The percentage of dropouts was high among girls at primary level in Rajasthan. Gangopadhyay found that there were more dropouts among boys and more repeaters among girls. The main cause for wastage and stagnation was the dropouts and repeaters' apathy to English and a dislike for mathematics, lack of educational guidance and poor study habits.

The wastage had a relation with student intelligence, socioeconomic status, parents' education and size of the family. Another crucial problem is absenteeism mainly in government schools where the percentage was higher. Absenteeism is related to poor family background and domestic life. The studies concentrated on empirical situations rather than on the causes and factors for stagnation except Rather's study which found a positive relation between dropout and the sociometric status of the child in the classroom. Future studies, emphasizing these di- mensions at micro-level would be useful to find out solutions to some of the problems.

EDUCATIONAL RESEARCH ON MANAGEMENT

Educational research on management, seems to be caught up in the syndrome of indifference and mutual exclusion. It is probably not yet seen as a professional activity. Educational management is still seen as basically an off-shoot of pedagogical skills at the school level and an overflow of content specialization at the higher education level. The situation is not different when one moves from institutional management to the management of areas and larger systems like districts, states and universities. The District Education Officers or the Joint Directors or the University Vice Chancellors or Registrars, are selected on the basis of their specialization either in the field of pedagogy or in the field of subject content. Education and training on management is not seen as a prerequisite for managerial positions and activities. Even when it comes to Directors of Education in the states and Deputy Secretaries onwards at the national level, such posts are offered to IAS cadre who have a record turnover rate, moving from labour to rural development to finance and what not. Educational management is, thus, not seen as a specialized area of activity.

Management education per se has matured in a significant way in this country with the establishment of the four Indian Institutes of Management, management departments in more than fifty universities, five IITs and a large number of specialized institutes in this field. Nevertheless, education is usually not an area of operation in such management institutes. In other words, the programmes and experiences would indicate that the total thrust of management education in this country has gone into business and industrial organisations. It would be evident from the above analysis that professional management and education have more or less remained mutually exclusive, and a reflection of this situation is seen in research on educational management. The Challenge of Education and the National Policy on Education, 1986 (NPE) brought this mutual exclusion into focus and emphasized the need for professionalization of educational management.

The NPE (1986) stressed the need for application of modem management science, including laying down specific goals of management, decentralization, participation, professionalization, autonomy and accountability. There were not many earlier studies in these areas so there is little to learn from past experience-which is a handicap. The situation warrants immediate undertaking of research in these areas.

Participative management

Participative management is increasingly gaining importance, whether at macro, meso and micro levels. There were no systematic studies conducted in this area. A block-level study conducted on Integrated Rural Development Projects revealed that lack of grassroots level participation in these projects resulted in poor performance.

Autonomy

Autonomy is another aspect dealt with seriously in the NPE, 1986. Not much research was done in this area beyond the study conducted on autonomous colleges in Tamil Nadu (NIEPA, 1986). The major findings of the study are: 20 colleges were given autonomy, out of which 16 were located in Tamil Nadu. The study found that the colleges are successful to a large extent in implementing the innovation. The courses have been restructured to suit societal needs. Teachers and community participation in the implementation led to success and solved many critical issues without much difficulty.

Another study also conducted in Tamil Nadu concentrated on one particular autonomous college and revealed more or less the same points as just mentioned. The study further observed that prior planning, teachers' participation in every phase of innovation, and mobilization of resources from other systems were key aspects of the success of the innovation in the college.

Structures

The role of certain structures in a given system like the Ministry of Human Resource Development, UGC, etc. and the organizational structure of an institution are the two broad areas of research. Out of 12 studies analysed in this category, one traced the organizational structure and role of the central Ministry of Education, seven studies were related to higher education, three were on school education and one dealt with Muslim educational organizations in Karnataka. It may be noted here that there is no study on organisational structures at state level. The studies in this category covered the states of Andhra Pradesh, Assam, Bihar, Kerala, Karnataka, Maharashtra and Punjab.

The organizational structure of the Ministry of Education of the Government of India was studied in a historical perspective, relating it to its functional components. Studies on structures for higher education have been on the role of the UGC and organizational and administrative structures of universities and colleges. The organizational pattern of libraries has also been an area of study. Sharma concluded that the University Grants Commission did not use its powers of inspection and stoppage of grants, with the result that maintenance of standards has taken a back seat. The study further revealed that the other drawbacks of the UGC were lack of evaluation and assessment of programmes and their impact, absence of mechanisms and methods (to some extent due to absence of powers) to see recommendations of various expert committees translated into actions. There mechanism for coordination with other bodies concerned with overall national planning and with other sectors of educational research was inade- quate.

The Federation of University (Service) Teachers' Association of Bihar (FUSTAB), in spite of various limitations, has been working for betterment of service conditions of teachers and qualitative improvement of higher education (Verma, 1985). On the other side, the age-old academic departmental structure was not found suitable for the changing objectives of the university. The respondents of Portia's study were in agreement concerning disjunction between university structure and the functions that the university was ex- pected to perform. The heads of departments felt that all faculty members could be consulted in academic matters but not in administrative matters. They further felt that the rigidity of rules left little scope for individual discretion.

The study conducted by Khan analysed the governance and administrative structure of Osmania University comprehensively. Another project studied the structure and functioning of colleges in Punjab. The study revealed that there was no representation of teachers in college managing bodies in Punjab. Khader studied college environment in six universities and found that university departments, constituent colleges and affiliated colleges, as institutions, varied to a large extent on intellectual orientation and monetary award and on institutional typology.

The study on organization of libraries in higher educational institutions in Kerala revealed that neither their structure nor their functioning was based on scientific principles. Fathima's study revealed that Muslim educational institutions were successful in fulfilling their obligation and realizing national objectives in the field of education. Single-teacher schools were setup in some parts of Assam without considering even the primary requirements of a school. Pathak studied the growth of administration and organization of in-service education for secondary school personnel in India. The study revealed that the apex body made gradual efforts to transfer the responsibility to states/local managements during the period from 1955 to 1971, and the goal was achieved in 1971.

Another interesting study on tuition classes revealed that the motive behind these was monetary gain. Not much attention was given to physical facilities in tuition classes. Unlike in the case of industrial and business organizations, professional management research on organizational structure and processes of optimization is totally missing in education. As a result, organizations are designed in an ad hoc manner. Even the national level institutes like, the NCERT, NIEPA, TTTIs, IIMs, IITs vary widely from each other in their organizational design. Organizational design and structuring is an open area for researchers on educational management

Behavioural Aspects

The attitudes, perceptions and morale of students, teachers and leaders of institutions are the key components which ultimately keep an institutions moving. These behavioural aspects play a dominant role in management of institutions. Revelations by a growing number of researches in this area in the last few decades are testimony to this. During the last four years, around forty studies were completed in this area. These studies can be grouped into three areas:

i. Organizational climate

ii. Leadership behaviour

iii. Job satisfaction and other issues

The studies on behavioural aspects have a wide geographical coverage. Another important region left out was the North-East Region except for one study on Nagaland. UP and Karnataka have the largest number of researches. It would be interesting to note that not many studies were conducted on leadership in higher education. The survey method was used in a majority of the studies. The instruments used were standardized tests like LBDQ by Halpin, OCDQ by Halpin and Croft, the Purdue Teacher Opinionnaire, attitude scales and tests and interview schedules in few cases. The SD, t-test, co- efficient of correlation, ANOVA, F-ratio and linear regression were the common statistical techniques used in data analyses.

Most of the studies on organizational climate are based on OCDQ. The studies included here reveal that the majority of the Indian schools have a closed climate, followed by open and autonomous climates. Teachers morale was comparatively high in open climates. Narula analysed the common factors of teacher morale. Five factors were ex- tracted, viz., (a) self confidence, (b) morale based on educational and social support, (c) human and social relationships, (d) service conditions, and (e) professional adjustment.

Most of these studies related organizational climate with a set of other variables like teacher morale, job satisfaction, performance of students, etc. The results are not consistent. They do not make much contribution in understanding the processes of improving management. A university climate was perceived by faculty in many ways irrespective of their age, level or position. Classroom climate was found to play a crucial role in student achievement. Sathappan found that productive and non-productive groups of college teachers did not differ on variables like professional attitudes and perceived organizational characteristics. Classroom climate was found to play a crucial role in student achievement.

Krishnaraj studied leadership at college level. Leadership behaviour was more or less the same in both affiliated and autonomous colleges; and centralization of authority was found in autonomous colleges at lower levels. Mukhopadhyay and others (in progress) recently completed a survey of leadership styles among school and college principals and district education officers. Very few respondents opted for delegation as a style. They preferred to labour themselves instead. Lack of trust in others was the predominant cause. School principals fared better in style flex and effectivity scores than college principals.

Teachers' job satisfaction is important for school organization and improvement. Teachers' job satisfaction significantly varies with organizational climate and it was higher in open climate schools. Kakkar found that women employees of different vocations differed significantly in their job satisfaction; and job satisfaction was positively related to occupational level. Another study revealed that the job intrinsic variable correlated positively and significantly with job satisfaction of professionals, viz., teachers, engineers, advocates and doctors.

Job concrete and job abstract dimensions of the variable had also been found positively and significantly correlated with job satisfaction. Tali examined and found that the quality of teaching and efficiency of high school teachers were adversely affected by poor job conditions and inadequate provision of facilities. Organizational characteristics, viz., esprit, thrust, consideration and total leadership behaviour were correlates of job satisfaction. Student activism had a rela- tionship with leadership of heads, teachers and improper methods of teaching.

Studies on behavioural aspects of management are large in number and important. In terms of statistical designs too they stand out, maybe because of easy-fit into multivariate designs. The studies, however, suffer from a few major limitations and gaps. These types of studies-design, tools, statistical analyses-were initiated in the early 70s at the Centre of Advanced Study in Education, Baroda.

Research on organizational behaviour derives its inspiration from the goal of organization development. Mukhopadhyay documented some experiments on organization development but no comprehensive research is available. In order to bring research on organizational behaviour in education to a professional level, researches have to be initiated in many of these crucial issues to bridge the existing gaps.

Four studies concentrated on utilization of incentives given to SC/ST, backward classess and merit students, one study examined the impact of physical facilities on primary education and another examined the procurement and utilization of financial resources in Nepal. Of the remaining two studies, one examined inventory management in engineering colleges and the other had focused on education financing and equity in Kerala and Haryana. These studies were carried out in the states of Assam, Maharashtra, Punjab, Himachal Pradesh, Gujarat, Kerala, Haryana and Nepal.

Facilities provided to students of backward classes were utilized to a large extent. However, most of the students did not know the details of the facilities available to them. Premi's study on ITIs also revealed that students were not aware of the facilities. Residential secondary schools were provided with adequate monetary and non-monetary inputs. However, utilization of these schools by scholars was dampened due to many other factors.

Gupta found in a comparative study that merit scholarship holders at college level were more numerous among students of Punjab than those in Himachal Pradesh. Das found a significant relationship between physical facilities in schools and the quality of education. Shortage of funds and delays in disbursing grants by the government were two serious problems in school education in Nepal.

Mukhopadhyay and Murthy conducted a national-level study on inventory management in engineering colleges. The study revealed a wide gap on per capita expense on consumables in central, state and university colleges. The centrally funded institutes were the most privileged. The study also revealed that, due to lack of proper utilization of resources, management cost of material was often higher than the cost of the material itself.

The study on education financing and equity conducted by NIEPA (1982) revealed that both Haryana and Kerala presented a picture of steady educational growth. Other findings of the study were: non- teaching expenditure was very small, indicating that the schools were running without needed equipments. Grants-in-aid rules need to be liberalized, particularly in respect of backward areas. There are no studies on resource mobilization and utilization. Although the studies referred to above make some contribution, the researches on resources are too meagre.

Legal Support

The NPE, 1986, recommended a statutory status for a few bodies like the AICTE and NCTE, after reviewing their functions, rules and regulations. Not many studies were conducted on statutes and rules. There was one study that analysed comprehensively the provisions and statutes in Osmania University. The study found that, to perform the variety of tasks in meeting the variegated responsibilities for the fulfilment of the objectives expected of it, the university was given an organisational structure by an act of legislature. The Vice Chancellor was the academic leader, ad- ministrative leader and fiscal manager.

There are widely differing practices vis-a-vis some of the management functions, like admission, instruction, examination and inventory control, in institutional and systems management in education. Although there are not many studies in this area it would, however, be useful to examine some of these studies. Mehta studied remedial teaching practice. He found that the programme of remedial teaching could be integrated with the programme of working holidays.

In the teaching-learning process, emphasis was laid on the acquisition of knowledge rather than on the application of knowledge to a new situation. An indepth study on inventory management in engineering colleges has revealed the pros and cons of this practice. The engineering colleges do not adopt a professional approach to inventory management despite the fact that this subject is taught in every engineering institution. Also, the institutions varied widely in their approaches.

Potdar suggested a multi-stage screening procedure for admission to the B.Sc. course. The semester system has been one of the issues under discussion ever since the early 70s. It was found that this system was adopted by many universities and discontinued in some others. The system made both teachers and students face a tight schedule. Another crucial problem of the university system concerned examinations-inaccuracies and delays in examination etc.

Management of change

Management of change is one of the fascinating problems of research on management. Since the beginning of research in this area in the mid 60s, most studies adopted a quasi-scaling approach on Roger's model, leading to identification of a cluster of variables that are related to change-related behaviour of educational personnel/ teachers and principals.

Diffusion of innovations was found positively and significantly related to the school climate. Innovative schools were found to have high change proneness. The gap between origin of innovation and diffusion always occurs due to many factors like ineffective communication, a tendency to keep new practices private and unpublished, conservatism among teachers, and lack of confidence and competence. Chauhan studied the characteristics of administrators. Innovative educational administrator had risk-taking capacity, self-confidence and willingness to innovate.

Kongrimai's study revealed that principals who visited innovative schools and studied improvement programmes were likely to accept new ideas and programmes without much resistance. Mukhopadhyay made a diagnostic study on management of change. On the basis of analysis of large number of Indian studies and a conceptual framework, the author concluded that management of change has not been one of the direct concerns of educational man- agers, leaving many gaps in the process of ensuring change. In another ongoing study, a series of cases have been developed on management of change at national, state and institutional level initiatives. Studies on successful innovative institutions and documents in the form of a case would help others to understand the criticality of the process of change and its management.

Administration of secondary education in Uttar Pradesh was adversely affected to a large extent due to dual control of government and managements. SC and ST students of Harijan and Tribal Welfare Department schools showed marked and developed personality characteristics in comparison with other caste students, except in punctuality School improvement plans were prepared in many schools of Rajasthan as recommended by the Indian Education Commission, 1966. Another study in Rajasthan was on the impact of study camps for talented pupils.

In India, very few schools have clear-cut schemes of self-evaluation. In few cases, it is carried out once in a while. In American and GDR schools self-evaluation is practised but it was not effective due to lack of adequate techniques and bureaucratic pressure. A study examined in detail the educational administration with reference to decentralization in Tamil Nadu. The impact of the Mid-day Meals Programme on enrolement and retention rate at the primary stage, particularly in rural areas, was found significant in an all-India study by Saxena and Mittal.

An in-depth study on monitoring and functioning of post-matric scholarships revealed that there was no uniformity amongst the state, particularly with reference to time-frame and disbursement of money to students. No systematic effort was made to streamline the functioning of the scheme. A study on special education revealed that integrated education for handicapped children was very useful, however at this stage the hurdles were non-availability of equipment, and teachers and lack of proper machinery to identify children.

A very massive project has been completed on evaluation of non- formal education in nine educationally backward states of India sponsored by the Ministry of Human Resource Development (NIEPA, 1987). This study revealed wide divergence in the process of implementation of NFE and levels of achievement of the scheme. Murthy evaluated administration of non-formal education in Andhra Pradesh and found that administrative machinery was inadequate both at state and district level.

Among the various levels of education, as usual, school education received the single largest amount of attention of the researchers followed by higher education and other levels. The reasons are not far too seek. Since most of the research workers who work for the Ph.D. belong to the field of teacher-education and their attention is directed essentially on school education, research on management automatically focuses on to school education. While there is no proof that other sectors are managed better, it is interesting to note that the management of the high-cost education sector, namely, higher education and technical and other professional education, has remained almost unexplored.

5

KOTHARI COMMISSION-1966

The Education Commission under the Chairmanship of Dr.D.S. Kothari, the then Chairman, University Grants Commission, began its task on October 2,1964. It consisted of sixteen members, eleven being Indians and five foreign experts. In addition, the Commission had the benefit of discussion with a number of internationally known consultants in the educational as well as scientific field.

The main task of the Commission was to advise the Government on the national pattern of education and on the general policies for the development of education at all stages-ranging from the primary to post-graduate stage and in all its aspects besides examining a host of educational problems in their social and economic context.

This House is of opinion that a Committee of Members of Parliament be appointed to go into the question on National Policy on education in all its aspects and to prepare a plan accordingly for the next three plan periods, and also to suggest suitable machinery for its implementation.

GOVERNMENT RESOLUTION SETTING UP THE EDUCATION COMMISSION, JULY 14, 1964

The Commission submitted its report to the Government on June 29,1966. It was laid on the Table of the House on August

29, 1966. The main features of the Commission's report were as follows:

(i) Introduction of work-experience which includes manual work, production experience, etc. and social service as integral part of general education at more or less all level of education.

(ii) Stress on moral education and inculcation of a sense of social responsibility. Schools should recognise their responsibility in facilitating the transition of youth from the work of school to the world of work and life.

(iii) Vocationalization of secondary education.

(iv) Strengthening of the centres of advance study and setting up of a small number of major universities which would aim at achieving highest international standards.

(v) Special emphasis on the training and quality of teachers for schools

(vi) Education for agriculture and research in agriculture and allied sciences should be given a high priority in the scheme of educational reconstruction. Energetic and imaginative steps are required to draw a reasonable proportion of talent to go in for advance study and research in agriculture science.

(vii) Development of quality or pace-setting institutions at all stages and in all sectors.

The Commission observed that mother-tongue had a pre-eminent claim as the medium of education at the school and college stages. Moreover, the medium of education in school and higher education should generally be the same. The regional languages should, therefore, be adopted as the media of education in higher education. The Commission further observed that the public demand for secondary and higher education had increased and would continue to increase in future. It was, therefore, necessary to adopt a policy of selective admissions to higher secondary and university education in order to bridge the gap between the public demand and available facilities.

The Commission was of the view that the social segregation in schools should be eliminated by the adoption of the neighbourhood social concept at the lower primary stage under which all children in the neighbourhood will be required to attend the school in the locality.

National Policy on Education Committee of Members of Parliament

A Committee of Members of Parliament on Education was constituted by the Government of India on April 5, 1967, with the following terms of reference:

(i) to consider the report of the Education Commission;

(ii) to prepare the draft of a statement on the National Policy on Education for the consideration of Government of India;and

(iii) to identify the programme for immediate action.

The Committee scrutinized only the major recommendations of the Education Commission along with the comments of the State Government and others thereon. The Committee's general approach to the problem differed from that of the Commission in three important ways. First, the Committee did not accept the recommendations of the Commission for the creation of five or six 'major' universities or for upgrading 10 per cent of the institutions at all levels to optimum standards.

The committee believed that better results could be obtained if efforts were made to maintain at least the minimum standards in all institutions and special additional assistance was offered, on the basis of proper criteria, to those institutions which showed high level of performance and promise. Secondly, they placed a greater emphasis on expansion of facilities than the Commission had done,especially at the school stage.

The Committee, therefore, did not agree with the Commission's proposal that a system of selective admission should be adopted at the higher secondary and undergraduate stages. They suggested methods for diverting a large proportion of students into different walks of life at the end of the higher secondary stage which would necessarily reduce pressure on access to higher education.

The committee further desired that every effort should be made to provide admission to institutions of higher education to all eligible students who desired to study further. Thirdly the Committee did not favour several recommendations of the Commission whose main objective was to create certain new administrative structure or changes in the existing ones. In the opinion of the Committee, such programmes would lead to increasing bureaucratisation and increase in unproductive expenditure.

Subject to the above observations, the Committee accepted several of the major recommendations of the Commission, some with modifications or changes in priority. They also added new recommendations in certain areas where the ground was not fully covered by the report of the Commission. The report of the members of Parliament was laid on the Table of the Lok Sabha on July 25, 1967.

The salient recommendations of the Committee are:

(i) The unhealthy social segregation that now takes place between the schools for the rich and those for the poor should be ended; and the primary schools should be made the common schools of the nation by making it obligatory on all children, irrespective of cast, creed, community, religion, economic condition or social status,to attend the primary school in their neighbourhood.

(ii) The development of a proper language policy can greatly assist in strengthening national unity. The key programme will be to develop all Indian languages and to adopt them as media of education at all stages.

(iii) At the secondary stage (classes I-X) the regional language should ordinarily be the medium of education. Adequate safeguards should be provided for linguistic minorities. In class XI_XII, a pupil should study at least one language of his choice in addition to the medium of education. While facilities to study languages , on an optional basis, should be adequately provided at the university-level, the study of no language should be made compulsory unless such study is an essential part of a prescribed course.

(iv) Hindi is already largely in use as a link language. The educational system should contribute to the acceleration of this progress in order to facilitate the movement of students and teachers and to strengthen national unity.

(v) Science education and research should be developed on priority basis. Great emphasis should be placed on the development of education for agriculture and industry. In technical education programmes of qualitive improvement should be stressed.

(vi) Work experience should be an integral part of general education at the school stage. Work with hands will help the young to develop insights into productive processes and use of science and inculcate in them respect for manual labour and habits of hard and responsible work.

(vii) There should be a broadly uniform educational structure in all parts of the country. The first step is to create the Ten Year School providing a common pattern of general education for all children. The national policy should be to ultimately make this period of ten years free and compulsory for all children. The next stage, the higher secondary should be uniformally raised to two years in all parts of the country under a phased programme. The duration of the course for the first degree in arts, commerce and science should be three years after the higher secondary stage.

(ix) Plans to accelerate the spread of literacy should be prepared and intensively implemented.

(x) Educational expansion should be accompanied by simultaneous efforts to raise substantially the standards of education and to keep them continuously rising.

(xi) There is an urgent need to upgrade and improve school curricula, to increase their knowledge content and to provide adequately for the development of skills,and the inculcation of right interests, attitudes and values. Similar steps are also needed at the university stage.

(xii) Regarding examination reform, attention should be concentrated on three major areas: reduction of the dominance of external examination; introduction of reforms which would make them more valid and realistic; and the adoption of a good system of internal evaluation.

The then Minister of Education on November,14 1967 moved Government Motions for discussion in Lok Sabha of the report of the Education Commission and the report of the committee of Members of Parliament. Participating in the discussion members stressed that the natural talent of the student could be unfolded only through his mother-tongue which had been recognised by the Commission.

The concept of the neighbourhood schools was also welcomed by some members. The emphasis laid by the Commission on work experience and compulsory service scheme was also commended. They considered it advisable that in the case of primary and secondary education the medium should be regional language all over the country. Members suggested that higher education should also be imparted through the regional language. For raising the quality of education, they pleaded for improving the quality of teachers. Promising people, they felt, would be attracted to the profession if the emoluments and the status of teachers were raised.

Replying to the discussion on December 6, 1967, the Minister said that one of the major recommendations of the

Education Commission was that the Government should issue a statement on the national policy on education which should provide guidance to the State Governments and local authorities in preparing and implementing educational plans in their areas. He informed the House that the Government had decided to give the widest possible opportunity to all concerned to express their views and opinions and after examining them critically to issue a comprehensive statement on the 'National Policy on Education'.

Resolution on National on National Policy

As a result of discussions on the recommendations of the Education Commission and the report of the Committee of Members of Parliament, a Resolution on National Policy on Education was formally issued by the Government of India on July 24,1966. The Resolutions enumerated seventeen principles to guide the development of education in the years ahead. These are:

(i) *Free and compulsory Education:* Free and Compulsory education for all children up to the age of 14 should be: "That this House takes note of the report of the Education Commission 1964-66, laid on the Table of the House on the 29th August, 1966 and that this House takes note of the report of the Committee of members of Parliament on Education (1967) - National Policy on Education laid on the Table of the House on the 25th July provided by the earliest possible date and suitable programme should be developed to reduce the prevailing wastage and stagnation in schools.

(ii) *Status, Emoluments and Education of Teachers:* Teacher education, particularly in service education, should received high priority. Teachers must be accorded an honoured place in society, their emoluments, and other service conditions should be adequate, and their academic freedom should be guaranteed.

(iii) *Development of Language:* The energetic development of Indian Language and literature is a sine qua non for education and cultural development. Unless this is done, the creative energies of the people would not be released; standards of education will not improve; knowledge will not be spread to the people and the gulf between the intelligentsia and the masses will remain, if not widen further. The regional language already used as media of education at the primary and secondary stages, should be urgently adopted at the university state. At the secondary stage every child should learn three languages; the languages of his region, Hindi or another Indian language if the language of his region is Hindi and English. Hindi should become the link language, a medium of expression for all the elements of the composite culture of India. For its cultural value the study of Sanskrit should be specially encouraged. Special emphasis needs to be laid on the study of English and other international languages. World knowledge is growing at a tremendous pace,especially in science and technology. India must not only keep up this growth but should also make her own significant contributions to it.

(iv) *Equalisation of Education Opportunity:* Regional imbalances should be corrected and good educational facilities should be provided in rural and other backward areas. To promote social cohesion and national integration, a common school system should be adopted; this should not, however, affect the minority rights guaranteed by the Constitution. The education of girls should receive emphasis, as should education among the backward classes.

(v) *Identification of Talent:* For the cultivation of excellence, it is necessary that talent in diverse fields should be identified at as early an age as possible and every stimulus and opportunity given for its full development.

(vi) *Work-experience and National Service:* The school and the community should be brought closer through suitable programmes of mutual service and support. Work-experience and national service including participation in meaningful and challenging programme of community service and national reconstruction should accordingly become an integral part of education.

(vii) *Science Education and Research:* These should receive high priority, and science and mathematics should be an integral part of general education till the end of the school stage.

(viii) *Education for Agriculture and industry:* This requires special emphasis. There should be at least one agricultural university in every State and the other universities selected departments may be strengthened for the study of one or more aspects of agriculture. Technical education and research should be related closely to industry. There should be continuous review of the agricultural, industrial,and other technical manpower need and a proper balance should be maintained between the output of the educational institutions and employment opportunities.

(ix) *Production of Books:* The quality of books should be improved and immediate steps should be taken for the production of high quality text-books for schools and universities. Efforts should be made to have a few basic text-books throughout the country. Special attention should be given to books for children and to university level books in Indian languages.

(x) *Examination:* A major goal of examination reform should be to improve the reliability and validity of examinations and to make evaluation a continuous process.

(xi) *Secondary Education:* Facilities for secondary education should be extended expeditiously to areas and classes which have been denied these in the past. Facilities for technical and vocational education needs to be increased, diversified and related closely to employment opportunities.

(xii) *University Education:* (a) The number of whole time students admitted to a college or university departments should be determined with reference to the laboratory, library and other facilities and to the strength of the staff. (b) New universities should be established only in case of proved necessity after adequate provisions of funds and with due care for ensuring proper standards. (c) The organisation of post-graduate courses and their standards of training and research need to be improved.(d) Centres of advanced study should be strengthened and a small number of clusters of centres aiming at the highest possible standards in research and training should be established. (e) Research in universities requires increased support,and the research institutions should, as far as possible, function within the fold of universities of in intimate association with them.

(xiii) *Part-time education and Correspondence Courses:* These should be developed on a large scale at the university stage and also be provided for secondary school students, teachers, and agricultural, industrial and other workers.

(xiv) *Spread of Literacy and Adult Education:* (a) The liquidation of mass illiteracy is necessary not only for promoting people's participation in the working of democratic institutions and for accelerating programmes of production, especially in agriculture, but also for quickening the tempo of national development in general. Employees in large commercial, industrial and other concerns should be made functionally literate as early as possible.....Teachers and students should be actively involved in organising literacy campaigns, especially as part of the Social and national Service Programme. (b) The education of young farmers and the training of youth for self-employment should have high priority.

(xv) *Games and Sports:* Playing fields and other facilities for developing a nation wide programme of physical education should be provided on a priority basis.

(xvi) *Education of minorities:* Every effort should be made not only to protect the rights of minorities but actively to promote their educational interests.

(xvii) *The Educational Structure:* A broadly uniform educational structure of ten years' general education in schools, followed by two years of higher secondary stage and three years ' course for the first degree should be adopted in all parts of the country.

The Resolution on National Policy on Education further stated: "The reconstruction of education on these lines will need additional outlay. The aim should be gradually to increase the investment in education so as to reach a level of expenditure of six per cent of the national income as early as possible".

The national policy on education, 1968 has been accepted by the Government as guiding principle for all educational development in the country supplemented by the guidelines adopted in the Sixth plan document.

The programmes spelt out in the national policy on education are being implemented by the Central and the state governments with such modifications and adjustments as are warranted from time to time by the socio-economic conditions in the country. Most significant of these programmes are universalisation of elementary education and eradication of adult illiteracy. Both these from part of Centre's minimum needs programme as well as the Revised 20-Point Programme.

For the discharge of its specific responsibility, the Union Ministry of Education has been acting directly by itself and through its institutions like the University Grants Commission, National Council of Educational Research and Training, etc. The aims and objectives of these institutions have been, by and large, to bring about improvement of standards of education and training at various levels or to promote specific areas of education like languages, production of books etc.

Priority has been given by the Government to the programme of universalisation of elementary education with emphasis on programmes for the weaker sections including girls, scheduled castes, scheduled tribes, etc. Another important priority area in education is promotion of adult education. In regard to other sectors, stress is being laid on qualitative improvement of education. Especially the technical and higher education, development of youth activities, vocationalisation of secondly education, development of regional languages, strengthening of the monitoring and evaluation machinery for the effective implementation of plan programmes, etc.

RECOMMENDATIONS FOR TEACHER EDUCATION

Professional preparation of teachers, being crucial for the qualitative improvement of education, should be treated as key area in educational development and adequate financial provision should be made for it, both at the State and national levels.

Removing Isolation of Teacher Education

In order to make professional preparation of teacher effective, teacher education must be brought into the mainstream of academic life of universities on the one hand and of school life and education development on the other.

To remove the existing isolation of teacher education from university life:

(a) Education, as distinguished from pedagogy, should be recognised as an independent academic discipline and introduced as an elective subject in courses for the first and second degree;

(b) Schools of education should be established in selected universities in collaboration with other university disciplines to develop programme in teacher education and studies and research in education,

To remove the existing isolation of teacher education from schools:

(a) Extension work should be regarded as an essential function of teacher training institutions and an Extension Service Department should be established in each institution - pre-primary, primary and secondary - as an integral part of it;

(b) Effective associations of alumni should be established to bring all students and faculty together to discuss and plan curricula;

(c) Practice-teaching for teachers under training should be organised in active collaboration with selected schools which should receive recognition from the Education Department as cooperating schools and special grants for equipment and supervision;

(d) Periodic exchange of staff of the cooperating schools and teacher training institutions should be arranged.

An intensive effort should be made to remove the existing separation among institutions preparing teachers for different stages of education or for special fields such as craft or art or physical education by:

(a) Implementing a phased programme of upgrading all training institutions to the collegiate standard with the ultimate objective of bringing all teacher education under the universities;

(b) Establishing comprehensive colleges of education in each State on a planned basis;

(c) Establishing a State Board of Teacher Education in each State to be responsible for all functions related to teacher education at all levels and in the fields.

Improving Quality of Teacher Education

The essence of a programme of teacher education is 'quality' and in its absence, teacher education becomes, not only a financial waste but a source of overall deterioration in educational standards. A programme of highest importance, therefore, is to improve the quality of teacher education. This can be done through:

a. Organisation of well-planned subject-orientation or content courses, in collaboration with University Departments (or postgraduate colleges), leading to insight into basic concepts, objectives and implications of subjects to be taught;

b. Introducing integrated courses of general and professional education in universities;

c. Vitalizing professional studies and basing them on Indian conditions through the development of educational research:

d. Using improved methods of teaching which leave greater scope for self-study and discussion and improved methods of evaluation which include continuous internal assessment of practical and sessional work as well as practice-teaching;

e. Improving practice-teaching and making it a comprehensive programme of internship;

f. Developing special course and programmes; and

g. Revising the curricula and programmes at all levels of teacher education in the light of the fundamental objective of preparing teachers for their varied responsibilities in an evolving system of education.

Duration of Training Course

The duration of professional courses should be two years for primary school teachers who have completed the secondary school course. It should be one year for graduate students but the number of working days in a year should be increased to 230.

The State Boards of Teacher Education should conduct a survey of teacher education programmes and curricula and initiate necessary revision. New professional courses must be developed to orientate headmasters and teacher educators in their special fields of work.

The postgraduate courses of education should be flexible and be planned to promote an academic and scientific study of education and to prepare personnel for specific fields requiring special knowledge or initiation. The duration of course should be increased to three terms. Quality is crucial at this stage and only institutions having properly qualified staff and facilities should be allowed to conduct them.

Improving Quality of Training Institutions

Early steps should be taken to improve training institutions for teachers on the following lines:

Secondary Teachers

a. The staff of secondary training colleges should have a double Masters degree in an academic subject and in education. A fair proportion of them should hold Doctorate degrees. They should all have taken induction or orientation courses in teacher education.

b. Qualified specialists in subjects like Psychology, Sociology, Science or Mathematics may be appointed on the staff even if they have not had professional training.

c. Summer institutes should be organised for in-service training of staff.

d. No student should be allowed to specialise in the teaching of a subject unless he has studied it for his first degree or obtained an equivalent qualifications prior to training.

e. States and Union Territories should adopt a rule that teachers in secondary schools will ordinarily teach only those subjects which they had studied for a university degree. If they are required to teach subjects other than those they have studied, they should take a special course either by correspondence or in summer institutes.

f. Attempts should be made to recruit first and good second class students to teacher training institutions and adequate scholarships should be provided for them.

Primary Teachers

a. Staff in institutions for training primary schools teachers should hold a Master's degree either in education or in an academic subject as well as B.Ed. and should have undergone special induction courses in teacher education at the primary level.

b. New appointments of primary school teachers should be restricted to those who have completed at least ten years of general education; exceptions may be made for women teachers and teachers in tribal areas.

c. Correspondence courses and liberal concessions for study leave should be made available to unqualified teachers in primary schools to improve their qualifications.

d. Special course should be organised for graduates entering primary school teaching.

e. Duration of the training course for primary school teachers should be uniformly two years for those who have completed the secondary school course. Teachers with different educational qualifications should be put through the same course.

General

It is necessary to introduce the following reforms in training institutions for primary as well as secondary schools teachers:

a. All tuition fees in training institutions should be abolished and liberal provision made for stipends and loans.

b. Every training institution should have an experimental or a demonstration school attached to it.

c. Adequate hostel facilities for trainees and residential accommodation for staff should be provided.

Libraries, laboratories, workshops etc. are very inadequate at present in most institutions, especially at the primary school teacher training institutions. These need to be improved.

Expansion of Training Facilities

Training facilities should be expanded on a priority basis. The objective should be to ensure that every teacher in a primary or a secondary school is either already trained at the time of his appointment or receives such training within three years of his appointment. From this point of view:

a. Each state should prepare a plan for expansion of training facilities in its area so that output of trained teachers meets the demand for teachers as well as the need for in-service education;

b. Part-time facilities and correspondence courses should be provided on a large scale and care should be taken to see that standards in full-time institutions are not diluted;

c. The backlog of untrained teachers should be cleared at an early date through measures of the type recommended in the Report;

d. The size of institutions should be fairly large and they should be located on a planned basis.

In-Service Education of School Teachers

A large scale and coordinated programme of in-service education for teachers should be organised by universities, training institutions and teachers' organisations for teachers of all levels. The target should be that every teacher will receive at least two or three months in-service education in every five years of his service.

The Programme of summer institutes of in-service training of secondary school teacher should be extended, with systematic follow-up and active collaboration among the agencies concerned.

Maintenance of Standards of Teacher Education

At the national level, the University Grants Commission should take the responsibility for the maintenance of standards in teacher education. The State Boards of Teacher Education should be responsible for raising standards at the state level. A substantial allocation of funds should be made available to the University Grants Commission in the Fourth Five year Plan for improvement in teacher education in Universities.

The University Grants Commission should set up a Joint Standing Committee for teacher education in collaboration with the National Council of Educational Research and Training. It should consist of competent persons from the profession and should be responsible for maintenance of standards in teacher education. The Government of India should make provision of funds in the Centrally-sponsored sector to assist State Governments to develop teacher education which is now outside the purview of universities.

6

YASHPAL COMMITTEE

A National Advisory Committee was set up on 1 March 1992 by the Ministry of Human Resource Development under the Chairmanship of Prof. Yash Pal, former Chairman of the University Grants Commission (UGC), to advise on the ways and means to reduce the academic burden on school students. The Committee submitted its Report to the Ministry on 15 July 1993.

On receipt of the Report of the National Advisory Committee, a decision was taken by the Ministry to set up a Group under the Chairmanship of Shri Y. N. Chaturvedi, Additional Secretary, Department of Education of the Ministry, to examine the recommendations of the Committee, give its views on the feasibility of implementing them and a time schedule of implementation. The Group was set up on 25 August 1993 and a copy of the Government Order giving the composition.

The. Group held two meetings on 23 and 24 September 1993 in which it examined the recommendations made in the Yash Pal Committee Report. The Group had the benefit of advice of Shri R.C. Tripathi, Adviser (Education), Planning Commission', also. In addition to participation by two senior functionaries of the National Council of Educational Research and Training (NCERT), the Group had the benefit of a detailed critique of the Yash Pal Committee Report prepared by the

NCERT. This was a particularly useful input in view of the role the NCERT plays in curriculum development, textbook preparation and other aspects of school education.

GENERAL OBSERVATIONS

The Group has observed with considerable appreciation the participative nature of the Yash Pal Committee Report about the load of curriculum on school students. While discussion on curriculum load has been extensive over the years in the mass media, it has been largely confined to the physical load of the school bag which a student has to carry. Many have felt that there has been a lot of generalisation in such discussions on the basis of the size of the school bag seen in metropolitan cities and particularly in regard to students studying in public schools even at the pre-school stage.

The Report has taken note in the beginning itself that "a survey conducted in Delhi revealed that the weight of school bag, on an average, in primary classes in public schools is more than 4 kg, while it is around 1 kg in MCD schools". This finding of the Yash Pal Committee is in tune with the information with the educational managers that firstly, the load of the school bag is not a forbidding one in schools in villages and in small towns and secondly, even in big towns, the problem is in its most aggravated form in regard to students of public schools and children of pre-school classes.

There are signs recently of the more enlightened public schools de-emphasising subject-matter learning at pre-school stage as also de-emphasising the need to prescribe a lot of books and exercise books at preschool stage. Since such schools are pace-setters, it is hoped that this example will soon influence other pre-primary schools. This Group is recommending subsequently some specific measures in pursuance of one of the recommendations of the Yash Pal Committee to accelerate this process.

The Yash Pal Committee has instead taken the problem at a more elevated plane by observing that in the present schools "a lot is taught but little is learnt or understood". it has, therefore, inferred that the load of non-learning or non-comprehension is the real load one should be concerned about. This approach of looking at the problem of academic burden has imparted to the Report of the Yash Pal Committee a great deal of significance.

Simultaneously, the Group noted that there are a few things to which the Yash Pal Committee could have given specific attention. The National Policy on Education (NPE) and the Programme of Action (POA) enunciate the need to have a national core curriculum and have spelt out some of the features of this. The policy also strongly enunciates a child-centred approach to education. It is in pursuance of this that the NCERT framed a curriculum framework for the school stage which has been accepted by all the states.

The NCERT has also developed the levels of competencies to be attained at the end of primary stage. These exercises with a lot of validity in them have been the basis for developing syllabi and textbooks for different stages of school education. While there may be some flaws in the syllabi and the textbooks prepared by the NCERT, it does not seem that they can be accused of being grossly unsuitable or overloaded in regard to curriculum load, the NCERT had carried out a study in mid-eighties which identified the physical overload of curriculum at some stages of school education and also pointed out that inadequate teacher competency, insufficient teaching days, and inadequate classroom facilities, transfer-the curriculum load to the students as well as indirectly to parents.

The Yash Pal Committee has not referred to this work and the facts stated in the preceding statements. While the main argument forming the basis of the Yash Pal Committee Report is eminently sound, with regard to the main thrust of its recommendations, some of the statements in the Report do not indicate the data or basis on which the Committee has relied.

Similarly, some of the recommendations like the one concerning affiliation of schools to the Central Board of Secondary Education (CBSE) are not accompanied by corresponding consideration in the main body of the Report.

In a few cases like in regard to medium of instruction in schools, the Committee has noted in the main body of its Report: "the educated sections of the society believe that command over English is key to upward mobility in social life... it is a well- known fact that young children studying in English medium schools mug the content of science and social sciences without understanding. It is an accepted principle of pedagogy that whatever is memorised without understanding proves burdensome on children.

Any language other than the mother tongue of the child, if used as medium of instruction, is a big source of academic burden on children". However, such strong statements do not have a corresponding recommendation. The Report also ignores the fact that for most of our students, medium of instruction is the mother tongue or regional language at all stages of school education.

Overall it is an important Report which has brought to the fore an understanding about curriculum load which one does not frequently come across. For this it is bound to raise the level of debate about the curriculum load to a qualitatively higher level. It is expected that this Report would lead to meaningful and adequate reform in curriculum formulation, textbook preparation, teacher training, etc.

The Group feels that the nature of the problem is different for each stage of school education but the Committee has not specifically referred to the distinct problems of each stage and ways of dealing with them. The views of the Group in regard to individual recommendations made by the Yash Pal Committee are given below.

RECOMMENDATIONS MADE BY THE YASH PAL COMMITTEE

Recommendation No. 1

A number of organisations and departments organise competitions at district, state and national level for students in various fields such as school subjects, exhibitions, essay writing, elocution, etc. Perhaps, the spirit behind these activities is to recognise and reward the talent in diverse fields. But, unfortunately this tends to produce somewhat unhealthy singling out of people for their brief moment of glory. Competitions where individual achievement is rewarded need to be discouraged since they deprive children of joyful learning. However, group activities and group achievements must be encouraged and rewarded to give a boost, to cooperative learning in schools.

Comments

The Group is of the view that group activity and individual effort are not mutually exclusive or antagonistic. Rewarding individual achievement does not take away the joy of learning and is also a means to motivate towards higher achievement. In the view of the Group, the educational system should promote performance of the students both as an individual and as a member of the group.

Recommendation no. 2 (a)

The process of curriculum framing and preparation of textbooks be decentralised so as to increase teachers' involvement in these tasks. Decentralisation should mean greater autonomy, within state-level apparatus, to district-level boards or other relevant authority, and to beads of schools and classroom teachers to develop curricular materials on their own, best suited to needs of local environment. All the schools be encouraged to innovate in all aspects, of, curriculurn, including choice of textbooks and other materials.

Comments

The Group noted that the curriculum and syllabi are designed by the NCERT/CBSE at national level and by the State Boards of Secondary Education/SCERTs at state level by involving teachers and through teachers. However, the number of teachers associated with this exercise is limited to the number of members of the Committee or the Board. The Yash Pal Committee has rightly underlined the need to increase teachers participation in curriculum development.

The Group feels that while the size of committees at national or state level cannot be increased beyond a limit, a meaningful way of improving teachers' participation would be for either the NCERT/CBSE/State Boards/ SCERTs to prepare the draft syllabus and finalise it after subjecting it to regional or district level consideration by a large body of teachers or, in the alternative, to get multiple syllabi developed at regional and district levels on the basis of which the final syllabi could be prepared at the state/national level.

The Group, however, does not recommend decentralisation in the preparation of syllabus or textbooks at the district or school level because it will be difficult to ensure adequate projection of national identity and of composite culture of India. Also, in such a situation, the adherence to even minimum standards in all parts of the country may become difficult. In regard to textbooks, the Group agrees with the Yash Pal Committee that the primary responsibility for preparing textbooks, particularly for the lower classes should be that of teachers. It may, however, be remembered that the involvement of experts since the early 1960s led to qualitative improvement in school textbooks. They helped in weeding out dead wood, brought in new perspectives in tune with contemporary knowledge. The Group, however, shares the concern of the

Yash Pal Committee that many textbooks presently tend to project predominantly the urban middle class life style. Therefore, the Group recommends that :

(a) The writing of textbooks, as far as possible, should be assigned to school teachers and to those who have developed professional expertise in the area. Subject-matter specialists should be engaged as consultants or advisers to vet the content and presentation of the subject-matter to ensure its accuracy.

(b) In states which have distinct socio-cultural geographical zones, different and parallel sets of textbooks with the same learning objectives should be prepared and used in schools for each such distinct socio-cultural geographical region.

(c) A conscious effort should be made by the textbook preparation agencies to take examples from rural areas for illustrating various points because a large majority of students are in rural areas.

(d) The textbook preparation agencies should undertake systematic review of all textbooks in a time-bound manner to ensure that any trivial matter which may have got included in the textbooks is weeded out. Similarly, such a review should also try to eliminate elements of repetitions of the topics covered in previous classes.

(e) The Group noted that, in some cases, the textbooks for subjects other than languages in some classes are written in a language which is considerably more complex and difficult than the language used in textbooks for that class. It, therefore, recommends that the group which writes a textbook should include one language teacher who should vet the manuscript to ensure that the degree of difficulty of the language used in the subject-matter is not more than the degree of difficulty designed for language competency for that class. In regard to curriculum transaction and teaching materials, the Group noted that there are no restrictions on schools and teachers to innovate. Indeed, the teacher training courses have consistently advocated this and many organisations have introduced special programmes to promote this. Needless to say that schools and teachers should be motivated to innovate to the fullest extent in regard to teaching methods and use of teaching materials.

Recommendation no. 2 (b)

Voluntary organisations with a specific commitment to pedagogical innovations within the formal or non-formal system be provided greater freedom and support in development of curriculum, textbooks and teacher training. A suitable and adequate mechanism be evolved for wider dissemination of the experiences of such organisations.

Comments

The Group fully agrees that voluntary organisations with a commitment to education should be encouraged in all possible manners. The Group also noted that the governments, both at the national and the state levels have, in recent past, made a substantial move to expand such cooperation. The process needs to be continued. However, for reasons mentioned in 2 (a), the Group does not favour decentralisation in curriculum development and textbooks preparation to the extent of entrusting it to voluntary organisations because of the sensitivity of the matter.

Recommendation no.2 (c)

We endorse the idea of setting up education committees at village, block and district levels to undertake planning and supervision of schools under their jurisdiction.

Comments

This is acceptable in principle. This has been strongly advocated in para 10.8 of the NPE, 1986. Following the Constitutional Amendment for decentralisation at Panchayat level, the Central Advisory Board of Education (CABE) has already constituted a Committee on Decentralised Management of Education to examine and recommend measures for effectively carrying out the desired involvement of the local committees. Therefore, this recommendation should be implemented in the light of the recommendations of the CABE Committee.

Recommendation no. 2 (d)

Sufficient contingency amount (not less than 10 per cent of the total salary bill of the school) be placed at the disposal of beads of schools for purchase, repair and replacement of pedagogical equipment.

Comments

This is acceptable. The State/UT Governments and autonomous bodies of the Central Government controlling their respective chain of schools (Kendriya Vidyalayas, Navodaya Vidyalayas, Central Tibetan Schools, Railway Schools and Sainik Schools and other schools run by the Defence establishments) should be urged to give this authority to the Principals/Headmasters of the schools to make repairs to school buildings, purchase, repair and replace pedagogical equipment and books and also to carry out innovative projects, subject to the control of the local education committees. The organisations controlling the schools and the State Governments should categorically specify that the Head of the school does not require approval of any higher educational authority and the School Management/ Advisory Committee for using the available money for these purposes.

Recommendation no. 3

The culture of writing textbooks be changed so as to involve a much larger number of teachers in the preparation of textbooks. The scientists and experts in various disciplines may be associated with the preparation of textbooks as consultants and not as writers of the books. Initiative in this regard should rest with groups of enlightened and innovative teachers who should be provided training in book writing.

Comments

The group agrees with the purport of this recommendation-greater involvement of teachers-and the views of the Group on this recommendation is included in the comments on 2 (a).

Recommendation no. 4

At least three parallel systems of school education (syllabus, textbooks and examination) are running concurrently in different states. In each state majority of schools are affiliated to the State Board of Education while a few are affiliated to either CBSE or ICSE. The schools affiliated to CBSE in the states other than Delhi enjoy the prestige of being elite schools. The CBSE curriculum becomes a trend-setter for the State Boards leading to heavier curriculum for majority of children. Therefore, the Committee recommends that jurisdiction of CBSE be restricted to Kendriya and Navodaya Vidyalayas and all other schools be affiliated to the respective State Boards.

Comments

The Group has been unable to appreciate the arguments put forth by the Yash Pal Committee in this recommendation. The choice of educational boards that the schools have is already very limited there is no free choice and it can be exercised only with the approval of the State Government. Therefore, if a school in any part of the country has the choice of affiliating with one Board or the other, it should be generally good for education. As for CBSE, it relies heavily on the NCERT for developing syllabi and preparing textbooks. The NCERT, in turn, operates- within the national policy framework and on the basis of guidelines contained in the National Curriculum Framework.

Rightly the NCERT keeps in view the existing standards in the country, the capability of students, and standards in developed countries because the syllabus and textbook must take note of all these. If there is unnecessary material in some of the NCERT books, it should be eliminated as the Group has suggested in the preceding recommendations. However, there is not adequate material on record to substantiate that CBSE syllabi or NCERT books per se are overloaded.

Also, the Yash Pal Committee has recommended that affiliation to CBSE should be restricted to Kendriya and Navodaya Vidyalayas with all other schools being affiliated to respective State Boards. If affiliation to the CBSE is good for Kendriya and Navodaya Vidyalayas it cannot be bad for other schools.

Recommendation no. 5 (a)

Appropriate legislative and administrative measures be adopted to regulate the opening and functioning of early childhood education institutions (pre-schools). Norms regarding accommodation, staff, apparatuses, play materials be laid down for the recognition of these schools. It should be ensured that these institutions do not perpetrate violence on young children by inflicting a heavy dose of 'over education' in the form of formal teaching of Reading, Writing and Numbers. The practice of holding tests and interviews for admission to nursery class be abolished.

Recommendation no. 5 (b)

Norms for granting recognition to private schools be made more stringent. This will prove conducive for improving the quality of learning on the one hand and arrest growing commercialisation on the other. The norms, thus developed, be made uniformly applicable to all schools including the state-run institutions.

Comments [5 (a) and 5 (b)]

The Group is in agreement with the recommendations. While the NCERT has prepared some norms for the staff, nature of curriculum and educational material for pre-primary stage, this sector of education in the country is largely unsupervised and unregulated it is also a known fact that most of these schools are loading the students with the burden of formal teaching of various subjects. The Group advised that an appropriate regulatory mechanism should be urgently set up in the country to ensure that learning at this stage is by playway method and formal teaching of subjects is scrupulously prevented.

Similarly, the Group agrees that recognition and affiliation of both private and government schools should be made more stringent so that schools lacking in minimum essential facilities are not allowed to function because it really means punishment to the students. Although there is a well set arrangement for recognition and affiliation of schools but due to extraneous pressures the standards sometimes are not observed. The Group would like to suggest that the possibility of having a legislation to, specify norms of facilities in schools and providing or powers to prevent opening of schools which do not have facilities should be seriously considered.

Recommendation no. 6

There is no justification for torturing the young children by compelling them to carry heavy bags of books everyday to schools. Textbooks should be treated as school property and thus, there should be no need for children to purchase the books individually and carry them daily to homes. A separate time-table for the assignment of homework and for the use of textbooks and notebooks be prepared by the school and be made known to the children in advance.

Recommendation no. 7

The nature and character of homework needs a radical change. In the primary classes, children should not be given any homework, save for extension of explorations in the home environment. In the upper primary and secondary classes, homework, where necessary, should be non-textual, and textbooks, when needed for work at home should be made available on a rotation basis.

Comments (6 and 7)

The Group has already agreed that there should be no formal teaching of subjects in the pre-school stage. The Group also feels that there should be no homework and project work at the primary stage (Classes I-V). However, it is an extreme point of observation that textbooks should be treated as school property. Besides the financial implications arising out of the burden on schools to purchase the textbooks and the concomitant responsibility on the schools to store the books when most of the schools of the country do not have either the financial resources or storage capacities, the children would be devoid of the opportunity to refer to the textbooks in their homes.

For an overwhelming majority of school students of the country, the textbooks remain as the only source of reading material. The Group recommends that the class routine for the upper primary, secondary and higher secondary stages should be drawn up in such a way that every subject is not required to be taught everyday. This should be included in the norms for compliance by every school which the Group has suggested in para. 5 (a) and 5 (b) above.

Recommendation no. 8

The existing norm for teacher-pupil ratio (i.e. 1:40) should be enforced and an attempt should be made to reduce this to 1:30, at least in the primary classes, as a basis for future educational planning.

Comments

The Group agrees with a higher teacher-pupil ratio with improved teaching and standards of education. It understands that in reality the existing teacher-pupil ratio is around 1:40 in most parts of the country. Attempts should be made to bring it to 1:30 over a period of time. Such change in ratio would have a very large financial implication because of the need to induct a large number of extra teachers and, therefore, this can be done only over a period of time. Efforts should be made to ensure that the class size does not exceed 40.

Recommendation no. 9

Greater use of the electronic media be made for the creation of a child-centred social ethos in the country. A regular television programme addressed to students, teachers and parents and possibly called 'Shiksha Darshan' be launched, along the lines of the 'Krishi Darshan' programme.

Comments

Greater use of electronic media for education is an essential part of modernising the educational system. A regular programme on TV addressed to students, teachers and parents would be very welcome. The Group took note of the fact that the Ministry of Human Resource Development, Department of Education, has already made a request for allocating one channel for education out of 15 or 16 channels which have recently become available with the commissioning of INSAT 2-

A. The Group strongly suggests that an educational channel should be operationalised at the earliest and this channel should include a programme of the nature suggested by the Yash Pal Committee.

Recommendation no. 10 (a)

Inadequate Programme of teacher preparation leads to unsatisfactory quality of learning in schools the B.Ed. programme should offer the possibility of specialisation in secondary or elementary or nursery education the duration of the programme should either be one year after graduation or three-four years after higher secondary. The content of the programme should be restructured to ensure its relevance to the changing needs of school education and to make it more practicum-centred. The emphasis in these programmes should be on enabling the trainees to acquire the ability for self-learning and independent thinking. Pre-service teacher education programme, being a professional course, has to be a rigorous, thorough and intensive programme. Therefore, B.Ed. degree courses by correspondence be derecognised.

Comments

There is a lot of merit in the argument advanced by the Yash Pal Committee for having a programme of B.Ed. aimed at elementary or secondary education. In metropolitan cities, a large number of teachers are actually getting recruited for preschool and elementary schools with B.Ed. qualifications. Recruitment in KVS and NVS is also, in practice, based on B.Ed. qualifications. Therefore, this reality needs to be taken cognizance of and the present practice of focussing on secondary education in B.Ed. needs to be given up by enabling B.Ed. to be pursued with either specialisation in secondary or in elementary or in pre-school education. In any case the existing arrangements, including the District Institutes of

Education and Training (DIETs) for preparing primary school teachers need to be continued and strengthened.

The recommendation of the Yash Pal Committee for derecognising B.Ed. degree by correspondence course is more problematic, while the National Council for Teacher Education (NCTE) has earlier made recommendations on these lines and the UGC has been interacting with the concerned universities during the last ten years on that basis, such courses are continuing. A recent expert committee of the UGC has expressed that for women candidates and for people from rural areas, B.Ed. correspondence course opens up valuable career opportunities. Also, in a large number of countries, B.Ed. through correspondence course is one of the prominent courses in distance mode. These arguments cannot be totally ignored. The Group understands that the matter is at an advanced stage of consideration in the UGC. Also the NCTE as a statutory body is expected to become operational in the near future. The Group recommends that this matter should be referred to the UGC and the NCTE for appropriate decision.

Recommendation no. 10 (b)

The continuing education of teachers must be institutionalised. The organisation of inservice education programmes and other activities aimed at professional growth of teachers be systematically designed and conducted imaginatively.

Comments

The emphasis given by the Yash Pal Committee to continuing education of teachers is totally unexceptionable. Thus DIETs are being set up in the country primarily to meet this need. Distance education system also is coming up in the country which can be used to meet the needs of inservice education. However, the progress in this regard has been slow. The Group fully endorses the need to set up arrangements for regular and periodic inservice training of teachers and recommends that the

DIETs should be operationalised as early as possible and the distance mode of education should be used extensively to strengthen inservice training of teachers.

Recommendation no. 11

The public examinations taken at the end of Class X and XII be reviewed with a view to ensure replacement of the prevailing text- based and 'quiz type' questioning by the concept-based questioning. This single reform is sufficient to improve the quality of learning and save the children from the tyranny of rote memorisation.

Comments

The Group feels that the Yash Pal Committee's reference to the concept-based questioning perhaps advocates greater importance to questions of higher ability. The Group agrees with this but it should be remembered that assessment should test various kinds of abilities and not just of one kind. The Group also feels that the Boards of School Education should emphasise Continuous and Comprehensive Evaluation (CCE) that incorporates both scholastic and non-scholastic aspects of education, spread over the total span of instructional time as stipulated in para 8.24 (iii) of the NPE, 1986.

Recommendation no. 12 (a)

A project team with a number of sub-groups be set up in each state to examine the syllabi and textbooks for all school classes, The sub- groups be required to decide the following:

(i) The minimum number of topics required to be taught.

(ii) The minimum number of concepts to be introduced within each topic.

(iii) The total time needed for teaching this minimum number of concepts comfortably by a teacher in the total working days realistically available in a year.

Comments

The Minimum Levels of Learning (MLLs) for language (mother tongue), mathematics and environmental studies for Classes I-V have already been prepared at the national level in 1990 and the NCERT, the Boards of School Education and the SCERTs have developed their resources to introduce the MLLs at the primary stage. Therefore, setting up another Project Team for the same purpose would amount to avoidable duplication. The Group feels that though in para 5.4.5 (vii) and para 21.3.1 (a), the POA, 1992 has called for laying down MLLs at the upper primary stage and in para 21.3.1 (b), the POA, 1992 has urged the Boards to lay down expected levels of attainment at Classes IX-XII, the reasonableness of laying down MLLs at the upper primary stage and above deserves a careful reconsideration since knowledge base is supposed to grow at a fast pace after the primary stage.

Moreover, with emphasis shifting to subject-matter learning at the upper primary stage and above, the idea of laying down uniform MLLs after primary stage does not seem to be a viable proposition. However, at the time of curriculum renewal and preparation of textbooks, the curriculum/textbook designers should systematically check that those can be covered within the instructional time available to teachers. The NCERT at the national level and the State Boards/SCERTs/SIEs at the state level may consider the desirability of reviewing the school curricula/textbooks to ensure that nonessential matter and repetitive treatment of concepts in subjects in different classes is minimised as far as possible without sacrificing the requirements of cognitive development.

Recommendation no. 12 (b)

Mathematics curriculum for primary classes in all parts of the country be reviewed with a view to slowing down the pace at which children are required to learn basic mathematical concepts, and broadening the scope of primary mathematics to include areas other than number work (eg. space- and shape-related concepts and problem solving). The tendency embedded in the syllabi and textbooks of primary mathematics to accelerate children's mathematical skills by teaching them mechanical rules at the expense of understanding and intelligent application ought to be discouraged in future syllabi and texts.

Comments

The Group endorses the recommendation that mathematics and syllabi for other subjects should be reviewed to assess whether they are overloaded. But it would not like to state at this stage that they indeed are overloaded. The MLLs adopted by the MHRD are now being tried out and the question of review should be considered only on the basis of the feedback. As has been referred to in the preceding recommendations, syllabi have to be designed keeping in view the existing standards, and capacity of students and standards in developed countries. However, the Group endorses the statement of the Yash Pal Committee that the syllabus should emphasise understanding and intelligent application rather than memorising without understanding.

Recommendation no. 12 (c)

Language textbooks should adequately reflect the spoken idiom., An attempt should be made in future textbooks to give adequate representation to children's life experiences, imaginary stories and poems, and stories reflecting the lives of ordinary people in different parts of the country. Pedantic language and excessive didacticism ought to be avoided.

Comments

These recommendations are acceptable. The NCERT and the Boards including CBSE and Council for the Indian School Certificate Examination (CISCE) should review their respective language textbooks from these angles.

Recommendation no. 12 (d)

Science syllabi and textbooks in the primary classes should provide greater room and necessity for experimentation than they do at present. In place of didacticism in areas like health and sanitation, the texts should emphasise analytical reflection on real-life situations. A great deal of trivial material included in primary- level science texts should be dropped.

Comments

The Group has already given its views that all the existing textbooks should be screened in a time-bound manner for eliminating trivial matter and repetition. The Group endorses the recommendation that there should be greater scope for experimentation at the primary stage. This should be systematically promoted through a large programme of inservice education of teachers.

Recommendation no. 12 (e)

The syllabi of natural sciences throughout the secondary and senior secondary classes be revised in a manner so as to ensure that most of the topics included are actively linked to experiments or activities that can be performed by children and teachers.

Comments

The Group is of the view that while experiments and activities at all levels are important, the selection of topics in science curriculum at higher stages cannot be determined by the criterion that they are linked to experiment, etc. Every effort should, however, be made to see that experiments and activities, as much as possible, depending on the nature of the topic, are made a part of science teaching even at higher levels.

Recommendation no. 12 (f)

Besides imparting knowledge of history and geography the social sciences curriculum for Classes VI-VIII and IX-X should convey the philosophy and methodology of the functions of our socio-political and economic system and enable the students to analyse,understand and reflect on the problems and priorities of socio-economic development. The repetitious nature of history syllabus should be changed. The history of ancient times should be introduced for systematic study in secondary classes (DC and X). The history syllabus for Classes VI- VIII should focus on the freedom struggle and post-independence developments. Me civics, as it is taught today, puts a great load on children's capacity to memorise. Therefore, it may be dropped in its present form and be replaced by 'contemporary studies'. The study of geography be related to contemporary reality.

Comments

As regards the Committee's suggestion that history syllabus for Classes VI-VIII should focus on freedom struggle and post-independence developments, the Group holds the view that a large majority of children drop out at the end of Class VIII, which is also the last year of compulsory education and, therefore, it would not be educationally sound to allow such a big section of our children to remain oblivious of the entire heritage of India before the freedom struggle. The Committee seems to have linked spiral approach (which is based on a well-established principle of curriculum construction) with repetition which leads to boredom and load and trivialisation of ideas'. The Group feels that in geography greater importance should be given to study of contemporary problems. The context or implications of the Committee's recommendation for replacing 'Civics' by 'Contemporary Studies' are not clear.

ADDITIONAL SUGGESTIONS OF THE GROUP

The Yash Pal Committee has made many thought-provoking

recommendations which the Group has tried to recommend for implementation in a more specific manner. if these are implemented efficiently, the standards of school education will undoubtedly improve and as the Yash Pal Committee has envisaged alienation of students from education and the burden of 'non-understanding' on them would effectively diminish. However, in addition to the recommendations made by the Yash Pal Committee, there are a few more issues which immediately present themselves for consideration While considering any exercises for reducing the load of curriculum. The Group would like to suggest these also for implementation.

1. *Age of Entry*

It is a known fact that in India children join school at a rather early age than their counterparts do in most of the developed countries. At the age of 4 and 5, a difference of one year in age makes a lot of difference in the mental capability of a child. A more mature child can easily cope with the learning requirements. The effect of early admissions of children in schools, particularly at the pre-primary stage, is that she/he is unable to cope with the demands that the syllabus makes and consequently she/he starts in a situation of personal inadequacy. This contributed significantly to the load of non-learning. It is, therefore, desirable that the minimum age of admission to pre-primary classes and in primary classes should be reconsidered for being raised by one year.

2. *Teaching Days*

Kothari Commission recommended 210 teaching days but the actual number of school days are 125-150. Since the syllabi are framed on the basis that 210 days will be available, this only means that either a part of syllabus is not covered by the teacher or that she/he covers the syllabus in a hurried manner which creates difficulty for students for being able to cope with a lot of content in a limited time. Effective action to increase the number of teaching days to 210 in a year would undoubtedly very substantially reduce the daily learning load and would also improve standards.

3. *Classroom Facilities*

In large number of schools in the country not only the facilities in the classroom but the classroom themselves are grossly deficient. This inevitably affects the quality of teaching and, therefore, of learning. The Yash Pal Committee has recommended and we have endorsed that recommendation earlier in this Report that norms for school facilities should be effectively and strictly enforced for recognition/affiliation. However, since government is the major funding agency for most schools, there should be a positive movement for improving availability of classrooms and improving availability of educational aids in schools.

For primary schools, the Government of India is implementing a large programme of Operation Blackboard and in the Eighth Plan it is being extended to cover upper primary classes also. At secondary level, the Government of India is implementing a scheme for assisting schools for improving science equipment. However, a much large effort needs to be made it would be imperative that the effort of the government is supplemented by individuals and philanthropic bodies because the requirement is large it would be appropriate that the governments and the school systems consider how best they can encourage such individuals and philanthropic bodies to help schools to develop.

4. *Strengthening of the Professional Support System*

An area which needs to be looked into is the qualitative improvement of professional bodies like the SCERTs, Textbook Bureaus and Boards of School Education who are primarily responsible for curriculum, textbooks and examinations. It is these bodies which will ultimately have to reckon with the problem of load. Under the centrally sponsored scheme of teacher education, there is a component of strengthening of SCERTs which should be taken up ion a priority basis.

5. *"...impact of examinations, admission to higher education institutions, including professional courses"*

This was one of the terms of reference of the Committee which has not been dealt with in the Report. The CABE may consider so refer this matter to a committee drawn from school and higher education. Another term of reference of the Committee related to the measures such as formal recongnition and weightage to sports and games and co- curricular and extracurricular activities..." A CABE Committee is looking into this matter and its report is expected to be presented to the CA-BE shortly.

TIME SCHEDULE FOR IMPLEMENTATION

As regards laying down a time schedule for implementation of the recommendations found feasible, the Group felt that the recommendations are of long-term nature. Moreover, the report of the National Advisory Committee as well as this report of the Group would be placed before the CABE in its meeting scheduled to be held on 15.10.1993. As such, it would be advisable to wait for the CABE's approval to Committee's recommendations and then draw up a time schedule for implementation of the recommendations accepted by the CABE.

7

POA 1992

Till 1976, according to the Constitution of India, education was the exclusive responsibility of the State Governments, although the Union Government was concerned with certain areas such as "Coordination and determination of standards in institutions for higher education or research and scientific and technical institutions". By the Constitution Amendment Act, 1976, the Seventh Schedule was amended making education "including technical education, medical education and universities... vocational and technical training of labour", a joint responsibility of both the State and Union Governments.

Though decisions regarding the organisation and structure of education largerly continue to be the concern of the State Governments, the Union Government has also a clear responsibility regarding the quality and character of education in general and that of the higher and technical education in particular. In addition to policy formulation, the Department of Education in the Ministry of Human Resource Development (MHRD) shares with the states the responsibility for educational planning. The Central Advisory Board of Education (CABE) set up in 1935, continues to play a leading role in the evolution and monitoring of educational policies and programmes. The most notable outcome of its activities was the formulation of the National Policy of Education (NPE), 1986 and the Programme of Action (PoA), 1986 drawn up within the policy framework. The NPE and PoA have been revised in 1992.

The NPE,1986 and the PoA,1992 envisaged that free and compulsory education of satisfactory quality should be provided to all children up to the age of 14 years before the commencement of the 21st century (See also Update). The government committed itself to earmark about six per cent of the Gross Domestic Product (GDP) for education by the year 2000 AD and 50 per cent of the outlay would be allotted to Primary Education. Both the targets however seem to be unachievable even in the distant future. The expenditure on education as a percentage of GDP could not even cross the 3.5 mark.

The system of education in India consists of three streams: (i) the School Stream, (ii) the University (including the College) Stream, and (iii) the Non-university Stream. The school stream (along with ITIs and Polytechnics) and the university stream may be called the formal sector of Indian education. The non-university stream consists, on the other hand, of both formal and informal sectors.

THE SCHOOL STREAM

The school stream comprises three stages: (i) pre-primary, (ii) primary (or elementary), and (iii) secondary. The pre-primary or pre-learning stage consisting of nursery and kindergarten schools terminates when the children attain the age of five years. At the age of six , they enter the primary stage. There are two levels at the primary stage - the primary (Classes I to V) and the upper primary (Classes VI to VIII). Students are expected to complete the primary stage at the age of 13 years and enter the secondary stage. Article 45 of the Constitution of India stipulates free and compulsory education for all the children until they complete the age of 14. In 1993, the Supreme Court, in its order in the Unnikrishnan case, has also declared education of children up to the age of 14 years to be a Fundamental Right. However, the target of universalisation of primary (or elementary) education is yet to be achieved.

The secondary stage, in turn, has two levels - the secondary (Classes IX and X) and the higher (or senior) secondary (Classes XI and XII). There is a public examination at the end of Class X called the Secondary School Leaving Certificate (SSLC) examination or the Secondary School Certificate (SSC) examination. This examination corresponds to the Matriculation examination of yesteryears.

Another public examination is conducted at the end of Class XII called Higher Secondary Certificate (HSC) examination or "10+2 examination". In some states, higher secondary education (Classes XI and XII) is also called the Intermediate education and the corresponding examination Intermediate examination. Secondary and higher secondary education are regulated by State Boards of Secondary Education and State Boards of Higher Education (or Boards of Intermediate Education) respectively.

In several States there is only one Board for both the levels. Secondary and Higher Secondary schools are managed by state governments as well as by private societies and trusts. The State Boards accord recognition to schools, formulate syllabuses and conduct public examinations. Besides the State Boards, there are two Boards whose jurisdictions extend all over the country, viz., the Central Board of Secondary Education (CBSE), established in 1929 by the Government of India, and the Council for the Indian School Certification Examination (ICSE). Any school in the country can get affiliated to these Boards. Both the Boards conduct Secondary School Certificate (Class X) and Senior School Certificate (Class XII) examinations.

There is yet another Board named the National Open School (NOS). It provides secondary and higher secondary education through distance learning mode, and conducts public examinations and awards certificates like any other Board. A brief account of the NOS has been given in Chapter 6 (Learning from a Distance). The Annexure gives a list of Secondary and Higher Secondary Boards. By the time students complete the higher secondary education, they should have attained the age of 17 years. The minimum age prescribed for admission to many post-higher secondary courses is, therefore, 17 years.

In addition, there is a parallel system outside the School Stream - Industrial Training (ITIs) and the polytechnics. Polytechnic education is of three-year duration after Class 10. These institutions, sponsored both by the government and private organisations, are under the control of the State Boards of Technical Education, and as such belong to the formal sector.

THE UNIVERSITY STREAM

In the Indian system, education imparted beyond the 10+2 stage, is called higher education (or tertiary level education). Education at this level is provided by universities and a network of colleges, affiliated to them but not exclusively. There is also a parallel Non-university Stream, the third stream of the Indian educational system which is also a significant component of higher education. The universities are established by State and Central Acts. Several States have consolidated the individual University Acts into a single Act, e.g., Karnataka State Universities Act, 1975, Andhra Pradesh Universities Act, 1991. Besides such universities, there are also two other categories of institutions of higher learning which enjoy university status - institutions deemed to be universities (or simply "deemed universities" and institutions of national importance.

The University Grants Commission (UGC) constituted under the University Grants Commission Act, 1956, is the apex body which oversees the standards of teaching, examinations and research in universities. It also looks into the financial needs of universities and allocates and disburses grants to universities and colleges. All the universities are members of the Association of Indian Universities (AIU), an autonomous inter-university organization. It liaises between universities and other official and non-official agencies in the field of education, both at the national and international levels.

The University Stream offers degree courses at three levels - first degree (or graduate degree, i.e., Bachelor's degree); postgraduate degree (i.e., Master's degree); and Doctoral and post-Doctoral degrees (i.e., PhD, DLitt/DSc). There is also a pre-Doctoral degree (M Phil). Besides, universities also offer certificate and diploma level courses. A brief overview of the duration of courses at these three levels follows. Bachelor's degree is obtained after three years of study in one of the streams - Arts (BA), Science (BSc), and Commerce (BCom). Most of the first degree professional courses are of four-year duration although there are variations. For example, in the case of medicine (MBBS), the duration is four and half-years, while the dentistry course (BDS) is of four-year duration. For both the courses there is a compulsory period of internship. The duration of Master's degree programme also varies. MA, MSc, MCom, MBA programmes are of two-year duration. In the case of ME/MTech, the duration is only one and half years; but the computer application course (MCA) needs three years of study. There are also postgraduate courses of one-year duration leading to the award of Bachelor's degree, e.g., BEd (Education), BLISc (Library and Information Science), BCJ (Communication & Journalism).

A further study of one-year leads to Master's degree in the concerned subjects. The duration of law course is three years leading to the award of a postgraduate degree (BL/LLB), although integrated BL/LLB programmes of five-year duration after 10+2 are also available. This decision perhaps, has led to the introduction of integrated Master's degree programmes in several subjects after 10+2. By and large, the students attain the age of 20 years when they obtain the first degree, and 21-22 years in case of first degree in professional courses. They are about 23 years when they complete the Master's degree programmes in most of the disciplines.

The MPhil course which is the preparatory programme for doctoral level(PhD) studies, is of one and half year duration. PhD programme takes two years or more depending upon individual students. There are also two higher post PhD degrees leading to the awards of DSc and DLitt degrees. Many universities and institutions offer part-time courses in selected subjects (mostly in management), the duration of which is more than that of a full-time programme. For example, a part-time course in management (MBA) needs three years of study instead of normal two years for regular courses. In addition to the degree courses, all the universities offer a plethora of diploma and certificate courses. Their range is wide and covers subjects from "Religious Dialogue" to "Computer Aided Design". Some are undergraduate diploma courses while some others are postgraduate courses. The duration, depending upon the subjects, varies from one year to three years.

NON-UNIVERSITY STREAM

Like the ITIs and polytechnics which function outside the School Stream, there are a large number of educational institutions which function outside the university stream. Most of them offer professional programmes, the largest concentration being in the management and information technology areas. While many of them are recognised by the concerned regulatory authorities, some are not. This stream is an important component of the national system of education and supplements the educational and training programmes offered by the university stream.

Regulatory Authorities

An important aspect of the Indian educational system is the role of the statutorily established regulatory authorities for the regulation and maintenance of uniform standards of education and training in professional subjects. Prior approval of these authorities are essential for starting new institutions, introduction of new courses and fixing the intake capacity in each course.

Distance Education

A recent development in the Indian educational system is the introduction of the system of distance education. As the name suggests, unlike face-to-face teaching, it is the mode of education wherein instruction is provided to students located at distant places, even the remotest areas of the country. The distance learning, all over the world, is now considered an important mode of delivering education at the door steps.

National Policy On Education

Educational policy and progress have been reviewed in the light of the goal of national development and priorities set from time to time. In its Resolution on the National Policy on Education in 1968, an emphasis on quality improvement and a planned, more equitable expansion of educational facilities and the need to focus on the education of girls was stressed. About a decade ago and a half later, the National Policy on Education was formulated which was further updated in 1992. The NPE 1986 provides for a comprehensive policy framework for the development of education upto the end of the century and a Plan of Action (POA) 1992, assigning specific responsibilities for organising, implementing and financing its proposals.

India's commitment to the spread of knowledge and freedom of thought among its citizens is reflected in its Constitution. The Directive Principle contained in Article 45 enjoins that " the State shall endeavour to provide within a period of ten years from the commencement of this Constitution, for free and compulsory education for all children until they complete the age of fourteen years". Article 29 (i) provides that any citizen having a distinct language, script, special care of the economic and educational interests of the underprivileged sections, particularly, the Scheduled Castes and Scheduled Tribes is laid down as an obligation of the State under article 46.

Though education is in the concurrent list of the Constitution, the State Governments play a very major role in the development of education particularly in the primary and the secondary education sectors.

STRUCTURE AND PROGRESS OF EDUCATION IN INDIA

The focus in on the broad dimensions and magnitude of the structure, organisation and progress in education. Further it also highlights growth and priority areas in education in India that point to the challenges of the future. There are about 888 thousands educational institutions in the country with an enrolment of about 179 millions. Elementary Education System in India is the second largest in the World with 149.4 millions children of 6-14 years enrolled and 2.9 million teachers. This is about 82% of the children in the age group.

Structure of School Education

A uniform structure of school education, the 10+2 system has been adopted by all the States and Union Territories of India. However, within the States and the UTs, there remains variations in the number of classes constituting the Primary, Upper Primary, High and Higher Secondary school stages, age for admission to class I, medium of instruction, public examinations, teaching of Hindi and English, number of working days in a year, academic session, vacation periods, fee structure, compulsory education etc.

Age Restriction For Admission

The minimum age for admission to class I of the Primary School stage is generally 5+ or 6+ years. In 22 States/UTs the minimum age for admission to Class I is 5+ years and in 7 States/UTs the minimum age for admission is 6+ years. There is no age restriction in the case of Mizoram. In Gujarat, the minimum age for admission is 5+ years (voluntary) and 6+ years (compulsory). In Lakshadweep, the minimum age for admission is 5 ½ years.

Number Of Working Days

The number of working days of School Education in a year is generally more than 200 days in all the States/UTs.

Academic Session

The academic session begins from different months of the year in the different States and Union Territories. However, in most of the States, the long vacation periods are availed in the summer season while in some of the hilly States, these fall in the winter months.

Compulsory Education

Compulsory education has been enforced in four States and Union Territories at the primary stage of education while in eight States/UTs there is compulsory education covering the entire elementary stage of education. As many as 20 States/ UTs have not introduced any measure of compulsion upto the year 1997-98.

Free Education

A majority of States and Union Territories have introduced free education in Classes I-XII of their schools.

Tution Fees Per Annum Per Child In Govt Schools

In the States/UTs where education is not free for classes IX and above, the annual fee varies considerably from the highest level of Rs. 360/- for classes XI and XII in the case of Meghalaya to the lowest at Rs. 48/- in the case of Assam.

Financing of Education

From 1968 onwards, goal has been to set apart 6% of National Income on education. In spite of resource constraints as well as competing priorities, the Budgetary expenditure on education by Centre & States as percentage of Gross National Product has steadily increased from 0.8% in 1951-52 to 3.3% in 1994-95.

Para 11.4 of NPE, 1986 states "that the investment on education be gradually increased to reach a level of 6% of the National Income as early as possible. Since the actual level of investment has remained far short of that target, it is important that greater determination is shown now to find the funds for the programmes laid down in this policy. While actual requirements will be computed from time to time on the basis of monitoring and review, the outlay on education will be stepped up to ensure that during the 8th Five year Plan and onwards it will uniformly exceed 6% of the national income".

The total budgetary expenditure on Education by the Education Departments of the Centre and States has increased from Rs. 644.6 millions in 1951-52 to Rs. 300,000millions in 1995-96. In terms of its share in total budgetary expenditure, it has increased from 7.9% in 1951-52 to 11.1% in 1995-96.

There are, at present 130 plan schemes in the Department with a total Eighth Plan outlay of Rs. 74430 Millions. The total plan outlay of the Department for the year 1996-97 is Rs. 33827 millions. There are 18 Centrally Sponsored Schemes which account for 65.7% of the total plan outlay. Mid-Day-Meal Scheme is the major Centrally Sponsored Scheme with 1996-97 outlay of Rs.14,000 millions. Other major Centrally Sponsored Schemes are Operation Blackboard, Non-formal Education, Teacher Education, Post Literacy and Continuing Education and Vocational Education with 1996-97 Outlay of Rs. 2790 millions, Rs. 1582.5 millions, Rs. 1170 millions, Rs. 755 millions and Rs. 820 millions respectively

Since independence, the central and state governments have been expanding the provision of primary formal and non-formal education to realise the goal of Universilisation of Elementary Education (UEE). The challenge now is to sustain and deepen current reforms in education and encourage local planning and management of strategies for expanding and improving primary education.

With a view to cushioning the impact of rising costs of text books and exercise books, the government has exempted writing and printing paper supplied to all State Text Book Corporations from excise duty. It is expected that this would make school text books more affordable for students from weaker sections of society.

Removal of systemic deficiencies in the implementation of UEE and forging ahead necessitates the creation of informed public opinion and a facilitative environment akin to that of the Total Literacy Campaign. This has to be achieved through effective and sustained advocacy, massive community mobilisation and consciousness building. With this perspective, a national programme of media publicity and advocacy has been planned. The programme will target: i) teachers and all those involved in education of children; ii) students and parents of students, particularly non-literate parents; and iii) community opinion leaders.

The Kasturba Gandhi Shiksha Yojana, a programme to establish residential schools for girls in all the districts which have a particularly low female literacy rate has been announced. A sum of Rs. 2500 million has been provided in this year's budget. The central government has also decided to grant financial incentives and scholarships for the girl child born in families living below the poverty line.

Several central and state level initiatives have been in operation from the early 1980s. While the design of these projects vary substantially, all of them address the objectives and strategies of the National Policy on Education 1986. They pay special attention to increasing girls' enrolment, improving educational outcomes, strengthening community involvement, improving teaching and learning materials and providing in-service teacher training. The status of some of these initiatives are discussed below.

Operation Blackboard

This scheme launched in 1987, is aimed at improving the school environment and enhancing retention and learning achievement of children by providing minimum essential facilities in all primary schools. The scheme has brought about a remarkable quantitative and qualitative improvement in primary education. In all, 523,000 primary schools have been covered as originally envisaged. These schools have been provided with central assistance

Decentralisation

Decentralised planning and management of elementary education is a goal set by the National Policy on Education, 1986. The Policy visualises direct community involvement in the form of Village Education Committees (VECs) for management of elementary education. The POA, 1992, emphasised micro planning as a process of designing a family-wise and child-wise plan of action by which every child regularly attends school or NFE centre, continues his or her education at the place suitable to him/her and completes at least eight years of schooling or its equivalent at the NFE centre.

The 73rd and 74th constitutional amendments provide for decentralisation of the activities and facilitate transfer of power and participation of the local self-government institutions or the Panchayati Raj Institutions. It has created a congenial ambience for the PRIs to play a more dynamic and proactive role. States are expected to evolve institutional arrangements both in rural and urban areas for undertaking these activities. These structures have been providing voice to women, Scheduled Castes and Tribes, minorities, parents and educational functionaries. They have also, been delegated with responsibilities with regard to location and relocation of existing primary and upper schools on the basis of micro planning and school mapping. In this regard, decentralisation of school management to grassroots level bodies is an important policy initiative.

During the 8th plan period several innovative efforts hove been made under the ongoing projects to establish decentralisation. For instance, the District Primary Education Programme has shifted the planning mechanism from the state to the district level, and Lok Jumbish has gone one step further by assigning decision making processes to a block level committee. At the village level, a VEC has the main responsibility for community mobilisation, school mapping, micro planning, renovation and construction of school buildings and improvement of pedagogical curriculum. In fact, the VECs of Shiksha Karmi schools have been activated as a result of the Lok Jumbish programme.

Since 1993-94, the scheme has been expanded to cover upper primary schools. More then 47,000 upper primary schools have been granted central assistance of Rs. 40,000 each for purchase of teaching- learning materials. Also, primary schools with enrolment exceeding 100 have been augmented with a third teacher. A Special Orientation Programme for Primary Teachers (SOPT) to facilitate optimum utilisation of materials supplied has also been launched to cover all primary school teachers in the country.

The total expenditure under the scheme from 1992-93 to 1995-96 has been Rs. 8,163 million. The outlay for 1996-97 is Rs. 2,910 million.

National Programme of Nutritional Support to Primary Education (School Meal Programme)

This scheme was launched on 15 August, 1995 to give a boost to UEE in terms of increasing enrolment, retention and attendance in primary classes by supplementing nutritional requirements of children attending primary schools. It is an ambitious scheme that has been operationalised throughout the country in a very short period. The programme envisages provision of nutritious and wholesome cooked meal of 100 gms of food grains per school day, free of cost, to all children in classes I-V by 1997-98.

During 1995-96, 378 districts, 225,000 schools and 33.5 million children have been covered with an expenditure of Rs. 4,412 million. In 1996-97, the scheme was extended to cover 55.4 million children with an expenditure of Rs. 8,110 million. The scheme has become fully operational in 1997-98 covering nearly 110 million children in primary classes. A positive impact on school enrolment and retention has been reported.

District Primary Education Programme

The DPEP launched in November, 1994 is conceived as a beachhead for overhauling the primary education system in India. The programme aims at operationalising the strategies for achieving UEE through district specific planning and disaggregated target setting. It draws upon the accumulated national experience of several state level initiatives that were started earlier. It moves away from the schematic piecemeal approach of the earlier programmes and takes a holistic view of primary education with emphasis on decentralised management, community mobilisation and district specific planning based on contextually and research based inputs. The basic objectives of DPEP are:

— To provide all children with access to primary education either in the formal system or through the non-formal education (NFE) programme.

— To reduce differences in enrolment, dropout rates and learning achievement among gender and social groups to less than 5%.

— To reduce overall primary dropout rates for all students to less than 10%.

— To raise average achievement levels by at least 25% over measured base line levels and ensuring achievements of basic literacy and numeracy competencies and a minimum of 40% achievement levels in other competencies by all primary school children.

The Government of India finances 85 % of the project cost as a grant to the DPEP State Implementation Societies and the concerned state government provides the rest. The central government's share is resourced by external funding. As of now, IDA has approved credit amounting to $260 million and $425 million under Phase-I and Phase-II respectively. The European Union (EU) is providing a grant of 150 million ECU. The ODA (UK) is extending a grant of $80.21 million. The grant from the Netherlands amounts to $25.8 million.

The first phase of the programme was launched in 42 districts in the states of Assam, Haryana, Karnataka, Kerala, Maharashtra, Tamilnadu and Madhya Pradesh. In the second phase, the programme has been launched in 80 districts of Orissa, Himachal Pradesh, Andhra Pradesh, West Bengal, Uttar Pradesh and Gujarat and in Phase I States.

DPEP has been able to set up project management structures at district, state and national levels, create the environment and capacity for micro planning, take up the challenge of pedagogical innovation, create a responsive institutional base which includes both government and non-government institutions, enhance community participation and strengthen the process of catering to special focus groups such as tribals, scheduled castes, women and other marginalised sections.

The first phase of the programme is under evaluation. The initial trends of impact studies are very positive. DPEP has made a decisive impact on increasing enrolment, reducing repetition rates and improving class room processes.

While the DPEP has been targeting backward districts with female literacy below the national average and where TLCs have stirred up a demand for elementary education, several state level initiatives have shown tremendous potential. These are directed at improving literacy levels in the five low literacy states of Andhra Pradesh, Bihar, Uttar Pradesh, Madhya Pradesh and Rajasthan.

BIHAR EDUCATION PROJECT

Bihar Education Project (BEP) was launched in 1991 with the express purpose of bringing about quantitative and qualitative improvement in the elementary system in Bihar. The project lays emphasis on the education of deprived sections of society, such as SCs, STs and women. Participatory planning and implementation are crucial ingredients of the project. A midterm review highlighted certain major achievements such as: a) a strong Mahila Samakhya component; b) organisation of VECs and community involvement in programme implementation at grassroots level; and c) non-formal education through NGOs. The review suggested:

— consolidation of the programme in the existing seven districts,

— establishing strong linkages between BEP and the education system in Bihar,

— giving greater focus to the primary stage of classes I-V,

— building better linkages with the activities in other states under DPEP and other programmes,

— providing more emphasis to MLLs and teacher training, and conducting periodic base line studies.

It has now been decided to extend the project to the second phase of two years duration. The total outlay for the second phase is estimated to be Rs. 613 million to be shared between UNICEF, Government of India and Government of Bihar as per the existing funding formula of 3:2:1. The total project outlay for BEP is Rs. 3600 million. It is proposed to merge the project with DPEP during the next five years.

UTTAR PRADESH BASIC EDUCATION PROGRAMME

A project "Education for All" prepared by the Government of Uttar Pradesh was approved by The World Bank in June, 1993. The project is currently in operation in 12 districts. It is planned to expand the coverage to 15 districts under DPEP-II. It has an outlay of Rs. 7,288 million spread over seven years. International Development Agency (IDA), the soft loan window of The World Bank, would provide a credit of US$163.1 million and the state government's share would be approximately 13 per cent of the total project cost.

The progress of implementation of the project so far has been satisfactory. The construction work of schools and Block Resource Centres is being completed as per schedule. Training materials for teacher trainers on DIETs have been prepared. The first cycle of in- service teacher training was completed in October, 1995. About 40,000 teachers have been trained.

Community Mobilisation and Participation

Many educational innovations of recent years are based on the strong foundation of community support and participation. When progress is discussed and analysed of different levels within the project, "people's acceptance and participation" is used as an indicator.

Mobilising the village community to take responsibility to ensure quality education for every child, is the core strategy of both Lok Jumbish (LJ) and Shikhsa Karmi Project (SKP) in their efforts to universalise primary education and deliver quality education. It would not be far removed from truth if we say that community involvement has been the key factor for the success of the two projects. LJ has had a positive effect on the empowerment of locally elected people, especially on female representatives at village level, who are often active members of the LJ core teams or women's groups. The Village Education Committees(VECs), carefully formed and trained though environmental building activities in the LJ programme, are actively involved in school matters.

SKP has constituted VECs in 2000 villages to promote community involvement in primary education and encourage village level planning. The role of the VEC is to mobilise resources for maintenance, repair and construction of school infrastructure. The VEC also helps in determining the school calendar and school timings in consultation with the local community and Shiksha Karmis (educational workers).

The positive impact of the LJ and SKP, focusing on supporting the teachers and the students by involving, the village community in taking responsibility for all educational activities of the village school, is serving as a demonstration of how deeply rooted problems of education in India can be addressed. Wide dissemination of these innovative approaches could inspire other educational programmes all over India and the world.

Andhra Pradesh Primary Education Project

The Andhra Pradesh Primary Education Project (APPEP), practised in the south central state of Andhra Pradesh, with a female literacy of just 34 %, adopts a two-pronged strategy of improving classroom transaction by training teachers and giving a fillip to school construction activities. The project has trained an estimated 80,000 teachers in 23 districts and more than 3,000 teaching centres have become operational. The project is assisted by the ODA with an estimated outlay of Rs. 1,000 million in the 8th Plan.

Shiksha Karmi Project

The Shiksha Karmi Project (SKP) is being implemented since 1987, with assistance from the Swedish International Development Cooperation Agency (SIDA). The project aims at universalisation and qualitative improvement of primary education in the remote and socio-economically backward villages of Rajasthan, with primary focus on girls. Since teacher absenteeism has been found to be a major obstacle in achieving the objective of UEE, the project uses the novel approach of substituting teachers in dysfunctional schools with local youth known as Shiksha Karmis who are provided with rigorous training and supervisory support. An important feature of this innovative project is the mobilisation and participation of the community in improving the functioning of primary schools.

The project is being implemented as an externally aided scheme with reimbursement of 90 % in Phase I and 50 % in Phase II, from SIDA. The project, with an outlay of around Rs.212 million in Phase I and Rs.490 million in Phase II, places strong emphasis on vigorous and continuous in-service training.

The SKP also runs non-formal classes called Prehar Pathshalas-schools of convenient timings. For girls' education, Angan Pathshalas are being run in three blocks. The programme at present covers over 150,000 students in 1,785 schools and 3,520 Prehar Pathshalas, involving over 4,271 Shiksha Karmis.

The project is known for its open participative style and continuous experimentation to achieve its objectives. The approach, strategies and achievements of the SKP have attracted national and international recognition. The project is slated for a major expansion with SIDA assistance in the 9th Plan. The total projections for the 9th Plan are estimated to be Rs. 4260 million.

Lok Jumbish Project

Barely five years old, Lok Jumbish (LJ) has made an indelible impression in the primary education landscape of Rajasthan. The coverage of the project has extended to 75 blocks, covering a population of approximately 12 million. Significantly, it has also achieved a major breakthrough in welding together government agencies, teachers, NGOs, elected representatives and the people into an interactive group effort to promote universalisation of primary education. The seven guiding principles of Lok Jumbish are:

— a process rather than a product approach;

— partnerships;

— decentralised functioning;

— participatory learning;

— integration with the mainstream education system;

— flexibility of management; and

— creating multiple levels of leadership committed to quality and mission mode.

Special focus has been given to environment building in all training programmes under LJ. This helps in the development of an understanding about issues involved in people's mobilisation, use of different media forms and clarity about the messages to be given to the people.

The first phase of the project was for a period of two years from 1992-94, with the expenditure shared between SIDA, Government of India and Government of Rajasthan in the ratio 3:2:1. The second phase stretches up to 1998, with the sharing modality remaining the same. The allocation for LJP is Rs.1100 million for Phases I and II and Rs.4000 million for Phase III. A Norwegian grant of Rs. 200 million is also available.

THE STATUS OF THE TEACHING STAFF

The role of the teacher has been well recognised in the traditional Indian thought through the centuries. The 'Guru' (teacher) was to be revered as an imparter of knowledge and a guide. In the present context, the role of the teacher remains as critical as ever. The teacher plays a major role in implementing the policies and schemes formulated to achieve a breakthrough in the quantitative expansion and qualitative improvement of education. Reflecting the crucial role of teachers in national development, the NPE 1986 called for a substantial improvement in the conditions of work and quality of teacher education The important determinants of the status of teachers could be identified as follows:

- — The academic and professional requirements for entry into the profession
- — The financial and other economic benefits
- — The freedom of teachers to take part in public affairs
- — The professional responsibility assumed
- — The degree of public recognition.
- — Growth of the teaching profession

The teaching profession has the largest number of members as compared to other professions in India. During 1994-95, about 4.3 million teachers were working in different levels of schools. Of these, 2.7 million [66 per cent] were engaged in primary and upper primary schools [grades I to VIII] of which 2,018,050 teachers were in government schools. Of the 1.5 million [34 per cent] in high/higher secondary schools [grades IX to XII] 609,121 were in government schools. During the period 1990-95, the total strength of teachers at different levels of school education increased from 4.0 million to nearly 4.3 million, marking an increase of 6.5 per cent. If this trend continues, the number of teachers, particularly primary and upper primary teachers, will grow significantly over the next decade.

A sex-wise analysis of the teacher force indicates that there are 3 times more male teachers than female teachers at all levels of school education. Although the number of female teachers has increased, yet, their share in the total teaching force is very small, particularly, in rural, remote and educationally backward areas. The number of women teachers in schools increased from 1,141,015 in 198788 129.4 per cent) to 1,343,667 in 1993-94 132.08 per cent).

System of teacher education

The NPE 1986, called for an over-haul of the Teacher Education System in the country. It emphasised the need for continuing education for teachers to meet the thrust envisaged in the policy. A new Centrally Sponsored Scheme of Restructuring and Reorganisation of Teacher Education was launched in 1987-88 which primarily envisages establishment of DIETs to provide pre-service and in-service training to elementary school teachers and to AE and NFE personnel. In addition, upgradation of Secondary Teacher Education Institutions into Colleges of Teacher Education (CTEs), establishment of Institutes of Advanced Studies in Education (IASE), strengthening of SCERTs and University Departments of Education through the University Grants Commission are components of this restructuring which has the basic objective of providing training and resource support to elementary and secondary education at the grassroots level. Central assistance is meant for the construction of buildings, procurement of books and equipments, additional expenditure on staff salaries and training programmes. In view of the high priority accorded to the achievement of the target of UEE, emphasis under the Teacher Education Scheme has so far been on setting up of DIETs. It was proposed to establish DIETs in 425 districts in the country (as per 1987-88 configuration when there were 451 districts in total) by the end of the VIII Five Year Plan. Against this target, 424 DIETs have been sanctioned as on 31 st March, 9h. Seventy three CTEs and 34 IASEs have also been sanctioned. Eighteen SCERTs have been assisted under strengthening of SCERT component of the scheme.

A Special Orientation Programme for Primary Teachers (SOPT) has also been taken up during the VIII Plan period 11992-971. Started in late 1993, this programme is aimed at orienting an estimated 1.8 million primary teachers in the country in the use of Operation Blackboard material and MLLs strategy. The NCERT is the apex body implementing this programme through state nodal agencies which are mostly SCERTs. Ministry of Human Resource Development releases grants to the NCERT based on the needs. Within the provision of the Centrally Sponsored Scheme of Restructuring and Reorganisation of Teacher Education, so far about Rs. 450 million has been released to the NCERT for the purpose.

According to the NCERT, State Governments have reported training of about 0.3 million primary teachers under the SOPT. Details on the implementation of Teacher Education Scheme have been presented earlier.

Qualifications and training

The minimum general qualification prescribed by some states for the recruitment of primary school teachers (teaching grades I-V} is 10 years of formal education (matriculation/secondary, whereas, it is senior secondary or 12 years of education prescribed in certain states (e.g., Haryana, Maharashtra, Tamil Nadu, Uttar Pradesh and Delhi). The minimum qualification prescribed by most states for the appointment of upper primary school teachers (teaching grades VI-VIII) is graduation (second level diploma) whereas in some states it is matriculation/senior secondary (first level diploma!. The educational qualifications of teachers have been gradually increasing.

According to the Fifth All India Educational Survey in 1986, as many as 2.1 million 177 per cent) primary and upper primary school teachers had been trained through first level diploma (under-graduation), 0.5 million (18 per cent) through second level diploma (graduation) and 0.1 million (5 percent) through third level diploma. All states in India require at least a graduation degree (second level diploma) for secondary school teachers (grades VI-X) and post-graduation degree (third level diploma) for higher/senior secondary school teachers (grades XI-XIII. As many as 58 per cent teachers teaching at the secondary and higher secondary levels had second level diploma, 33 per cent had third level diploma and only about 9 per cent had first level diploma (under-graduation).

Pre-service teacher training

The Fifth All India Educational Survey indicates that about 87 per cent primary and upper primary teachers are trained, that is they have acquired a primary or elementary teacher training certificate of one or two years' duration or bachelor's degree in education. There are, however, significant regional variations. The percentage of trained teachers at primary and upper primary level is more than 99 per cent in the states of Haryana, Tamil Nadu, Chandigarh and Delhi. It is less than 50 per cent in Arunachal Pradesh, Meghalaya, Sikkim, Nagaland and Tripura.

The Centrally Sponsored Scheme of Restructuring and Reorganisation of Teacher Education taken up in 1987-88 in pursuance of NPE 1986 envisages, on the one hand, strengthening of institutional base of teacher training and, on the other, takes up special programmes for training of teachers in specified areas and other non-institutional programmes of orientation for teachers. The Scheme provides for the setting up of DIETs to provide training and resource support to elementary education (both formal and non-formal) and AE systems at the grassroots level. The scheme for establishing the DIETs envisaged raising the general education of primary teachers to 12 years of schooling. With the establishment of DIETs, almost all states are now moving towards a two-year diploma in education for those teaching at the elementary level following 12 years of schooling.

Of the total number of teachers working in high or higher secondary schools, approximately, 90 per cent are trained, i.e., they have acquired a bachelor's degree in education (B.Ed.). The percentage of trained teachers at both the levels is the highest in Chandigarh and lowest in Assam. A comparison between male and female teachers indicates that the number of male untrained teachers is more than that of female teachers at all school levels in the country.

The National Council for Teacher Education

The NCTE was established in May, 1973 by a Government resolution to advise Central and State Governments on all matters pertaining to teacher education, with its Secretariat located in the NCERT. The NCTE's status and role till 1993 have been purely advisory and it did not have statutory powers to enforce its guidelines. As per the provisions laid down in the NPE 1986 and the Programme of Action for its implementation, the NCTE has been conferred statutory status as per the NCTE Act No. 73 of 1993 passed by the Parliament and assented to by the President. It has come into existence with effect from 17th May, 95. The Act provides for establishment of the NCTE with a view to achieving planned and coordinated development of teacher education system throughout the country, regulation and proper maintenance of norms and standards in the teacher education system and for matters connected therewith.

Programmes and activities taken up by the NCTE so for include:

— Preparation of a framework for competency-based curriculum for elementary teacher training institutions.

— Restructuring of pre-service teacher education curriculum for all stages.

— Human Rights and National Values- preparation of materials and orientation of teacher educators.

— Preparation of a video film on teacher training in physical education.

— Preparation of a project proposal on Teacher Education in States/UTs-current status, issues and future projections.

— Development of material for teacher educators on specific subjects.

Instructors in NFE

In the NFE system, the instructor is the key person. The instructor is a nominally paid volunteer who is usually employed on a part time basis. He/she could be an educated housewife, a girl from the village, an educated unemployed youth, a retired teacher, a qualified social worker, an anganwadi worker or even a professional semi-skilled person. Among the qualities expected of an instructor are dedication to work, and volunteerism. Girls' NFE centres have only lady instructors. The minimum qualification of the instructor is class 10 pass. But studies show that the qualifications of instructors vary from class 8 to Master's degree with a professional degree in education. In fact, there are many remote areas-rural and tribals-where individuals who have studied beyond class 8 are not available. In such cases, the VEC is empowered to relax the minimum qualification of the instructor. In the case of lady instructors, this problem is even more acute.

The basic skill which an NFE instructor is expected to have or develop is multi-class teaching as the group of learners he/ she has to deal with is a heterogeneous one. The methodology of teaching at the NFE centre has to be different from the one used in formal schools. Therefore, to orient the instructor in the teaching methodology and also to acquaint him with the content of the learning materials, a four-tier system of training has been developed.

During the first year, the minimum training period for the instructor is 30 days and in the subsequent year it is 20 days. The first phase is usually divided into three phases and focused on training in pedagogy! content, evaluation and monitoring. The second phase of training is devoted to discussion focused at finding solutions to the problems faced by the instructors while teaching at the centre. Various packages. of training materials have been developed to cope with the needs of training. The training of instructors at the district level is done through DIETs. The overall responsibility of training NFE functionaries at the state level rests with the SCERTs.

In the NFE centres, the instructor is the link between the centre and the community and is expected to perform a more dynamic role. He is also expected to take care of the individual needs of the learner and help him/her in solving day-to-day problems. The responsibilities of instructors include the organisation of the daily activities of the centre, identification of out-of-school and non-school going children, the selection of the site for the centre in consultation with the VEC, organising teaching-learning activities by drawing on supervisors, primary school teachers, TLC volunteers, ECCE Centres, the community, nearby voluntary agencies, mobile village library, Block Development Office, Primary Health Centres, etc. The monitoring of the NFE programme is done on a continuous basis at all levels viz. village, district and state through the VEC, DIETs, SCERTs and Directorate of Education.

The teachers working under TLCs are volunteers and are not paid any salary for their services. Since the qualification of these volunteers is not fixed, any educated person capable of working as a volunteer is appointed and trained. The responsibility of training volunteers of TLCs is that of the State Resource Centres (SRCs).

Conditions of work

Salary

Good conditions of work play a significant role in attracting and retaining the right type of persons in the teaching profession and enabling them to function efficiently. The working conditions include teacher's salary and benefits, availability of o suitable school building and essential facilities in the school, teacher's workload, method of recruitment, availability of teaching and non-teaching materials and opportunities for promotion.

Today, teacher's pay is probably the most important element affecting the quality of education. The calories of different levels of teachers ore established separately by each state and are determined on the basis of academic qualifications, training and experience. In addition to salary, price-index linked 'dearness allowance' is given to all teachers Various other allowances are also granted to all categories of teachers to compensate them for the special stress under which they work.

These allowances are: city compensatory allowance, house rent allowance, hill allowance and other special allowances such as winter allowance, backward, remote and tribal area allowance, island allowance, etc. These allowances differ from state to state and within the state from stage to stage of education. Entry level salaries for trained primary teachers are only slightly higher than those for untrained teachers. The maximum salary for a trained teacher is 3 to 4 times his/ her entry salary, and is achieved only after 1 & 20 years of service in most states.

In the majority of states, the salary scores of trained and untrained graduate teachers in upper primary/middle schools are at par with those in secondary and higher/senior secondary schools. Teachers with a Master's degree working in higher/ senior secondary schools hove separate salary scales and ore designated as post-graduate teachers (PGTs) or "Lecturers". There is a provision of selection grades for all categories of teachers. Twenty per cent of senior teachers of different categories get selection grades after 10 to 15 years of service.

In addition, most states provide fixed medical allowance or reimbursement of medical expenses, advances for house building and purchase of conveyance, and free education for the children of teachers, as well as retirement benefits of pension, gratuity and group insurance. In the majority of states, there is also a provision of incentives for some special categories of teachers. For instance, in Assam, Bihar, Gujarat, Maharashtra and Tamil Nadu, a certain percentage of elementary (primary and upper primary) women teachers working in rural and remote areas are given residential accommodation. In some states, physically handicapped teachers are offered conveyance allowance.

Working environment and facilities

Working conditions for primary school teachers are different from secondary and higher secondary school teachers, particularly, for those in primary schools in rural areas.

According to the fifth all India educational survey 56.25 per cent primary schools, 69.36 per cent upper primary, 72.97 per cent secondary and 89.39 per cent higher secondary schools are housed in buildings. There is a tremendous demand in provision of more facilities such as classrooms and instructional materials. Library facilities are available in only one-fourth primary schools as against 90 per cent in secondary and higher secondary schools.

A plan provision of Rs.500 million has been made in the budget for the year 1996-97 for financing a new Teacher's Housing Scheme under the Central Plan which will be implemented through the State Governments. It has been observed that teachers serving in remote and inaccessible areas do not have suitable residential accommodation. As a result, they have to commute to their schools from a distance and this affects their punctuality and attendance, adversely. The provision made in this year's budget could be utilised for construction of residential accommodation for teachers in such areas

Teaching material

Recent studies at primary level in selected educationally backward districts have revealed that charts, maps and globes were available in the blocks covered by the Operation Blackboard (JOB) Scheme introduced by the Central Government to provide some minimum infrastructure to primary schools e.g., two classrooms, a kit consisting of some teaching-learning materials and provision of an additional teacher. Teachers in remote areas now handle 2-3 classes, whereas, earlier they used to handle 4-5 classes Thus, it is evident that the minimum essential facilities needed for a smooth school functioning and a teaching-learning process need to be upscaled at all school levels, particularly, at primary level.

Other conditions of work

Some of the problem areas identified in the teaching field arc teacher absenteeism, non-availability of adequate housing facility, frequent transfers, etc.

The workload of teachers is often judged in terms of amount and type of work done by them. More than 60 per cent of teachers teach about 50 students on an average, 34 per cent teach between 51-100 and about 5 per cent more than 100 students. This means that on an average about 39 per cent teachers teach more than 50 students in the primary school. At high/higher secondary levels, however, the teacher-pupil ratio was 1:16 in 1994-95. It is evident that there is too much stress on primary school teachers, specially those handling multi-grades. Education codes in different states specify the number of class or periods teachers at different levels have to teach. In middle schools, nearly half of the teachers teach 31-40 class periods a week, whereas, 12 per cent teach more than 40 class periods.

Besides teaching, elementary and secondary school teachers have to spend a fair amount of time on co-curricular activities, specially in private schools. In addition, teachers have to do clerical work and other miscellaneous work like organising relief work, collecting census data, participating in family planning campaigns, and population control drives, helping in the smooth conduct of elections, etc.

Promotional prospects for teachers

In most states, the promotion of teachers in government primary and secondary schools is either on the basis of seniority or seniority-cummerit. Acquiring higher qualifications also helps in promotion provided a departmental vacancy exists which suits the qualification of the candidate. In the case of teachers working in private and aided schools, the chances of promotion are rare because in privately managed schools there is a shortage of senior positions and so only one or two persons have the opportunity to reach the level of headmaster/head teacher In secondary and higher secondary schools, a Trained Graduate Teacher (TGT) may become a PostGraduate Teacher {POT) provided he gets some higher qualifications i.e. a Master's degree in any school subject and depending upon the availability of a vacancy in the school. It may well be that teachers in private aided schools or privately managed recognised schools or public schools remain in the same post from the beginning to the end of their service of 30 to 35 years.

Teachers in government schools can aspire for higher administrative posts in the Education Department of the Government of India. Though a certain percentage of posts in the. higher categories of education are reserved for teachers, yet, avenues of promotion in the teaching profession are comparatively more limited than in other sectors such as industry, commerce and business.

Teacher support material

A number of agencies such as the NCERT, NIEPA, SCERTs and Departments of Education in universities have developed documentation services for teachers. A number of educational journals addressed to school teachers are published by national and state institutions such as NCERT, SCERTs, Boards of School Education, Teachers' Associations, NGOs and private publishers to disseminate research findings and information regarding innovations attempted by teachers, teachers' educators or researchers in different settings. Materials (multi-media packages, self-learning materials, etc.) for training and upgrading the knowledge and skills of teachers/functionaries of minority institutions through Distance Education are prepared by the NCERT, IGNOU, NIEPA and NOS, etc.

Some leading newspapers also sometimes bring out supplements or special editions on education. In addition, several institutions and NGOs bring out educational material in audio and video format. Professional associations have also made their contribution in this field. The UGC supports these efforts at the higher education level through a chain of EMRCs (Educational Media Research Centres) and AVRCs (Audio Visual Resource Centres). These efforts are coordinated through a Consortium of Educational Communications (CEC) The IGNOU also has a media programme service. These programmes are telecast throughout the country under the programme 'Country-wide Classroom'. Even though the programmes are targeted at students, teachers are also able to upgrade content and methodology-related delivery and evaluation techniques. Computer software has also been developed to upgrade the knowledge content in various school subjects. At the school level, the CIET in the NCERT and the SIETs which have been set up in six states are responsible for producing these programmes. Besides these, broadcasts and telecasts cater to regular and out-of-school children and teachers at the primary and secondary level. Several other technological aids and other audio-visual aids have been developed to help teachers in their instructional tasks. A large number of films have also been produced on teacher training, including the teaching of difficult concepts and content areas to children. The films produced include films on the methodology of teaching science, and the needs of children with special problems. Science kits, too, have been developed to enable children to perform experiments related to the prescribed syllabi.

Influenced by the advent of new technologies of communication, the teacher's role has been changing rapidly and teacher education curricula have been revised periodically reflecting this. Interpersonal skills for making instruction interactive and the two-way communication effective have become an integral part of the changes. These curricular reforms have provided teachers an opportunity to participate in the designing of instructional material using locally available resources. A number of newspapers and magazines extend support to teachers in their work. Many teachers, through their writings in newspapers and magazines, provide additional material to students. School broadcast and school telecast programmes addressed to students of different levels are organised with the help and cooperation of practicing teachers. Teachers participate in the planning, organisation and evaluation of these programmes. Since, these programmes are meant to provide syllabus-based enrichment material to children, they supplement the work of teachers. The government provides a satellite channel to educational and development programmes, the telecast of which is available to students in all parts of the country. This would also give a boost to the development of educational software

Motivational efforts for teacher development

Private educational establishments-government-aided and government recognised but unaided-make special efforts to maintain their teachers' motivation. Both incentives and disincentives are used. Good work in these institutions is rewarded by giving additional responsibility which is often linked with monetary incentives. In government schools, this is not possible as the head of the institution is not empowered to extend monetary incentives to teachers. Teachers in private education establishments have relatively less security of service. It is relatively easier to dispense with their services if their performance is not found satisfactory. In government schools, though teachers are accountable, teachers' unions make it difficult to enforce accountability, and it is extremely difficult to dispense with their services.

Teachers are involved in the formulation of education policies, development of curricula, syllabi and instructional material. They are also represented on decision-making bodies of universities, boards of school education, SCERTs and DIETs.

Moreover, teachers are autonomous in the management of their own classes. They are encouraged to undertake experimentation and action research and are provided incentives both at the state and national level. Every year, the NCERT conducts an All India Competition of Innovations and Experiments undertaken by school teachers and Teacher Educators. Teachers are invited to submit papers on the basis of the work done by them in their schools and as many as 50 primary school teachers and 20 secondary teachers are given national level awards. Similar awards are also available for elementary and secondary teacher educators. In the management of educational institutions, teachers at some places enjoy partnership in decision-making. The School Education Acts in vogue in some states have a provision for the membership of teacher representatives on the managing committee of the institution. For example, in the Delhi School Education Act and Rules, 1973, teacher representatives have to be on the managing committee of every recognised school. In the last few years there has been a move that even government schools should have an advisory or managing committee with representatives of the teachers working in the school as members.

To ensure parental support, many schools have either Parent Teacher Associations or Mother Teacher Associations. Parents are invited periodically to the school to discuss the performance of their children with the teachers. In some schools, particularly private schools, parents support the teachers in the organisation of co-curricular activities, art education activities and work experience activities by providing the materials required for these activities. In the DPEP, large scale efforts are underway to facilitate a constructive involvement of parents and the community with the school through the formation of grassroot structures such as VECs, Mother Teacher Associations and Parent Teacher Associations. Another aspect of enhancing motivation is through the institution of on annual Teachers' Day, on September 5. This day is observed in all the schools throughout the country, according a special place to the teacher. Under the aegis of the Ministry of Human Resource Development, a National Foundation for Teachers' Welfare has been set up. This Foundation provides facilities for teachers' welfare.

Similarly, with the objective of raising the prestige of teachers and giving public recognition to teachers, the Scheme of National Award for Teachers was launched in the year 1958-59. Primary, middle and higher secondary school teachers are eligible under the scheme. Each award carries a certificate-of merit, cash payment of Rs. 10,000 and a silver medal. In 1993, the number of awards given was raised from 296 to 302.

HIGHER EDUCATION

The enrolment in universities has been on the rise over the past years, with approximately a teaching staff of 0.301 million, catering to a student population of 6.1 1 million students. The pay scales of university teachers have been revised periodically and are considered to be on par with the highest pay scales of civil servants. Benefits include provident fund, residential accommodation (depending on seniority), retirement benefits. etc. Various incentives exists for teachers to improve their qualifications during their service by way of training and research. They are sent abroad under bilateral programmes of research, area studies, conferences, etc. There are fellowships and scholarships offered by various countries besides travel grants to go abroad. Approximately, 250 scholars visit various countries under these programmes.

Involvement of teachers in decision making is also a vital component of teachers' service conditions. University and college teachers, are involved in the formulation of curricula and the management of university/college affairs They are autonomous in planning their research. In Autonomous Colleges, teachers have been given the freedom to formulate and teach their courses of general curricula and evaluate their students. A scheme of Academic Staff Colleges provides training programmes in various subjects as a support for professional development of University and College teachers.

Teachers in technical education

With a large network of technical institutions established and developed since independence, and the programmes and initiatives launched in India during the successive plan periods, the technical education system has made significant contributions in producing one of the largest reservoirs of technically trained manpower which has been a source of strength for scientific and industrial development. The role of teachers in technical education is quite central and crucial. To be effective in their task, the technical teachers have to maintain fine balance between their professional competence and teaching potential. The job of technical teachers is multifarious, "to guide and inspire the students, to enrich self-discipline, to foster the area of specialisation by keeping abreast of the latest technologies and changing trends and, ultimately, to provide services and expertise to the industry and community for finding solutions to real life problems".

The Government of India, over years has taken a series of steps for developing the overall performance of the technical teachers. Significant among them are mentioned below:

Quality Improvement Programme (QIP)

The programme was launched in 1970 with an objective of upgrading the expertise and capabilities of the teachers of engineering colleges and polytechnics in the country. The aspect of upgradation of academic qualifications is achieved with the help of seven major centres located in the IITs, University of Roorkee, IISc., Bangalore and 18 other centres through which the engineering college teachers can acquire their masters and doctoral degrees with full salary and allowance. They are also paid a monthly stipend. Over the years, about 2,000 engineering college teachers have acquired and about 1,700 teachers have acquired masters degrees in engineering/technology.

The ISTE, a national professional body in technical education conducts summer/winter schools for improving the knowledge, skills and capabilities of engineering college teachers as well as polytechnic teachers. The ISTE conducts a large number of short term courses and programmes at various institutions and industries in the country. The teachers are provided travelling and other allowances as per the rules. So far over 25,000 college level teachers have participated in such programmes and over 4,500 polytechnic teachers have been benefited under such programmes. In addition, QIP centres in the IITs, IISc., Bangalore and University of Roorkee also have established curriculum development centres for upgrading curricula of engineering colleges with the help of teachers and experts.

The statutory AICTE has also launched some innovative schemes for teachers of technical institutions which include:

— Travel Grants Scheme

— Seminar/Conference grant

— Career award for young teachers

— Emeritus fellowship

— Professor of Eminence.

Under the scheme of continuing education programmes, presently handled by AICTE, the working professionals in the industry are provided knowledge-based skills and training with the help of teachers of various technical institutions, both at the degree and diploma level. Continuing education has been a very significant aspect of the World Bank assisted project for polytechnics as also the CIDA funded Canada India Institutional Cooperation Project for 12 polytechnics in Southern India. Despite several measures taken so far, the overall position of filling up the sanctioned posts and attracting competent engineers/ technologists to the teaching profession has been a matter of concern and debate. Efforts are, therefore, afoot to launch some new schemes and programmes for attracting brilliant young ,teachers by taking them up at a young age and sponsoring them for acquiring higher qualifications. At the same time, designing some new scientific methods of selection and providing adequate research facilities and challenges so as to keep the teachers motivated, professionally satisfied and result-oriented. Several new measures are also required in order to fill up the existing vacancies and the vacancies likely to be created because of mass scale retirement in the near future, especially, in the old reputed technical institutions. The aspects of providing need-based training and also to engage eminent experts as visiting faculty and contract faculty are also being encouraged.

UNESCO-ILO recommendations on the status of teachers in the Indian context:

The recommendations concerning the Status of Teachers adopted on 5th October, 1966 by the Special Inter-governmental Conference on the Status of Teachers convened by UNESCO, Paris in cooperation with ILO in 1966 recognised that the document was a unique instrument which recognised that education is fundamental to development and that teachers are the key to educational process. In the Indian context, the major aspects of the recommendations viz. the guiding principles recognises the importance of education and the fact that the status of teachers should be given its due regard in society. This is already incorporated in the NPE. As far as the educational objectives and policies are concerned the items concerning the interface between the world of learning and the world of work in the field of education is well recognised and has been implemented in India. In fact, the EFA commitment speaks of a financial commitment to the extent of 6 per cent of the GDP by the turn of the century for the education sector.

In the recommendations concerning Preparation for programmes, Educational objectives and policies and Preparation for the profession, there is evidence that there is widespread availability of teacher training facilities as well as comprehensive selection and recruitment facilities for each in the country. The various incentives that are given to employment and career opportunities to teachers have also been well documented. The security of tenure is particularly well established in government run schools. In the domain of the Rights and Responsibilities of teachers, the Indian context enjoins a fair degree of freedom and flexibility based on a framework outlined by the respective state governments on the issue of freedom of association. In every state, teaching and non-teaching personnel have their unions/associations. These organisations have powers of collective bargaining to secure teeter service conditions for their members.

State level organisations have joined together to form federations of educational organisations for primary, secondary and college stage of education. These federations negotiate with the central government to secure teeter pay scales and other service conditions. The central question under Indian laws is whether a "teacher" can be equated to a "workman", the latter being defined in the Industrial Disputes Act 1947. Various suggestions in this respect are being considered by the Ministry of Labour to amend the Industrial Disputes Act and initiate reforms to grant teachers the same protection as other workers. On the question of the rights of teachers, (in particular, salaries), these are structured as per government norms as laid down by the government from time to time.

On the Conditions for Effective Teaching and Learning, due consideration has been given in the context of the Indian teachers incorporating the recommendations of ILO. According to NPE 1986, development of Teachers' Code of Professional Ethics has been the responsibility of National level Teachers' organisations and they have themselves evoled such a code. On the issue of Teacher Shortage and Social Security, there are provisions for various benefits and salary revisions commensurate with inflationary trends that protect the pay of teachers.

It is also a fact that with the expansion of enrolment brought about by active interaction of the government, the requirement of teachers is constantly assessed, monitored and shortages are filled up through regular recruitment procedures. In short, it may be seen that the spirit and letter of the ILO recommendations have been incorporated in the Indian context and that the status of teachers in India is under constant review to keep pace with the growing and expanding reach of educational opportunities.

8

EDUCATION FOR EMPLOYMENT AND SOCIAL DEVELOPMENT

Education is a core sector for achieving the objective of employment, human resource development and bringing about much needed change in social environment, leading to overall progress through efficient use of resources. An appropriate education system cultivates knowledge, skill, positive attitude, awareness and sense of responsibility towards rights and duties and imparts inner strength to face oppression, humiliation and inequality.

LITERACY

A person who is able to read and write with understanding in any language is recorded as literate. Literacy is the best possible barometer to judge the level of educational awakening in a state, leading to a minimum capacity for self-learning. In Punjab, the literacy rate has been rising. It was 58.51 per cent in 1991 and increased to 69.95 per cent in 2001, an increase of 11.44 per cent points during the last 10 years.

Punjab has fared well in reducing the gap between male and female literacy, which decreased from 15.25 per cent in 1991 to 12.08 per cent in 2001. Male literacy rate increased from 65.66 per cent in 1991 to 75.63 per cent in 2001 and female literacy rate from 50.4 per cent to 63.55 per cent. Female literacy rate has increased by 13.14 per cent points and male literacy by only 9.97 per cent points during the last decade. Female literacy rate in Punjab is also considerably higher than that of India where 54.16 per cent of the females are literate.

According to the 2001 Census, rural literacy rate is 65.16 per cent and urban 79.13 per cent signifying that the gap is not very wide. There has been a reduction in the rural-urban literacy gap, from 19.31 per cent points in 1991 to 13.97 per cent points in 2001. In spite of these positive trends, there are still 94.35 lakh (including 0-6 population) illiterate in the state (Census of India, 2001). It is also a matter of great concern that in spite of having improved its literacy rate figure, the rank of Punjab went down from the 12th position in 1971 to the 16th in 2001, when compared to other states and UTs in India.

At present, Kerala has the highest literacy rate of 90.92 per cent while Bihar has the lowest of 47.53 per cent. The literacy rate of the non-Scheduled Castes is quite high (65.10%) as compared to the Scheduled Castes (41.09%). The female literacy rate of the non-Scheduled Castes (57.6%) is almost double than that of the Scheduled Caste women (31.03%). Hence, it is obvious that the total literacy percentage of the state has been adversely affected by the Scheduled Caste population. The literacy rate of Scheduled Caste women is really pathetic in the pockets of Bathinda (12.84%), Faridkot (15.78%), Ferozepur (15.09%) and Sangrur (17.02%). Government should, therefore, give priority consideration to improve the literacy rate of the Scheduled Castes and especially females in the identified pockets.

ADULT LITERACY

The adult education programme was being run under 100 per cent Centrally sponsored Rural Functional Literacy Programme and Social Education Scheme until the beginning of the nineties. After the abolition of these schemes in June 1991, the adult education programme remained neglected in the state for two to three years. It was again revived by NLMA and given a new name, Total Literacy/Post Literacy Programme.Total Literacy Campaign (TLC) The objective of this campaign is to provide basic knowledge of reading, writing and numerics. All 17 districts have already been covered under TLC in Punjab.

Hoshiarpur, Faridkot (including Moga and Muktsar) districts have completed this campaign. Of the total illiterates in the 15-35 age group in 1991, during enlistment under TLC, only 20,74,679 person were identified between 1994-98 and only 55.24 per cent enrolled. Post Literacy Campaign (PLC) The objective of this phase is to develop basic skills amongst neoliterates. There is a book called Post Literacy Primer (PL-I) which is taught during this programme. Six districts, namely, Hoshiarpur, Faridkot (including Moga and Muktsar), Ropar and Nawanshehar have been covered under PLC. Hoshiarpur and Faridkot (including Moga and Muktsar) districts have already completed this programme, but it is continuing in Ropar and Nawanshehar.

CONTINUING EDUCATION (CE)

During the Tenth Five Year Plan, it is proposed to introduce Continuing Education (CE) to impart functional literacy to all illiterates in the age group 15-35 years. For adult learners, only Hoshiarpur district has qualified for the CE programme. However, except for some districts, the TLC programme has not functioned well. It is going on at a very very slow pace. There has been no progress for the past 2-3 years in the Patiala, Fatehgarh Sahib and Gurdaspur districts.

Post-literacy campaigns need greater emphasis to ensure the realisation of the gains of TLC. Withdrawal of school teachers, lack of funds and enthusiasm at all levels of society have been reported by most of the districts as the cause of the very slow pace or failure of the programme. It is strongly recommended that there should be regular monitoring at the state and district levels. The adult literacy programme can now be merged with SSA for effective functioning and optimal utilization of resources, as there is a very easy convergence of adult literacy programmes with EGS (Education Guarantee Scheme), AIE (Alternative Innovative Education) under SSA.

PRIMARY, ELEMENTARY, SECONDARY AND SENIOR SECONDARY

'Elementary education is the most crucial stage of education spanning the first eight years of schooling and laying the foundation for the personality, attitudes, social confidence, habits, learning skills and communicating capabilities of pupils. The basic skills of reading, writing and arithmetic are acquired at this stage. Values are internalized and environmental consciousness sharpened. The crucial role of universal elementary education for strengthening the fabric of democracy, through provision of equal opportunities to all for the development of their inherent individual potential, was accepted from the very inception of our Republic in Article 45 under the Directive Principles of State Policy in the Constitution, which provides for free and compulsory education to all children until they complete the age of 14 years. This was iterated in1968, by the Resolution on the National Policy on Education'.

Problems of School Education

Punjab is in the most unenviable position with respect to literacy and education. There has been an increase in total literacy rate by 11.4 per cent points between 1991-2001. Male literacy has improved by 9.97 per cent points, female literacy by 13.1 per cent points and rural literacy by 12 per cent points during this period. Although the absolute number of illiterates has decreased from 70.43 lakh in 1991 to 63.80 lakh in 2001 (excluding the 0-6 age-group), the number continues to be alarmingly high.

The state has universal access at the primary level. It has a significantly high ratio of primary sections. Except some remote areas/new habitations with small populations, there is a government primary school in almost every village. However, there are 61 per cent villages without a middle section. In fact, 16 per cent habitations do not have an elementary school even within the norm of 3 km. Nearly one-fourth of the children are either not enrolled in schools or are in unrecognized schools. Further, there are still about 2.97 lakh children of 6-14 age group who are out of school. Among those enrolled in schools, the dropout rate is very high.

Out of 100 children enrolled in class 1, only 22 reach senior secondary level. The condition of facilities and infrastructure available in the primary schools is pitiable. More than 1,000 schools do not have buildings of their own. Even such basic necessities as drinking water and toilets are conspicuous by their absence in a large number of schools. Students do not have proper sitting arrangements and teachers do not have sufficient numbers of black-boards to teach and chairs to sit on. Apart from physical inputs, the most glaring weaknesses are lack of motivation, outdated teaching methodology and unskilled teachers.

Although Punjab has a respectable teacher-pupil ratio of about 1:42 at primary level, a one-way dialogue between teachers and students has remained the norm and learning by rote the only methodology. The prevalent teaching-learning process is inadequate for the first generation students, who are not supported by the home environment. Further, there is lack of relevance ofeducation to day to day life. A commitment to create specific and stated levels of learning and competence at different stages of education, is absent. At present, there is no reliable system of concurrent monitoring or evaluation at the state level.

Planning is vague and indicative, with no commitment to fulfillment of stated specific targets. The main stress has only been on formulation of schemes and almost no action-research to discover what will work. Total lack of accountability towards pupils and their performance is further hindering educational development. The time has indeeed come for introspection and diagnosis, consolidation of existing resources and planning for bridging the gaps.

Education Policy and Plans

The Government of India's National Policy on Education, 1986 (modified in the year 1992) is a forthright statement on education as an empowering agent. While making certain modifications in NPE (1986) in 1992, the Central Government took a significant decision to direct the State Governments to have their own state programmes of action for implementing the thrust areas of the policy, keeping in view local conditions as also the spirit of NPE.

NPE gives priority to universalization of elementary education (UEE) and identifies it as the major goal. It, inter alia, lays emphasis on the following aspects of education:

(i) universal access;

(ii) universal enrollment and universal retention of children upto 14 years of age;

(iii) a substantial improvement in the quality of education.

The policy relating to secondary education implies:

(i) Providing access to secondary schools in the unserved areas.

(ii) Establishing open schools for children who cannot attend full-time schools.

(iii) Enhancing the options by ensuring a vocational stream along with the three streams of humanity, science, commerce in higher secondary schools.

(iv) Consolidating the facilities:

a) Improvement in curriculum and evaluation methods.

b) Improvement in infrastructural facilities, such as building, classrooms and playgrounds, etc.

Adhering to the national policy, Punjab aims to achieve the goal of universalization of elementary education. For this, separate Directorates of Primary Education and Secondary Education have been set up. Till now, we had been adhering to the national policy. This is, however, for the first time that Punjab has initiated its own policy wherein the major objective is to universalize implementation of the national policy. A perusal of the Five Year Plans of Punjab reveal that although the First Five Years Plan did recognize quality as the key area of concern for educational reforms, the pressures for expansion were such that most of the development expenditure was consumed for opening new schools and appointment of additional teachers, rather than in making concentrated efforts to improve the quality of education.

Moreover, opening of new schools and appointment of additional teachers were more attractive as a populist measure. Statistically too, the data on the number of schools reveal that the maximum increase was during 1970-80.It was only during the Seventh Plan (1985-90) that the focus shifted from expansion and upgradation of education to consolidation of qualitative improvement. However, during the Ninth Plan (Punjab), the main focus was on both qualitative improvement and expansion and upgradation of schools, to meet the target of universalization.

During the Tenth Plan, it is envisaged that the main stress will be laid on providing/upgrading infrastructural facilities in the existing schools by providing buildings/furniture. It will also cater to decentralization to the village level, training of manpower, which includes teaching personnel and leadership. The focus of the state administration in the Tenth Plan is mainly on improving the quality of education.

In the Eighth and the Ninth Five Year Plans, although there has been a marginal increase in the outlay i.e. it increased to 2.62 per cent in the Eighth Plan and 2.89 per cent in the Ninth Plan, but the percentage is still very low as compared to the Fourth Plan and even the Fifth Plan. Hence, it is obvious that the education sector is not being given as much priority as it was given earlier. However, the expenditure during the Ninth Plan, i.e., from 1997 to 2000 has really exceeded the given outlay. Rs.60,947.61 lakh has been spent on education in 1997-2001 as against the allotted amount of Rs. 41,310.49 lakh.

The main reason was the implementation of the recommendations of the Fifth Pay Commission, wherein again the major amount was spent on salaries/state liabilities rather than educational development. In the Tenth Plan a major jump to Rs. 1,41,089.77 lakh is envisaged for the education sector and the state government claims that besides meeting the state liabilities, during this plan period, care is being taken to ensure that the money released is utilized to meet the objectives of development.

In spite of the fact that educational expenditure continues to be the highest item next only to defence, the resource gap for educational needs is still one of the major problems. Punjab is spending 2.88 per cent of the SGDP on education in comparison to 3.62 per cent at the national level. However, this percentage is really less, as there was a clear indication in the NPE 1986 that the investment on education should reach six per cent of the national income. Not only is the allocation for education very low, but, according to present data, 99 per cent of the expenditure at the primary level and 90 per cent at the secondary level are spent on salaries.

The expenditure on salaries at the primary level has increased from 97.8 per cent in 1992-93 to 100 per cent in 1995-96. It dropped to 97 per cent in 1996 but has again increased and reached 99 per cent in 2000-01. At the secondary level, the expenditure on salaries has been consistently rising from 83 per cent in 1992-93 to 87 per cent in 1995, 89 per cent in 1998 and has finally reached 90 per cent in 2000-01. Such a high percentage of expenditure on salaries clearly reveals that very little is left for development of education itself.

Progress of Education at Different Levels

According to the 1991 Census, 51 per cent of the population in Punjab were completely illiterate. Nearly one-fourth of the population had studied only up to the primary level or below, nine per cent up to the middle level and 10 per cent up to matriculation. Only three per cent of the total population had studied up to graduate level or above. These figures are alarming and show that the overall picture of education in Punjab is very poor. Another fact revealed is the failure of the education system at the secondary level, as the desired dispersal to the various streams has not taken place, which is obvious from the low figures of diploma holders.

The status of education at different levels, i.e., primary, middle, secondary and senior secondary, has been discussed under the umbrella of the major goals identified by the National Policy of Education, i.e., to ensure access to school, universal enrollment and retention of children up to the age of 14 years and improving quality of school education.

GOALS AND ACHIEVEMENTS

Goal I: Ensure Access to Schools

In Punjab, the state government manages 90.8 per cent of the recognized educational institutions; nine per cent are non-government, aided and/or recognized institutions and only a negligible number comes under the control of the Centre. The number of non-governmental but recognized institutions is however higher in the case of high schools and senior secondary schools than primary and middle schools, i.e., one-fifth of the high schools and one-fourth of the senior secondary schools are non-governmental institutions.

Punjab Government has made great strides in expanding access to education by opening new schools at all levels. The total number of schools increased from 8,891 in 1966-67 to

18,998 in 2001. The data reveal that the most massive expansion of schooling facilities took place during the 1970s-80s in Punjab, when the number of schools jumped from 9,394 to 16,050. Although there has been a gradual increase in the number of institutions from the 1980s to 2000, the expansion has not been that significant as in the period 1970-80.The number of primary schools increased tremendously in the past. It rose to 7,256 in 1970 and reached 12,383 in 1980. At present it has already reached 13,076.

The number of middle schools was 1,498 in 1980-81, increased to 2,545 in 1996-97, and is at present 2,534. High schools numbered 919 in 1969-70, 1,275 in 1974-75,1,912 in1980-81, 2,249 in 1990-91 and 2,199 in 2000-01. It is evident that the number of schools really increased only during 1970-80. Senior secondary schools too increased to 1,189 in 2000-01 from 520 in 1990. The data of the survey conducted in 12,625 villages by the Education Department reveal that except for some remote/unserved areas, there is a primary school in almost every village. There is likelihood of shortage of primary schools in Mand/Kandi/Border and Bet areas of Punjab, because of their difficult terrain. However, at the other end, the data also show that there are only 39 per cent of villages, having elementary sections and only 21 per cent which have secondary sections.

Even if we consider the distance norm as laid down by government, there are only 84 per cent habitations which have a middle school within three kms. which means shortage of elementary sections in 16 per cent habitations. Similarly, there is also a shortage of secondary and senior secondary schools in 10 per cent and 20 per centhabitations, according the distance norm of five kms. and eight kms. respectively. The assessment of the number of schools reveals that though the state is progressing well and there has been a quantitative expansion of educational institutions in Punjab, the real increase in the number of schools has been just at the primary level.

However, according to the present data, following the norm that there should be one secondary section for every 1.8 elementary section, the shortage comes to nearly 6,000 secondary schools. This indicates that even if all the secondary schools are upgraded upto the senior secondary level, there will still be a shortage of nearly 3,000 schools.

Alternate Schooling

Non-formal education for children in the 6-14 age-group: In pursuance of the National Policy on Education, 1986, the Central Government provides help for the establishment of non-formal education centres. But in Punjab, neither the government, nor NGOs, nor voluntary agencies run any such centres. Non-formal education was carried on until 1991, but there are no data available. However, since 1991, Punjab has no facility for non-formal education at the primary or upper primary level for children in the age group 6-14.

In only one district of Amritsar, a Chandigarh- based NGO applied to the Centre for starting NFE centres in 90 slums of the district. This project has been approved. But at present, no non-formal educational centre is operational. It is, however, proposed that under the Sarv Shiksha Abhiyan, in the Tenth Plan, the Education Guarantee Scheme and alternative innovative education will be initiated. The National Policy 1986, had proposed alternative education/open schools at the secondary level to provide access to dropouts, working children and girls. However, the state's effort so far has been to bring the children to mainstream/ formal schooling, and hence not much work has been done on open schools, though the large number of school dropouts warrant such an initiative.

Punjab started the open school programme in 1992, as an integral part of Punjab School Education Board as a centre of open learning to cover the gap at the secondary level. PSEB is operating the programme with 175 centres and 16,000 students. It has not developed any separate set of operational procedures except providing flexibility in the number of chances for passing examinations. In 1994-95 the open school was converted into a correspondence course, as a distance education programme. It has the same curriculum, examination and certification process as in formal schools. Except for this programme at the matriculation level, there is no alternative schooling in the state at present for the out-of-school children in the 14-8 age group.

The open school in Punjab is dependent only on student fees. In the absence of any financial support and requisite publicity, it has not realized its full potential. Recently, the state government claims to have formed VEDCs in the villages to check drop-out rates under SSA. However till date, Punjab Open School has hardly been able to cover even one per cent of the out-of- school children at the matriculation level. The open schools in fact have lost their orientation and become a haven for unrecognized schools which wish to expand up to the secondary level of education and get their pupils certified through these open schools.

To restore the essential character of the open schools, steps have to be taken urgently to rescue these from the stranglehold of commercially-run private schools. Further, Central funding is required to subsidize the study material and offset publicitycosts. At present, the number of study centres is far short of the requirement. Central assistance is essential for the extension and upgradation of the study centre network. But the best way will be to utilize the existing school infrastructure (buildings and teachers) innovatively for such non-formal education.

Goal II: Universal Enrollment and Retention of Children up to the Age of 14 Years

Enrollment in primary classes in government and recognized schools has remained almost static for 15 years, i.e., the number of admissions has increased from 4.49 lakh to only 4.80 lakh during 1984 to 1998. The growth at upper primary, high and senior secondary levels seems to be quite healthy, but in reality the picture is not that rosy, as it is based on a smaller base. Total enrollment of students in recognized institutions increased from 30.6 lakh in 1980-81 to 36.61 lakh in 1991. However, the increase in the next nine years was not that significant. It touched only 39.48 lakh in 2000.

Further, enrollment of Scheduled Caste students too has been rising in the age groups 6-11, 11-14 and 14-18. The increase was from 7.9 lakh in 1980 to 10.2 lakh in 1991 and has touched 14.31 lakh in 2000-01. The real expansion in enrollment of SCs is, however, a recent phenomenon. Their numbers grew the maximum in 1990-2000. However, the share of SCs at the primary level was 43.84 per cent of the total students in 2000-01, which came down to 32.89 per cent at the middle level and to 21.18 per cent at the secondary level. This has emerged as a very important intervention area for the government, as the data reveal a high dropout rate among Scheduled Castes as they move to higher levels of education.

In the last decade or so, there has also been a rapid increase in the number of unrecognized private schools in Punjab at the primary level. The enrollment of children in these unrecognized schools in Punjab has reached 25 per cent of total enrollment at the primary level, although the number of such unrecognized schools is negligible at the middle and high level.

The share of recognized schools in total enrollment is marginally increasing and has gone up to 9.21 per cent from 8.89 per cent in 1996-2000. Larger growth is in the unrecognized schools, which has gained 24.50 per cent points from 19.24 per cent points. It reflects the diminishing confidence of the public in government-run schools, which not only lack such basic infrastructure as buildings and furniture, but also motivation and commitment of the teachers. Hence households with comparatively higher income prefer to send their children to private schools, which they perceive as imparting qualitatively better education.

However, without undermining their role in enrolling children in small mohallas, who might otherwise have been out of school, the government has recently started the policy of enlisting the unrecognized schools so that these are also brought under some kind of check and control, and also to enable the educational data of these schools to be included in the education statistics of the state.

According to the Constitution of India, primary and elementary schooling have to be provided free of cost to all citizens. However, except for tuition fees, parents continue to bear the expenditure on other kinds of fees, books, stationery, uniforms, etc.On an average, at the elementary level (including private schools), the household expenditure per child is annually Rs. 670 (1994) in Punjab. It has increased from Rs.612 in 1992. This is despite the fact that free elementary education has been declared as a fundamental right. Household expenditure is quite high when compared to the national level, where the per pupil expenditure is Rs.378.

Household expenditure per child is Rs. 479 in government schools and Rs.1,398 in private schools in Punjab, as compared to Rs. 317 in government schools and Rs.742 per annum in private schools at the national level. Punjab ranks third (only after Haryana and Himachal Pradesh) so far as household expenditure on elementary education is concerned. It was reported that a major chunk of the household expenditure on education was also spent on private coaching/tuitions, apart from transport, uniform and books. The state government also spends quite a large budget on school education. About 1,15,855 teachers and 19,554 support persons work in the department. There are three Directorates functioning under the aegis of education. There are four accepted levels of education - Primary, Middle, Secondary and Senior Secondary.

Retention in Schools

Household and state expenditure per child show that huge amounts are spent in educating every single child. Therefore, enrollment by itself is no panacea if children do not continue education beyond a few years. Dropout is in fact an indicator of wastage in education. The dropout rate at the primary level of education in Punjab declined from 31.42 per cent in 1992-93 to 21.74 per cent in 1993-94 but thereafter it increased marginally and has again declined to 20.36 per cent at present, which is less than the dropout at the National level (42.39%, 1998-99). Surprisingly, the dropout rate for boys (21.96%) is more than that of girls (18.53%) at the primary level.

Although at the elementary levelthe drop-out is less in Punjab than at the all India level (56.82% in 1998), it continues to be at 37 per cent, as it was in 1991-92. The male and the female dropout rates are almost similar at the elementary level. At the secondary level, the dropout rate increased from 48.54 per cent in 1993-94 to 54.01 per cent in 1994-95, but thereafter it consistently declined till 1999 and reached 35.54%, but recently it has again risen to 40 per cent (2000-01). In spite of the government's initiative to reduce the dropout rate, the figures continue to be very alarming.

It is a matter of great concern that 20 per cent of the children drop out of schools at the primary level, 37 per cent by the time they reach the middle level, 40 per cent at the secondary and 78 per cent at the 10+2 level, i.e., 78 per cent of the children in class I dropout by the time they reach senior secondary classes. It is a matter of serious concern that out of the total students enrolled in class I only 22 per cent reach class XII.

According to the survey conducted by the Directorate of Education, there are 1.69 lakh children in the 6-11 age group and 1.28 lakh children in the 11-14 age group in the state, who do not attend school. According to the data available, 2.97 lakh children in the 6-14 age group and 10.52 lakh children in the 14-8 age group are out of the school network.It may be observed that 76.91per cent of the out-of-school children belong to the SC or OBC population. Even the remaining 23.09 per cent, though may be coming from upper social classes but belong to the economically weaker sections.

Further, the Directorate of Education also confirms that out of the 2.97 lakh children not going to schools, 1.13 lakh (37.91%) are engaged in one or other kind of labour activity and the majority of them are in the age group 11-14 years. Besides working as labourers or assisting their parents in work, the other reasons for children remaining out of school/or dropping out of school, identified by the Directorate of Education are: 1) poverty, 2) large family, 3) lack of inspiration/ interest/awareness or disinterest among parents and children, 4) illness/death/desertion/ emigration of either of parents, 5) lack of teachers/ infrastructure in schools, 6) study curriculum uninspiring/ dull/difficult, 7) teachers uninterested/uninspiring/ dull/rude, 8) timing not convenient and 9) access to school/ difficult/far away, etc. In addition to the reasons mentioned above, field studies also suggest that many parents still hesitate to send girls to co-educational institutions and are particularly averse to those in which there are no women teachers.

In Punjab there are 48 per cent such schools. Thus, state intervention becomes important in not just providing sound education, economic incentives and committed teachers, but also in tackling the socio-cultural impediments.Further, it is not only important to initiate schemes but also to ensure its regular monitoring, e.g., the scheme for providing scholarships for attendance to the SC girls is being promoted as an economic incentive, but field visits to different schools in various districts in Punjab revealed that money for disbursement under this scheme is not remitted regularly. Scholarships are not paid in time, if paid at all, was the common complaint of the school authorities. Many a time, the scholarships were received after the students had passed out of the Institution.

Goal III: Improving Quality of School Education

Heavy obsolete syllabus, outmoded teaching methods and inappropriate examination system: Overall improvement in curriculum, teaching practices and examination methods were the core targets for secondary education, envisaged even in the year 1986 as mentioned in the National Policy of Education. However, at present, the quality of school education and the creativity of students are being adversely affected by the heavy syllabus prescribed and the system of examination and awarding marks in the schools. Although, Punjab Government claims that it is striving to make the curriculum more relevant to local specificities, many studies, including the one conducted by CRRID in Faridkot and Lambi Blocks in Punjab, reveal that the parents are not satisfied with the syllabus taught, as they feel that it does not give their children access to skills that are related to the employment available outside.

Empirical studies reveal that people felt that what their children learnt in schools were not relevant for everyday life. It was also suggested by the teachers of different schools that the curriculum framework should be based on both compulsory and flexible subjects. Except languages, arithmetic and general science, all other subjects, such as algebra, geometry, geography and even history were not of practical value in day to day life and hence could be listed as optional subjects. It is important to make the curriculum more relevant and flexible.

It is also strongly felt that present methods of teaching are quite outmoded especially in the rural areas. The percentage of rural enrollment to total enrollment is as high as 75 per cent at the primary level and 70 per cent at the middle level. Quite often, the teachers encourage memorizing the contents of books and rote learning. There is also very little stress on value-education in the curriculum. Teachers and curriculum have been reported as uninspiring. This has been a major reason for school dropouts. The level of satisfaction of children/parents can be imagined from the fact that out of 100 students enrolled in class I in Punjab, only 60 per cent reached class 10 and 22 per cent reached class 12.

Further, urban-rural disparities emerge because of the privately managed English-medium institutions, generally located in urban areas. Although Punjab Government has decided to introduce English language in all government schools in the class 3 itself (according to the latest Education Policy, 2002), it, however, seems that this will create more problems than solve them.One notices that nearly 98 per cent expenditure at the primary level and 90 per cent at the secondary level are incurred on salaries of teachers and administration, leaving very little for socially useful work programmes, excursions, games and hobbies, science equipment and kits or even simple blackboards, chalks, posters and charts. In these circumstances, even an inspired teacher, with the best of training would have no choice but to encourage rote-learning of texts.

The present mode of teaching/learning is a matter of concern when one considers that in Punjab only 75 per cent of the school-age children ever go to recognized primary schools and only 58 per cent appear for the 10 th standard public examination. The pass percentage in the matriculation examination is only 49 per cent for regular students and 33 per cent for those appearing privately. Pass percentages have deteriorated over the years both among regular as well as private students.

Low examination results at grade 10 clearly indicate the weakness in the knowledge and understanding of the subjects among the students. It is a direct indicator of the low quality of teaching in schools. Otherwise how could one explain nearly 50 per cent failure rate in Board Examinations at the matriculation level?. Since the parents and the state have invested such huge amounts for a period of 10 to 12 years in the education of children, is not this an expression of the failure of the entire education system? It is, therefore, suggested that while classroom learning is important, what the child learns by self-observation outside the classroom is equally important. The child must become an active participant in the process of learning through observation, field studies, experiments and discussions. The child's individuality and creativity needs to be given due importance.

Innovations in curriculum, which should be based on the needs of the learners and related to the local environment, are required. It has been strongly recommended by educationists that there should be no textbooks upto the fifth class and the curriculum should be totally activity-based. Priority also needs to be given to reorientation in the outlook of the teachers, which at present is getting highly commercialized, as reflected in the number of tuitions being encouraged by them. There is also need for overhauling the examination system, so that it recognizes and evaluates creativity and new thinking rather than mere memorization.

Schools must change from mere education shops to centres for imparting knowledge and building skill levels. Teachers will perhaps have to play the most important role to enable the coming generations to develop capabilities to cope with a profoundly change-oriented world. But for this, teachers, education/training will have to be adopted as the first area of intervention.

Teacher-pupil ratio: The teacher-pupil ratio is also an important indicator of the quality of school education.In Punjab, the teacher- pupil ratio is 1:42 at the primary level, 1:26 at the middle level, 1:23 at the secondary and 1:28 at the higher secondary level. However, notwithstanding this overall satisfactory position, there are significant inter-district disparities, especially in primary schools. In some districts, such as Muktsar, Mansa, Moga and Sangrur, the teacher-pupil ratio is more than 1:50 at the primary level.Surprisingly, at the primary level in Punjab there are 242 schools, which have only one sanctioned post for a teacher. Shockingly, there are 746 schools (6%) where there is no sanctioned post of a teacher/head teacher/or a centre head teacher and this is especially true in Gurdaspur, Sangrur, Ferozepur and Patiala districts.

The rationale behind some schools not being sanctioned a single post of a teacher and the others being sanctioned eight posts to teach five classes is not known. Frequent transfers of teachers is another area of concern. Further, field visits in the blocks of Punjab have shown that, in rural areas, even where there are teachers, there is the persistent problem of absenteeism. This becomes even more serious in single-teacher schools. Panchayats could, therefore, be given the role of monitoring absenteeism among teachers. During field visits, it was also observed that teaching by proxy teachers existed in areas off the main roads.

Lack of options: The major challenge of education to achieve the ends of equity, documented in the policy perspective, is to ensure the availability of facilities for studying science and vocational subjects in all secondary schools so that everyone would be able to exercise equal freedom of choice with regard to the professions that they would like to pursue in future.

Vocationalization of higher secondary education was the major objective of the reforms envisaged in the Education Policy. It however seems that attempts made so far have not borne fruit and enrollment in the vocational stream, which was expected to reach 50 per cent at the 10+2 level, has remained rather marginal as only six per cent have opted for it in both rural and urban areas.

Further, in Punjab only 12 per cent of the students opt for science as compared to 32 per cent in Kerala, 47 per cent in Madhya Pradesh, 56 per cent in Meghalaya and 44 per cent in Andhra Pradesh. Similarly, children opting for commerce are less in Punjab than in other states. The state is also far behind Kerala in vocational education. The main reason for it is the outdated syllabus, with no relevance to the technical requirements in the employment market. Hence this stream is less popular as it fails to prepare the child for work and for upward mobility. The committed expenditure on teachers with knowledge limited only to a particular outdated field, already in employment with no students opting for it is a burden on the state.

As pointed out by the government itself 'many experienced teachers have stated that vocationalization within the secondary school system has been a casualty at the hands of educational planners who have no insight into the opportunities of employment, or the type of expertise required, for vocational employment. Consequently, lack of professionalism characterizes every initiative in the planning of training of teachers, preparation of curricula, selection of courses, infrastructure and other prerequisites. For future planning, therefore, while laying stress on vocationalization of education, adequate financial resources have to be allocated for starting viable activities in this field.

Adequate infrastructure and manpower prerequisites have also to be sorted out. The total non-enrollment of the children at the secondary level (45%), their dropout rate (48% at the secondary and 78% at the higher secondary level), their results (50% failure at the matriculation level), all show that the secondary and senior secondary levels have remained a terminal stage for the child to stop education. Perhaps this is considered as the time for the child to start working. Actually, secondary education was never considered a goal and this was perhaps the major drawback of education planners. It is only now that the state is moving towards secondary education and is preparing itself for universal secondary and senior secondary education by the year 2015.

Lack of infrastructural facilities in schools: For the child, the school is one of the main agencies of socialization, and the first prerequisite of schooling is availability of good quality infrastructure for imparting education. Hence a school must be attractive in terms of its environment. However, the data in the tables that follow do not give a very positive picture of the infrastructure facilities available in the schools of Punjab. The data in Tables 27 and 28 reveal that there are 676 schools (5%), at the primary level without their own buildings; 78 per cent require more toilets, 36 per cent boundary walls, 28 per cent verandas and 45 per cent require usable playgrounds. Further, there are only 76 per cent school buildings in good condition.

The remaining one-fourth of the buildings require urgent repair. Drinking water, which is a basic necessity, is also not available in 20 per cent of the schools. Further, only 31 per cent of the Government Primary Schools have the facility of toilets for girls and boys. At the middle level, 13 per cent of the schools require buildings, 48 per cent boundary walls, 47 per cent verandas, 49 per cent playgrounds and 66 per cent require toilet facilities.

Although provision of such infrastructural facilities, as buildings, playgrounds, etc., at the secondary level were the priority areas to be met during the Seventh Plan itself, there are still eight per cent of secondary schools which require buildings of their own, 37 per cent require toilets, 32 per cent verandas and 29 per cent playgrounds. Similarly, at the senior secondary level, five per cent of the schools are without buildings and 26 per cent require toilets. Even at the 10+2 level where the children are grown-up and need to have privacy, there are no separate toilets for girls in a number of schools.

Further information and data collected from the Directorate of Education too indicate that many of these buildings are in depilated conditions and have been declared unsafe for use as classrooms. The majority of the schools also face problems of shortage of classrooms. The data reveal that 60 per cent of the primary schools and 58 per cent of the upper primary schools require additional classrooms. Further, 69 per cent of the secondary and 73 per cent of the higher secondary schools too are short of classrooms, although a programme for the construction of additional classrooms, to the extent they were deficient, was declared a major target in the National Policy 1986.

The total number of additional classrooms required is 18,002 at the primary level, 4,150 at the upper primary, 4,091 at the secondary and 3,239 at the higher secondary level. There is also shortage of such basic necessities in the schools as blackboards, chalks and dusters. Nearly one-fourth of the sections do not have furniture even for the teachers. In 14 per cent of sections in the schools, the furniture/mats supplied for students are inadequate and in one-fourth there is absolutely no furniture, i.e., desk, bench, patre or even a mat for students. The data speak volumes about the state of infrastructure available in the schools.

In a nutshell, the condition of school buildings, basic amenities, availability of blackboard, furniture and playgrounds reveal that infrastructural facilities available at present in the schools of Punjab are poor. It is high time that our focus shifts to providing/upgrading/ optimally utilizing the existing infrasructural facilities in the schools. A look at the current status of education in Punjab in terms of the national goals reveals that, in spite of a specific provision in the Constitution to endeavour to provide free and compulsory education up to the age of 14 and several explicit commitments with regard to the achievement of universal elementary education and improving secondary education, the progress so far has been way behind the target.

In spite of the Policies on Education at the National Level and Programme of Action, the status of education in Punjab is not very impressive. In many cases, measures of reform could not be initiated because of lack of commitment, a positive attitude, planning and implementation. Further there were faults at the stage of policy planning itself. The policy framework lacked the specificity required for evolving implementation strategies for a vast variety of situations existing on the ground. Hence, the commitment, which was to be fulfilled by the seventies/eighties, is still to be realized.

There has been an uneven development of education not only between states but also between different castes and gender. Present schemes have not yielded significant results. A great many people, particularly educationists, feel that a large majority of the goals of the 1968 National Policy on Education still remain merely goals, even after the formulation of the 1986 and 1992 National Policy on Education.

DEVELOPMENT OF HIGHER EDUCATION

Independent India inherited a higher education system with strong colonial legacies. The planners of India were, therefore, faced with the immediate challenge of bringing about a basic transformation in its educational system to fulfill the developmental needs of the country. The educational planners had recognized the bi-directional linkages between education and development.

Considerable emphasis was also given to higher education to strengthen the educational system as a whole, and particularly to scientific and technological components therein, so as to meet the requirements of high-level capabilities in the realm of knowledge as well as skills. To achieve these objectives, the University Grants Commission (UGC) was set up as the apex national organization concerned with the establishment and maintenance of standards in higher education. The UGC acts as a vital link between the policy-making bodies of the government and institutions of higher education. Some of the recommendations of different commissions on education which have influenced policies, planning and development:

— Report of the University Education Commission, 1948-49.

— Report of the Education Commission, 1964-66.

— National Policy on Education, 1968.

— National Policy on Education, 1986.

— Education Reforms Commission, Punjab, 1985.

The broad areas and recommendations on higher education and their institutions concerned, covered by these commissions, are:

(1) aims and objectives of institutions of higher education;

(2) their management and governance;

(3) assuring quality and standards in these institutions;

(4) achieving equity and access through them;

(5) their funding pattern; and

(6) reforms in the existing system and distance higher education, etc.

National Policy on Education (1968) reinforced the recommendations of the Education Commission (1964-66) on reconstruction of education to relate it more closely to the life of the people, in the context of (a) continuous efforts to expand educational opportunities; (b) a sustained and intensive effort to raise the quality of education; (c) emphasis on development of science and technology; and (d) cultivation of moral and social values. Later, the National Policy on Education (1986) visualized that higher education should become dynamic with the (a) consolidation and expansion of institutions, (b) development of autonomous colleges, (c) re-designing of courses, (d) training of teachers, (e) strengthening research, and (f) improvement in efficiency and management.

Basic Problems of Higher Education

As higher education in the country, as well as in Punjab, grew in size, its problems and prospects too increased both in numbers and size, and its relevance to development and especially to the socio-economic needs of the society increasingly became issues of debate. Comparing the situation of higher education in other states and at the all-India level, its development in Punjab is seen to be relatively superior.

But there are problems, such as imbalanced and unplanned institutional growth, lack of infrastructural facilities, excessive and discriminatory system of admissions, financial constraints, placement of degree holders, irrelevant course content and gap between general and professional courses. Hence, there is need for various changes, modifications, adaptations, orientations and innovations.

Punjab has a long history of higher education-whether formal or non-formal-of a traditionally progressive and forward-looking educational system. The reorganized state of Punjab has experienced a large number of changes in its size, social fabric and economy. These are directly linked with the development of education in the state. The structure and system of higher education in the state has followed the national pattern, such as college and university education in general and professional degrees. The current position of higher education in Punjab, although, considered as the core sector for achieving the objective of employment for an individual, is also oriented towards socio-economic, environmental, and human resources development.

Punjab Agriculture University at Ludhiana is well known for its contributions to education, research and extension services in the field of agriculture. Punjab Technical University at Jalandhar, Punjab Medical University at Faridkot, and Punjab Veterinary University at Talwandi Saboo are in the process of being established exclusively for technical education, medical and veterinary sciences. In addition, there exists another institution offering higher learning in medicine, namely, the Postgraduate Institute of Medical Education and Research, Chandigarh.

These universities and institutes are autonomous bodies, created by Acts of State/Central Legislatures. Punjab University and the Postgraduate Institute of Medical Education and Research, Chandigarh, are both in a slightly different position, in respect of their governance and financial aids or grants. Since, they also serve Punjab, as such, it would be legitimate for us to include a reference to these matters in the discussion here.

In quantitative terms, the increase in the number of institutions of higher education in Punjab has been spread equally across universities imparting arts/sciences/commerce, technical and professional education. The facilities they provide, however, appear to be inadequate to meet the present requirement, especially for the population of rural areas, as these are all located in urban areas. In qualitative terms, standards of attainments of most of these universities are comparable with that elsewhere.

Nevertheless, there is need and scope for further improvement in respect of their goals and pursuit of excellence. Views of the members of the faculty, administrative staff and students of different universities highlight great scope for introducing changes in higher education, for improving the performance of the system and making it more relevant to the needs of the day. The structure of governance of the universities in Punjab has followed the pattern evolved by other universities in the country, and based on the model developed in Europe. Hence here is no need to suggest any change in the university structure, but it is imperative to follow a pattern, which has international acceptance.

Colleges

There are a sufficient number of colleges in the state and most of them are affiliated to one or the other of the seven universities of Punjab. Undergraduate teaching is mostly undertaken in the affiliated colleges (whether government, private aided or private unaided). Though these colleges mostly confine themselves to undergraduate teachings, some also offer postgraduate courses. Besides, some universities also provide education facilities at graduate and postgraduate levels, through correspondence courses and evening colleges.

STATUS OF TECHNICAL AND PROFESSIONAL (VOCATIONAL) EDUCATION

The Department of Technical Education and Industrial Training looks after 16 engineering colleges (13 government and three affiliated private and three private), 41 polytechnics/ institutions including Pharmacy (diploma level institutions), and Hotel Management institution and about 129 industrial and vocational centres at the ITI level. Every year a total of about 2,800 engineers, 5,300 diploma holders and about 16,800 craftsmen at the certificate level are being trained by these technical institutes. Besides, three engineering colleges, seven polytechnics and 33 new industrial training institutes are in the pipeline at various levels of establishment in the state.

The Directorate of Medical Education and Research, Punjab, governs medical education and research in the state. The directorate was set up to develop medical manpower and to ensure that medical education and teaching hospitals received adequate attention and proper facilities for research in various branches of medicine. To develop superspecialists, teachers from the level of senior lectures and above are sponsored to the Post-graduate Institute of Medical Education and Research, Chandigarh and the All India Institute of Medical Sciences, New Delhi, for postgraduate courses. These developments indicate that the Government of Punjab considers professional education, and especially industrial training, as high priority.

In the circumstances, action needs to be initiated on different fronts to make the technical education system responsive to the needs and requirements of industry. Participation of the private sector needs to be encouraged for continuous up-gradation and expansion of HRD facilities. Keeping in view the expansion of technical higher education, besides the promotional activities of Punjab Technical University in the field of professional education it is necessary to establish a higher-level apex body like IIT as a separate unit.

Hence, there is need to restructure the admission system in different courses to improve the status of employability of graduates and postgraduates. Besides, there should be two streams of courses-vocational and general-at the firstdegree level, at least for the next two decades or so, as an interim measure. This endeavor may help in reducing the unwanted rush of students for higher-level arts/sciences courses. Provision for offering courses of functional utility, with a vocational bias, may be helpful to those who wish to end their studies with a pass degree and are not willing to pursue further education.

Vocationally motivated students could then find gainful employment or be self-employed in vocations of their own choice after the completion of +2 school stage. If they wish to continue their education, they may go in for general education, or may proceed to polytechnics for diploma or certificate courses in technical, professional or any other skill-formation courses. Therefore, vocational courses at the first-degree level need to be enriched and diversified. By this effort, government or private institutions would definitely reduce the educated unemployment level and equip students for self-employment, while giving the highest priority to vocational sectors.

Concerned with higher education and placement of students, the Education Commission 1964-66 recommended the need to strengthen linkages between higher education and productivity, which leads to socio-economic development. There is no follow-up record of higher-level degree holders available in published or unpublished form; therefore, it is difficult to assess the social and economic relevance of higher degrees. The existing educational system has not undergone any change, nor has it any direct linkage with the socio-economic needs of the people.

Relevance and Access

The Education Commission (1964-66) rightly stated, 'Indian society is hierarchical, stratified and deficient in vertical mobility. The social distance between the different classes, particularly between rich and poor, the educated and the uneducated, is large and is tending to widen ...' Similar is the situation in Punjab, and this complex character of the population affects the socio-economic development of the state. People living in rural areas, and especially Scheduled Castes and Backward

Castes and other economically weaker sections of society, are exploring the same educational opportunities as the other castes, because of lack of financial support.

Although the number of women students in all the subjects at the higher level is increasing relatively in successive decades, the equality of women and men remains an issue of debate in relation to higher education. This demands immediate attention. In this context, the National Policy on Education has rightly emphasized the need for removal of disparities and equalization educational opportunities for all sections of society.

In Punjab, the Scheduled Castes population is more than 33 per cent, but comparatively, their enrollment at postgraduate and graduate levels is significantly low. Their enrollment in different courses of studies is quite uneven, such as 86.27 per cent in arts/sciences/commerce, 2.93 per cent in teachers' training, 4.30 per cent in medical and paramedical sciences, 0.54 per cent and 5.03 per cent in agriculture and engineering. It is evident that despite government's efforts, the enrollment of women and Scheduled Castes students is still far behind that of the general castes. Reasons for the educational backwardness of women and Scheduled Castes are mainly: (i) economic and social status of the families; (ii) lack of interest and inadequate backup by family or society; (iii) medium of instructions imparted in colleges and universities; and (iv) negative attitude of the students. Although the proportion of women and Scheduled Castes availing higher education has increased in relative numbers, there is still need to encourage them to go in for higher education.

EFFICIENCY, STANDARDS AND QUALITY OF HIGHER EDUCATION

Higher education contributes to the development of every area by providing educated and trained manpower for its economic and industrial set-up. Thus, higher education and economy are closely related and have a direct impact on each other. The efficiency of the system is, therefore, judged by the quantity and quality of the product at the given cost. Efficiency can be considered, as to (1) whether the out-turn of graduates and postgraduates of university education is upto the mark both in terms of quantity (number passed) and quality (level of academic achievement), or (2) whether the graduates and postgraduates are equipped with skills and capabilities required by the existing economy, or whether there is a mismatch between the training imparted and the skills needed. This can be assessed by examining extent to which graduates and postgraduates are absorbed in the job market. The present position of higher education in regard to efficiency and quality reveal the level of wastage and the number of failures at the first-degree stage or passes in third division. This adds to the number of educated unemployed. This is a major issue, which must be tackled.

The quantitative expansion of higher education in the state has been unplanned and unbalanced. The expansion has taken place not by choice but by compulsion. Some times it has been in order to satisfy social and political demands. While the system has expanded in terms of institutions and enrollments, there has been no change in the basic infrastructure facilities for meeting the educational needs of the growing number of students. One of the obvious implications of this numerical growth, without qualitative improvement, is that students do not get the education desirable, related to the demand. The colleges do not have adequate space, classrooms, and playgrounds, libraries and laboratories.

Inadequate infrastructure facilities contribute to low academic standards in the affiliated colleges, where more than 80 per cent of the enrollment is concentrated. The problem is particularly acute in urban areas where, due to political and social pressures, colleges have to enroll students beyond the allotted number of seats, strength, or unqualified or, below average students. Overcrowding in the affiliated colleges has almost made it impossible to produce quality pass-outs or to introduce any change or innovation. Even the condition of the professional colleges is not very healthy, where admissions are also made after charging heavy fees in the form of endowment funds. In these cases the merit and capabilities of the candidates are generally ignored. In such circumstances, retention of the quality and standards of education is impossible. This state of affairs demands serious attention.

Support for Research

Research, the highest academic endeavor, is either compulsory, or an optional subject, directed by different departments of different universities, especially in post-graduate courses. Obviously, research at this level cannot be expected to have a high standard of quality and the findings might not be accepted as valid to be considered for any policy or plan. M.Phil research is in partial fulfillment of degree requirements and in many cases, it can be extended to Ph.D Most research work at a higher educational level does not seem to be thematic; it is fragmentary and lacks precision of thought and technique, as reported by the Education Reforms Commission Punjab, 1985. The report did not under-estimate the scope of fundamental research in education, but suggested that, to solve current educational problems, applied research, including action research, is equally important. Research must not be restricted merely to universities departments, but has to flow to other institutions too, and should be linked with the policy and planning strategies of the state.

TEACHERS, TRAINING AND TEACHING

The State Council of Education Research and Training, Punjab has laid the main stress on pre-service and in-service teachers training. For giving in-service training to the already working secondary teachers, 12 In-service Training Centres have been functioning at District headquarters in the state. In addition the State Institute of Science Education imparts in-service training to science and mathematics teachers. To impart training in the latest advances in educational technology, SCERT organizes seminars for teachers through the educational technology cell. The main objectives of these institutions are to:

(1) bring about qualitative improvement in the existing educational system of the state;

(2) provide pre- and In-service education for teachers and educational supervisors;

(3) monitor and develop educational programmes;

(4) introduce and implement new education policies of the Central and State Governments.

Education Reforms Commission, Punjab, 1985, had also given importance to preservice or entering-service training programmes. It maintains that existing training programmes have no relevance to the present-day teaching and learning situation. A sense of professionalism is often lacking among teachers and no attempts are being made to arouse it. Institutions imparting teacher-education have superficial links with the existing system of education, whether in schools or in universities, therefore, the dominant thrust areas of teacher-education should be value-oriented education to strike a balance between the concomitants of advances in science and technology and humanistic values.

As for vocationalization of education, teachers should be sensitized to acquire skills to link educational activity with work and employment, so as to create an urge for continuing professional education. In the current technological environment, there should be a special training programme package in the pre- and in-service training programmes. Teachers' training institutes should have their own practicising schools. Information technology needs to be introduced in the course of the training programmes.

To raise the quality and standards of education among pupils, it is absolutely essential to produce better-quality teachers and this can be done by providing better quality of training programmes. The state has no training programmes for teachers. It is necessary to initiate pre-service and in-service (condensed courses) training programmes for teachers, teaching in colleges and universities. The quality of teachers needs to be evaluated in terms of academic achievement, professional training, and the desirable attitude towards teaching as a profession.

The present observations on Punjab's teachers highlight the lack of a system of ensuring accountability of the teachers in terms of the quality of their teaching work. There is no system of evaluation of the teacher's output with regard to teaching, research, innovation, and regularity at higher levels; hence, there is urgent need for the department of education to consider these issues seriously.

Courses and Examinations

Examination is an integral part of the total educational process, as it has linkages both with teaching and learning. The examination component of the educational system has two broad objectives, namely, (a) to serve as a feed-back mechanism with regard to the effectiveness of the teaching-learning process, and (b) to classify the students at the end of a pre-determined period for purposes of class-promotion. In the present circumstances, examinations are being held mostly for the classification or promotion of students. The assessment is the basis of evaluating the performance of the students in a public examination, generally held annually. This system of examinations is almost identical in Punjab.

In 1981, the UGC brought out a monograph on education reforms, which iterated the deficiencies, as a number of committees and commissions had earlier pointed out. On the basis of the recommendations of the committees and commissions, efforts have been made to remove the glaring shortcomings of the examination system. Basically, the whole system in the state has become examination-ridden. Mass copying (somewhere and sometime) is also prevalent at graduate and post-graduate levels. Some universities have introduced a semester system to reduce the burden of examinations on the students, but this effort has not produced significant results. Internal assessment, introduced in order to make evaluation of education an integral part of the teaching-learning process, has not produced much positive result. There is very low correlation between marks obtained by students in internal assessment and in external examination.

The Education Reforms Commission, Punjab, 1985, has maintained that the existing method of holding examinations in the state is not satisfactory. The use of unfair practices is on the rise. Teachers are not voluntarily coming forward to share responsibility because of various reasons. Hence the credibility of the existing examination system is fast disappearing. The report has suggested measures and approaches for overcoming the shortcomings of the examination system.

OPEN LEANRING SYSTEM

With the advancement of science and technology, the concept of imparting higher education has undergone a tremendous change. The conventional concept has given way to that of distance education. The new approaches to teaching and learning combine together correspondence with different communication media, such as television, audio-video recorder, computer and even satellite, etc. The system aims at extending facilities of education to all individuals regardless of 'who and where'. During the last decade, distance education has spread (correspondence courses and Indira Gandhi Open University system) throughout Punjab.

The Open University system is an outgrowth of the development and wider acceptance of the concept of distance education. This includes use of non-print media as supplementary material, such as television, computer and satellite. Although Punjab has no open university, the Indira

Gandhi Open University provides opportunities for higher education even here. Moreover, Punjab Technical University, Jalandhar, provides a franchise system of education for those, who are not enrolled in conventional institutions. The other universities, such as Punjabi University, Patiala, Guru Nanak Dev University, Amritsar, and also Punjab University, Chandigarh, provide facilities through correspondence courses with print material and contact courses, mainly in Arts and literature subjects.

In fact, the Directorate of Correspondence Courses and the Open University system have made significant progress in imparting higher education. Despite all efforts, this system of education mostly reaches the economically well-off upper class families, because of high fees. If the system of distance education has to develop into a viable and effective alternative to make education reach the most deprived and most needy population, then it has to provide education at nominal charges and introduce such subjects as are available in the conventional system of education.

Financial Resources

In regard to the financial position, there is some difference in allocation of funds to government and non-government colleges. Statistics in previous tables revealed that the quantitative growth in higher education is noteworthy, but the flow of financial resources into the system of education is slow, insufficient and unevenly distributed.

Financial resources are divided into two parts: (i) General Education and (ii) Technical and Professional Education.The general trend of resource allocation shows that a major part of the expenditure is on salaries of teachers. The proportion of expenditure on staff salaries has been continuously rising over successive decades in Punjab. This leaves little for expenditure on enhancing the quality of education. This has an adverse effect on developmental objectives.

Besides funds allocated by the state government, there are several other bodies, apart from individuals and business undertakings, which contribute directly or indirectly to the expenditure incurred by educational institutions. These include the Central Government, University Grants Commission, universities, etc. The trend of expenditure by such institutions, however, cannot be projected for future years.

FUTURE SCENARIO

There are serious difficulties in presenting a comprehensive projection of the future because of inadequacy of data and lack of clarity about the overall future scenario. However, it would be adequate to present a broad picture, which might yield some insights into policy planning. Although it was projected that enrollment would slightly decline in the initial years, i.e., till the year 2001, but if the governments started to take action and seriously implemented their plans and policies, 'there will be acceleration of the programmes for the universalization of elementary education, which will increase the enrollment rate by 2006-07'.

Increase at the primary level will be only just more than marginal, but at the upper primary and secondary levels, it will be substantial. Increased incentives will further attract the children to government schools'. In spite of the increasing craze for private schools in Punjab, if the government improves the quality of school education according to the recommendations made in the pages that follow, i.e., making education useful and relevant for children through curriculum revision, child-centred teachinglearning methods, improvements in educational provisions, value-education, teachers' training, teacher empowerment, change in the examination system and improving the infrastructural facilities, enrollment in government schools will be at least 70 per cent of school-age going children by the year 2007.

'The enrollment in only government schools is likely to increase from the present 30.19 lakh (2001) to 35 lakh in 2006 or 2007. The increased enrollment and retention at all levels will also increase the output of more secondary graduates. The share of private schools in total enrollment is not likely to reach more than 30 per cent from the present 25 per cent'. However, the government has to depart from 'tokenistic' planning on models provided by the national planners and others and take initiatives involving experimentation with specific objectives at the grassroot, institutional and district levels. It is also necessary to develop an authentic system of monitoring, appraisal and evaluation to achieve our present targets and also to cater to the projected education scenario of the future.

Achievements In Literacy and School Education

- The literacy rate has increased from 58.51 per cent in 1991 to 69.95 per cent in 2001, a rise of 11.44 per cent points during the last 10 years.
- The gender gap in literacy rate has decreased from 15.25 per cent points in 1991 to 12.08 per cent points in 2001. Female literacy has increased 13.14 per cent points as compared to only 9.97 per cent points in the case of males in the last decade.
- The rural-urban gap in literacy rate has come down from 19.31 per cent points in 1991 to 13.97 per cent points in 2001.
- There has been a quantitative expansion of educational institutions. with the total number of schools increasing from 9,394 in 1970 to 16,038 in 1980 and further to 18,998 in 2000-2001. Data suggest that the most massive expansion of schools has taken place at the primary level. At present, except for some remote areas, all villages have access to primary schools.
- Enrollment of students in recognized institutions has gone up from 30.6 lakh in 1980-81 to 36.61 lakh in 1991 and

the figure touched 39.48 lakh in 2000. Enrollment of girls has shown considerable improvement

— Enrollment of SC students has consistently been increasing. Their numbers increased from 7.9 lakh in 1980 to 10.2 lakh in 1991 and 14.31 lakh in 2000-2001.

Lliteracy and School Education

— Allocation of resources in education is only 2.88 per cent as against the target of six per cent of the SGDP.

— At present 99 per cent of the expenditure on education at the primary level and 90 per cent at the secondary level is being spent on salaries, leaving very little for development in other spheres of education.

— Punjab's rank in literacy rate has come down from the 12th position in 1971 to the 16th position in 2001. There are still 95 lakh illiterates in the state (2001 Census)

— Except for few districts, the TLC programme has not functioned well in Punjab.

— The literacy rate of the Scheduled Caste population is very low, i.e., 41.09 per cent. Female literacy rate of Scheduled Caste women (31.03%) is almost half that of non-Scheduled Caste women (57.6%). The literacy rate of SC women is as low as 12 per cent in Bathinda, 16 per cent in Faridkot, 15 per cent in Ferozepur and 17 per cent in Sangrur. Government should, therefore, give priority consideration to female Scheduled Caste in this pocket in Punjab.

— According to the 1991 Census, nearly one-fourth of the population had studied in the primary level or below, nine per cent upto middle level and 10 per cent upto matriculation level. Only three per cent of the population had studied upto graduation or above.

— Sixty-one per cent of the villages do not have an elementary section. 16 per cent habitations do not have access to a middle school even within the norm of three km. If we have to achieve our aim of universalizing elementary education, 100 per cent accessibility to elementary schools will have to be provided. Further, there is also shortage of secondary and senior secondary schools within the normative distance.

— One-fourth of the children in the 6-11 age group and more than 31 per cent in 11-14 age group are still not enrolled, or are enrolled in unrecognized schools.

— Share of government schools in total enrollment in primary classes in gradually decreasing and has come down from 71.86 per cent (1996) to 66 per cent (2000), whereas there has been a larger growth in the share of unrecognized private schools, which has now increased from 19 per cent to 25 per cent in the last four years. It reflects the discontent of the public with government run schools.

— Although Punjab has reduced the dropout figures to some extent, this rate is still very alarming, as 20 per cent of the children dropout at the primary level, 37 per cent at the middle level, 40 per cent at the secondary level and 78 per cent at the 10+2 level. It is a shocking fact that out of 100 children enrolled in class I, only 22 reach senior secondary level.

— The percentage of Scheduled Caste enrollment at the primary level is 43.84 per cent of the total students. It has come down to 32.89 per cent at the middle level and to 21.18 per cent at the secondary level. This reflects a very high dropout rate among Scheduled Castes, as they move to higher levels of education.

— The number of out-of-school children is also quite high. At present 2.97 lakh children in 6-14 age group and 10.52 lakh children in 14-18 age group are out of school.

— There is no non-formal education centre at present for children in the age group 6-14 and no alternative schooling in the state for out-of-school children in the age group 14-

18 years, except for one at the matric level. That is why in Punjab open school has hardly been able to cover one per cent of the out-of-school children.

— There are significant inter-district disparities in teacher- pupil ratio. In some districts, such as Muktsar, Mansa and Moga, the teacher-pupil ratio at the primary level is more than 50 students per teacher as compared to other districts where the ratio varies between 31 to 40. Further there are many schools in Punjab where there is no, or only one sanctioned post of a teacher, head teacher or centre head teacher.

— The quality of teaching in schools can be judged by the poor results of the students. At present there is 50 per cent failure of students at the matriculation level.

— There are lack of infrastructural facilities and civic amenities in the schools. The heavy syllabus prescribed and the system and examination of awarding marks in most of the school are adversely affecting the quality of school education and the creativity of students. Schools with no, or a single post sanctioned for a teacher and problem of teachers' absenteeism are other threats to quality of school teaching.

— Five per cent buildings are required at the primary level, 13 per cent at the middle, eight per cent at the high and five per cent at the senior secondary level. Besides the building-less schools, there are many other schools where buildings, need urgent repair. Many of these buildings are in dilapidated conditions and have been declared unsafe for use as classrooms. The majority of the schools are also facing the problem of shortage of classrooms, toilets, playgrounds, boundary walls, verandas etc.

To achieve the targets of elementary and secondary education, we need to take the following steps:

1. Optimal upgradation of primary schools to elementary level and secondary schools to senior secondary level: The state has nearly achieved universal access to primary schools, except in certain Mand/Border/Kandi and Bet areas.

Special strategies like the Education Guarantee Scheme (EGS) should be envisaged for these remote areas without accessibility to basic primary education. The focus should be now on achieving universalized accessibility at the elementary level and easy accessibility at the secondary level, by optimally merging the number of schools under two categories instead of four, i.e., one at the elementary level and the other at the secondary level.

The government should make efforts to upgrade the maximum number of primary school to the elementary level and the secondary schools to senior secondary level, rather than creating totally new infrastructure. The expansion in the number of schools should be middle upwards. This has also been recently accepted as a major target by the state government (Punjab Education Policy, 2002). But how far it is implemented, is the real issue.

2. Rationalization and redistribution of staff: At present, a major chunk of the expenditure on education is on salaries/ state liabilities, leaving very little for actual development in education. The state government should try to utilize optimally the expenditure. Staffing in Punjab needs to be redistributed, restructured and rationalized. It is very important to upgrade the primary schools to middle level, so that the shortage of teachers at the former is compensated by the excess at the latter, the teacher-pupil ratio being lower at the middle level than at the primary level.

   The merging of the two levels will help in rationalizing the manpower required upto the elementary level. The secondary level should also be optimally upgraded to the senior secondary level. It seems that the total number of teachers recruited is not so much of a problem, the need is to ensure their proper and rationalized deployment. The convergence and merger of the four branches of education into two will reduce the workload of the education department and help in redistributing the number of teachers required at different levels.

3. Focus on pre-service/in-service teachers' training: The government should enhance the competency and skills of the teachers by promoting pre-service and in-service training for them. DIETS (District Institution of Education and Training at elementary level)/GISTC's (Government In-service and Training Centres at secondary level) and other training institutions must be optimally utilized for this purpose. Such pre-service and in-service training programmes should be constantly reviewed and strengthened, as its quality has a direct bearing on the quality of education in the state.

4. Rationalizing teacher transfers: Transfer of teachers in Punjab is not merely an administrative problem but also hits at the very core of the quality of education. One of the reasons for non-enrollment/dropouts is the single-teachers and teacher-less schools and persisting absenteeism. Influential teachers get themselves transferred to convenient locations, leaving behind a bunch of schools which do not see the face of a teacher for months/years. So the need of a rational and transparent transfer policy cannot be over emphasized. The new education policy released by the state sets guidelines for teachers' transfers for the first time. These guidelines, which are pragmatic and practical, must be adhered to and implemented by the state.

5. Focus on teacher empowerment: The critical role of teachers in the entire education set-up must be realized. Emphasis should be made to address their professional development needs. Processes should be set up to initiate a participative mode for the teachers in the development of curriculum, text-book, teaching-learning material and methodologies. However, simultaneously the teachers have to be made more responsible and performance-oriented.

6. Setting up an academic council: There is need for an autonomous multimember academic authority to undertake sample studies to collect data about the functioning of institutions and learning capabilities of students. It is

necessary to make the education system more transparent. Action-research and policy development should be other concerns of this council. Members should include educationists, PRIs and school representatives, preferably teachers.

7. School heads: It is strange to note that there is no post of a headmaster in a middle school and some of the primary schools also function without any head. Apart from the non-availability of the post of a head, it is also the aptitude/ attitude and vision of the school head which has a direct bearing on the quality of education. The present system of promotion for school headship is outdated. Teachers at the fag end of their service, when they prepare themselves for the bliss of retirement, get promoted to school headship. By that time they neither have the zeal nor the stamina to make any impact on the school under their charge.

   Moreover from teaching they are just thrown into an entirely new field of work which requires altogether new skills. So, not only must every school, have its head, but they must be sufficiently young, with enough years of service ahead in which they may translate their vision of the school into reality. The new education policy of the state has come out with such a programme, which must be implemented without delay.

8. Revamping the curriculum: There should be a special thrust to make education at elementary level useful and relevant for children. At present, it is highly regimented with uniform courses. The state has been blindly following the national curriculum without considering the special conditions at the grassroot level of Punjab. Hence modernization of the syllabus with more flexibility in the choice of subjects is recommended. Curriculum framework should be based on compulsory and flexible subjects, wherein the children have the choice to opt for the subject of their interest.

   It will help in reducing the weight of the school bag. It is recommended that the subjects, which do not have practical value in day to day life could be listed as optional. In fact there should be a continuous review of the utility of the curriculum from time to time. Further, there is need to emphasize on moral values and iterate their importance in everyday life.

9. Need for reforms in examination/evaluation system: It is important to review the current examination system and consider possible alternatives of bringing reforms in it. At present, the emphasis in education is on theory which is encouraging rote-learning without basic understanding. More practical work and activities should be encouraged, which would also discourage mass copying and rote-learning. It will be appropriate to adopt a regular grading system and emphasize on the year-long classroom work, instead of evaluating only on the basis of annual examinations. This will increase the attendance rate and the knowledge of the students.

10. Provision of infrastructure/optimum utilization of the existing infrastructure: Efforts should be made to bridge the infrastructural gaps. Schools should raise resources through voluntary organizations and panchayats, with the state government providing matching grants. The state should also endeavour to optimize utilization of existing infrastructure in schools, by merging the school education at two levels-elementary and secondary-which would help in maximizing the utilization of the existing infrastructure. Introducing a shift system and using the existing buildings and teachers for open learning/nonformal education in the evening are the other methods of utilizing the existing infrastructure.

11. Changing the mindset of parents: As far as the social and cultural handicaps of enrollment and retention of girls in schools is concerned, the NGOs and PRIs need to be associated effectively to initiate an attitudinal change in the parents of the girl child.

12. Enhance incentives to all children in government schools: The various incentives being provided by the government

should be for all children, irrespective of caste criteria (as being adopted today) to achieve the goal of universalization of education.

13. Promoting free lunch: Interaction with the parents in the various districts of Punjab and the government machinery of the departments concerned have led to the recommendation that, although the mid-day meal scheme is not achieving the desired results and encourages the children to sell off wheat on the way from the school to their homes, it is felt that some sort of packed, cooked and nutritious food should be supplied to children to attract them and retain them in the schools.

14. Adult literacy programmes should be merged with SSA: This will help in effective functioning and optimum utilization of resources. There should be timely release of the Centre's and the State's share of funds and regular monitoring of these programmes at the state as well as district level.

15. English should be started in class 6: According to the new Education Policy of the state, the English language has to be started in class 3 in government schools. But it is strongly felt that it is difficult for the child to bear the burden of an additional language at such a tender age. His understanding capacity is limited in the formative years and, therefore, it is strongly recommended that English should be started in class 6 and not in class 3. The English language cannot be avoided, but emphasizes needs to be given to the mother tongue, especially in the formative years.

16. Village as unit of planning: To initiate a community-based approach, village should be the lowest unit for planning education. Village plans should converge to form the District Educational Plans.

17. Decentralization and community participation: The state government should take effective steps to encourage transfer of elementary educational institutions to the PRIs

and urban local bodies, in a bid to empower the community and other stakeholders. It is essential that control of schools and teachers should be transferred to local bodies, which have a direct interest in teachers' performance. Efforts should be made to involve the community in education development through VEDCs.

The state's efforts at decentralizing powers to VEDCs for running the SSA programmes in villages should be replicated in other educational programmes too. Decentralization will actually be achieved only when the panchayats, VEDCs and UEDCs become fully autonomous, with full financial powers to plan, manage and control the school affairs. It is also important to enlarge and strengthen the role and participation of PTAs/MTAs in schools.

18. Increased allocation/resource mobilization for education: The state should substantially increase public investment and encourage and private investments in education, so that it rises to six per cent of the national income by the year 2007. It is, however, important that money is spent on increasing access to schools, infrastructure, monitoring, inspection, management and development of education rather than merely on salaries.

19. Private initiatives have to be facilitated: In recent times, a tendency has developed in people to send their children to private schools. There is need to facilitate and encourage private bodies to share the responsibility with government. It is, however, very important to ensure that minimum standards of quality of education are maintained in the private schools.

20. Monitoring and evaluation: An institutionalized mechanism has to be set up for regular inspection, monitoring and follow-up. A school gradation and evaluation system, initiated by the state from this year, is a welcome step, which needs to be institutionalized. A similar system of appraisal of teacher and school heads must also be put in place. One needs a local-level body or institution to monitor the performance of teachers.

21. Participative field studies should be undertaken: At present not much research on education is being undertaken in Punjab, at the grassroots level. So, to identify the requirements of planning, measure the effectiveness of various schemes, evaluate the measures undertaken by the state to improve quality of education and curriculum, it is important to expand research, which will reveal the ground realities. Government should also probe into such areas as relevance of education in daily life and public perception of government schools.

9

WITHER INDIAN EDUCATION SYSTEMS

In a poor country like India, illiteracy of the majority continues to pose a serious challenge. The central and state governments have promised to wipe out illiteracy and have engaged in many projects to achieve that goal. The ruling establishment has sought local and international financial support to eradicate illiteracy. While the policies and pronouncements have been ambitious, many marginalized communities have gone from bad to worse.

The framers of the Constitution were well aware of the debilitating effect on society of discrimination against the weak. Thus, they made constitutional provisions to remove all forms of such centuries-old discrimination. Article 14 of the Constitution provides: "The State shall not deny to any person equality before the law or the equal protection of the laws within the territory of India."

Article 46 mandates:

> "The State shall promote with special care the educational and economic interests of the weaker sections of the people, and, in particular, of the Scheduled Castes and the Scheduled Tribes, and shall protect these from social injustice and all forms of exploitation."

In the last five decades, attempts have been made to improve education for all and for the weak sectors in particular, to improve their economic and social standing. Over 30% of the allocation on education was spent to improve education of scheduled castes and tribes. Many factors, however, operate to deny the weak sectors of their right to education and to prevent them from fully participating in various educational efforts.

The introduction and impact of the New Education Policy needs to be examined from this background. Many educationists argue that a class-divided system of education has played a central role in molding the patterns of uneven development and disenfranchisement in postcolonial India.

In much of urban India, there are two systems of education-English medium (the upper tier of English-medium schools in cities) and vernacular medium (often state run). At the individual level, English-medium education has been a ticket to vertical mobility in Indian society.

At the societal level, English-medium education has played a critical role in producing what Kothari calls a modernized technomanagerial elite that continues to have disproportionate influence in shaping the discursive terrain of development and the policies that affect the social fabric. Less visibly, English-medium education widens fractures in society by creating and reinforcing a social, cultural, economic and discursive divide between the English educated and the majority. This is not tosay that the vernacular medium is egalitarian or free of political agenda.

State intervention in education is closely associated with, if not anchored on, the distinction between producing leaders who will contribute to nation building and engaging the masses in rural reconstruction. While education continued to favor the urban rich, some public pronouncements were made for the rural masses.

Anil Sadgopal argues that the Kothari Education Commission (1964-1966) advocated the common school system along with the transformation of schools-government, aided, or private-into neighborhood schools, which will be open to all children residing in a given area, irrespective of their socioeconomic background. The common school was a policy imperative in the first National Policy on Education 1968 (NPE 1968).

Parliament twice made a commitment to the goal of building a common school system-first in the 1986 policy and again in the revised version in 1992 (NPE 1992). This commitment was violated twice by the 1986 policy itself-first, through its proposal to set up the Navodaya Vidyalaya (New Enlightenment Schools) as a layer above the government school system for the rural elite; and second, through the establishment of another layer of nonformal centers below the government school system for child laborers.

A careful look at the education reveals two dominant trends from 1998 onward. First is the ongoing process of communalization of education in the name of "Indianizing" or nationalizing education. "Casteization" of education is also on the agenda under the slogan of spiritualization. Although noble ideals are projected, the ultimate aim is to thrust upon the citizens the agenda of Hindutva force, or the right-wing Hindu nationalist force.Another trend is the "marketization" of education.

Neoliberal agents, or market forces, have been trying to highjack education for their own vested interest. The Ambani-Biral Report on Education,submitted to the trade sector of the Prime Minister's office, is a clear indication of the growing nexus between the ruling establishment and the business class. Among socially conscious citizens, the cause for concern is not just the attempt to tinker with the educational system, but the objective of the forces behind it.

The Sangh parivar, or the right-wing Hindutva force, is hell-bent on introducing change in the educational system with the stated objective of "Indianization, nationalization, and spiritualization." The right wing will attempt to manipulate and alter the basic structures of society and polity to serve its objective. The corporate sector wants a steady market and is hobnobbing with the ruling class to fundamentally change education. In the long run, these changes will uphold and maintain the hegemony of the dominant caste, the upper class, and retain a skewed, hierarchical, and patriarchal social order. This process seems to be gaining upper hand, but citizens and civil society are trying to work for a democratic, plural, egalitarian, and just social order.

In 2001 another trend was observed in education. On 28 November, Parliament passed the 93rd amendment, making education for the 6-14 year age group compulsory. This step has been widely welcomed, but the amendment has shortcomings that may work against those who have till now been excluded from schools. A large number of child laborers are denied not merely education but also their right to childhood.

The amendment makes education compulsory but not free, and imposes on parents a fundamental duty to send their children to school while not obliging states to invest in making education accessible to all. The minister for human resource development says the states will be encouraged to make such investment in the 5-year plans.

Allocation for education, especially at the primary level, is biased against the rural poor. Geetha Nambisan analyzes the financial alloca-tion for educational activities: "Financial allocations for important programs of elementary education funded by the central government are revealing. In 1992-1993 the budget estimates for Non-Formal Education (NFE) include-centers (US$9 million), NFE for girls (US$6 million), and grants to voluntary agencies to set up centers (US$4 million). This works out to around 32.3% of the total allocations for elementary education estimated for 1992-1993. Allocations for NFE are almost equal to that for Operation Black Board, which is meant 'to provide minimum essential facilities to all primary schools in the country.'

Much-publicized programs such as the Bihar Education Project, Lok Jumbis, and World Bank-assisted projects also have sizeable nonformal components and receive considerable external assistance."These facts again raise questions about the reality and the government's rhetoric on education. Vaidyanathan and Gopinathan discuss education policy pronouncements and implementation: Eradication of poverty and illiteracy figured prominently in the political rhetoric of the Indian nationalist movement even before independence. Achieving universal elementary education within 10 years was included as one of the Directive Principles of State Policy in the Constitution of Indian Republic. The rhetoric continues but the goal remains elusive even after 50 years of planning.

Governments, both at the center and in the states, irrespective of their ideology, have not pursued this objective seriously and with vigor. Resources allocated to education have been woefully inadequate and, with higher education absorbing a rising proportion of allocations, elementary education has remained on a semi-starvation diet. The idea of making elementary education legally compulsory for all children has not evoked much enthusiasm. Some states have enacted the necessary legislation but none has exerted itself to get the law enforced.

EDUCATION DISCUSSION GROUP

A group of educationists, academicians, activists, and concerned citizens met and discussed the issues that ail the education system, and formed the Education Discussion Group (EDG) in September 2001 to discuss, debate, and evolve strategies to address the current crisis in school education. EDG held its First National Consultation on Education in Delhi in December 2001. Participants from 10 states included teachers, social activists, educationists, and policymakers.

While the immediate focus of the consultation was on the communalization of education, the running theme was the need to evolve a broad perspective. The participants identified regional issues in education and decided to focus on them, while EDG agreed to be a national watchdog. To advance the discussion and evolve alternative long-term state-level and national strategies, the group decided to hold a more intensive consultation in April 2002.

Three broad themes were identified for the consultation:

— monitoring of textbooks to see how much they reinforce gender hierarchies, social inequalities, and communalism;

— ways and means of ensuring equal access to education; and

— issues related to pedagogy in curriculum formulation and teacher training.

The response was overwhelming. Three days of intense, heated discussions raised awareness of the educational crisis. Wide-ranging, stimulating presentations persuaded participants that this exercise would be a long-term process, not a sporadic event. They agreed that they should build networks of communication to exchange ideas, share experiences, develop short-term and long-term strategies for educational interventions, and engage in dialogue and debate.

The national consultation focused on the issues raised by the National Curriculum Framework (NCF), released by the National Council ofEducational Research and Training (NCERT) on 14 November 2000,as a "gift" to the children of India. The participants felt that on Independence Day the values enshrined in the Constitution should be reaffirmed so that future generations can realize the long-cherished dreams of true independence.

National Consultation

The national consultation began with a lecture by Krishna

Kumar of Delhi University, who focused on the implications of state education policies. He raised fundamental issues, emphasizing the need for continuous enquiry and evaluation of state policies, and for interventions. He pointed out that the government, instead of upholding constitutional provisions, was violating them in a variety of ways, most obviously in handling the carnage in Gujarat, and in the formulation of NCF.

First Session

NCF evoked widespread criticism, discussion, and debate among educationists, teachers, and parliamentarians. Instead of taking their concerns into account, NCERT went ahead and issued syllabi in line with NCF in January 2002. The Central Advisory Board of Education (CABE), which includes representatives of all states, was not consulted in formulating NCF. A few eminent concerned citizens appealed to the Supreme Court, through a public interest litigation, the first ever pertaining to curriculum. The petitioners argued that NCF violated constitutional provisions that guaranteed secularism and democracy, including equal opportunities.

Ironically, most teachers and principals were just concerned with immediate problems, including lack of textbooks. The participants also made reference to wider political scenario. In a sense, there was a parallel in the way the policies of economic liberalization were adopted in the 1990s-no consultation, discussion, or debate; suppression of dissent; and presentation of a fait accompli.

The government extended this process to education, which was not surprising as the Bharatiya Janata Partywas the only political party with a deep interest in education, with a network of 26,000 schools all over the country. Unfortunately, virtually all political parties, including Congress and the left, put low priority on education. The Ministry of Human Resources Development portfolio is not a prized ministry, unlike defense, external affairs, or finance.

Although the National Policy on Education (1986) was drafted under the Congress government, it showed no interest in implementing its own policy. Past appointments to educational bodies (NCERT, UGC, ICSSR, etc.) had been based on getting people who were willing to do the bidding of political bosses. Thus, the interest of the nation and citizens of the country was mortgaged for party interests.

In the 1950s and 1960s, the education policy was committed to generating a scientific spirit. In the 1970s, the vision was one of common schooling and education in the mother tongue. All these have been relegated to the background. As time went on, the educational system was brought under the purview of political vested interests.

Four major commissions have inquired into education since Independence. Of these, the Secondary Education Commission, (1953) and the Prof. Yashpal Commission (1990-1992) raised issues on curriculum and pedagogy. They suggested that curriculum must be grounded in the world of the student, to lend the lessons a vibrant reality, since it is in the classroom that children imbibe morals, values, and skills.

Examinations are regarded as the end of all education. Worse, teachers' unions are disunited. The program on universalizing primary education has produced the so-called parateacher, who is paid a pittance. Para-teachers, hundred thousand today, are not well equipped to educate. Teachers have virtually no role in writing textbooks and are, at best, given token representation in the process, which is usually undertaken by experts who have no experience in classroom realities. Often, textbooks are simply stuffed with facts. As the writer R.K. Narayanan said,

> education has become the national sport of teaching children facts they cannot digest. Most poor children are thus severely disadvantaged while middle-class children have access to information. For poor children, going to school becomes a demeaning experience, and fear of failure often forces them out of the system.

The quality of textbooks is shocking. While government reports are printed on art paper, schoolbooks are printed on newsprint, and not for lack of resources. Even states such as Karnataka, which try to project themselves as "modern," use poor-quality books. NCF emphasizes values education. The values are supposed to be derived from religious traditions, not from the Constitution.

Values education thus undermines the constitutional values of secularism and democracy. Historical records bear testimony to this fact. In 1939, when Gandhiji was questioned in Wardha as to why his Nayi Taleem did not mention values education, he pointed out that values could not be taught, they could only be acquired by seeing how others practiced them. Thus, values education attempts to impose one religion in a country historically known for its pluralism. What the future holds for students, parents, educationists, and society is a big question.

The participants of the First National Consultation on Education have become painfully aware that educationists are contemplative rather than activist, regardless of the deep national crisis. Any attempt to rework the curriculum must address the problem of a nation in tatters, where the minorities and the marginalized face the gravest threat to their existence since Independence.

Issues in the Second Session

The second session was devoted to an analysis of textbooks. The participants raised issues of stereotypes, including stereotyping of gender roles, caste, and tribal or indigenous identities, communal identities, and treatment of class. Focus was on social science books and language books, including Hindi, Sanskrit, and Bengali. Although the discussion was meant to be on textbooks, a number of participants raised important issues of context, including the nature of educational institutions, leading to a rich discussion.

In language, the terms used for men are markers of respect, while those used for women (and lower castes) are less formal, suggesting a clear-cut hierarchy. Illustrations accompanying the text show women to be passive and men to be active. The Sanskrit books used in the Delhi region reinforce gender roles and stereotypes by praising girls who cook, clean, etc., suggesting that they will be rewarded. This type of formulating textbooks reinforces gender bias.

Seema Ghosh pointed out that the Bengali books used in Assam lay down the norms for girls. They "grow up" when they are 4 or 5, must stop playing when they are 8 or 9, and must obey rules when they are 10 or 11. Boys of the same age are at liberty to play football. Females are shown to be nervous, while males are shown to be in control of any situation. The role models for women are Sati, Savitri, Gargi, and Mother Teresa.

A teacher from Madhya Pradesh pointed out that Sanskrit books present Sita as a role model for girls, with special emphasis on her loyalty to Ram until the very end, when she disappearsinto the bosom of the earth. Through such models, the qualities of subservience, selfeffacement, and sacrifice are inculcated among girls. In Hindi books from Uttar Pradesh, women figure in approximately 25% of the lessons. In more than half of these, women are shown as mothers of "great men." Even when "great women" such as the Rani of Jhansi are mentioned, they are shown as having greatness thrust on them, unlike the men who are shown to be born great. Even when women are nonconformists, they are depicted as conforming to norms.

The Constitution envisages a secular state, but the participants raised questions on the secular credibility of the textbooks. Many schools prescribed a weekly for supplementary reading that serialized the story of Mughal rulers, who were represented in a very poor light. Even in textbooks, most characters are given Hindu names. Use of Christian or Islamic names is rare. The only festivals discussed are Hindu.

While books in the formal school system in West Bengal tend to be secular, the existence of Vidya Bharati schools in a number of districts points to ominous trends, which the state government has not addressed. Abdur Rauf focused on the question of madrasas, or Muslim educational centers, in West Bengal, of which there are three kinds: those that follow state curriculum, await recognition, and khariji madrasas, which impart religious instruction. The last type is often stereotyped as breeding ground for terrorism.

However, it was pointed out that the fundamentalists or communalists usually come from "modern" backgrounds, and that the students of khariji madrasas may be backward but they are not fundamentalist. Mr. Rauf also pointed out that secondary school textbooks in West Bengal contained stereotypical notions about Islam and jihad, although they were written by "progressive" leftist scholars. He suggested that this was because most of these scholars were upper-caste Hindus, biased against Muslims, whom they regard as low-caste converts.

Poorva Bhardwaj drew attention to the implicit communalism in Sanskrit books used in Delhi. Sanskrit is referred to as dev bhasha, the language of the gods. Besides, metaphors and analogies are drawn from Hindu mythology, and dates that are identified as important are drawn exclusively from the Hindu calendar of festivals. This type of exclusivism deeply affects the mental make of the children.

Dipta Bhog and Archana Dwivedi focused on Hindi books in Uttar Pradesh, pointing out how they were concerned with "history," especially constructing a glorious Hindu past, and emphasized patriotism. Even the two Muslim characters represented in more than 90 lessons were shown as patriotic in spite of their religion. Muslim rulers, such as Akbar, are represented as outsiders, and the battles with them as "national struggles." This type of distortion of history contributes to the spreading communal crisis.

Other religious traditions are appropriated and brought under one religion. For example, Buddhism and Sikhism are portrayed as mere offshoots of Hinduism. Damayanti Modi pointed out an attempt to create a glorious Hindu past in social science books in Gujarati. Thus, the Arthasastra is projected as a text that is unique in the entire world, and Rana Pratap is now projected not simply as a Rajput but as a Hindupati (Lord of the Hindus).

The iron grip of the caste system is unaltered. The attitude of the dominant castes toward the lower castes, as spelled out in textbooks, reinforces the exploitative nature of the system. Rama Panchali pointed out that in MadhyaPradesh Sanskrit books predominantly focused on Brahmins and their rituals, and represented the so-called lower castes as unworthy of a dignified existence. Participants pointed out that most book characters continue to be upper caste Hindus.

In West Bengal, however, lowercaste characters are now represented in social science and mathematics books. Dipta Bhog and Archana Dwivedi pointed out that the Hindi books used in Uttar Pradesh contained a biography of Dr. Ambedkar,but even this did not address the issue of caste discrimination. The problems he faced were projected as arising out of backwardness or orthodoxy.

Tribal peoples are also shown as backward, ignorant, and even cannibals. The bias against the tribal population in textbooks reflects the same bias by the political establishment. The government has refused to acknowledge that the tribal population is similar to indigenous peoples in other parts of the globe, thus thwarting attempts by indigenous peoples to build international solidarity.

There are clear indications of communal bias in many books, which is against the Constitution.

— .Representation of marginalized sections of society, whether women, minorities, dalits, or tribal people, is grossly inadequate. If ever, they are represented derogatively, or as a segment of the population that needs to be brought into the mainstream.

— Generally, the distinction between myth and reality is blurred, preventing a critical examination of the past. Warfare and militarism are glorified, contributing to acceleration of social conflict.

— While lip service continues to be paid to democracy, secularism, and equity, the images in textbooks do little to nurture these ideals among children, and even produce the opposite results.

Issues of Pedagogy

The government of Maharashtra had introduced a 30- minute session in schools on values education, which had become a mere formality. Guruji Pratishthan envisions inculcating values such as peace and gender equity among students. The participants were open to explore the place and role of values education in schools, but there were a lot of questions.

For one, promoting values education had become a new mantra, a new slogan to enforce ones views. For another, there is a need to know what values are to be inculcated, and for whom? Are textbooks devoid of values? Can values be imparted through textbooks? Are values caste or class neutral? Another question raised was, Is our schooling system conducive to democracy?

Pradip Borthakur argued that the schooling system is inherently authoritarian. Knowledge is presented by teachers, with little scope for dialogue or reasoning. Democracy rests on dialogue, and schools do not equip children to develop skills and abilities to engage in dialogue and evolve a consensus. Since "managing" or "administering" the school is the overarching concern, discipline leads to authoritarianism.

Lachman Khubchandani emphasized that the medium of instruction, content, and accessibility were related issues and could not be examined in isolation. Language is vital in communication, and it is important to emphasize plurality and diversity. Language policy since Independence has been elite-centered.

Abhijit Pathak made a passionate plea to envision learning as a dynamic, aesthetic process by transforming the learning process. At least three critical problems exist:

— Education has reproduced and reinforced social inequality instead of reducing or contesting it.

— What is regarded as worth knowing is closely related to the political economy. Commerce is thus preferred over science.

— The process of learning, or the pedagogy, is oppressive, regimented, and deeply conservative.

For instance, Gandhi's vision of decolonization was linked to an alternative vision of education. Tagore's vision of education was related to a cosmopolitan ideal that went beyond narcissistic nationalism. Freire envisaged dialogic education as a means to create an egalitarian society. He advocated daily, continuous innovation in the classroom. He suggested that teachers move beyond the text to enable the child to question its sanctity. Teachers should be empowered to develop a symbiotic, dialogic relationship with students, instead of the mindless brutality of most classroom situations. Learning can be a joyful, aesthetic experience instead of a source of oppression.

Third Session: Exploring Alternatives

The National Consultation also explored alternative forms of learning, preparing, and presenting curriculum and syllabus, and of making education responsive to society and society accountable for the educational system. Some of the experiments that were examined as alternatives to the present educational system are as follow:

The Ekalavya Experience

The experiment began about 30 years ago, in the Hoshangabad Science Teaching Programme (HSTP). This was initiated by a group of scientists who approached the Madhya Pradesh government with a proposal to develop alternative materials for teaching science in government- run schools. This experiment contributed immensely to the creation of a space for nongovernment initiatives. However, it has never been replicated. Even the space for this kind of initiative has been shrinking.

The Eklavya effort was an innovative experiment to bring about an interaction between the state, curriculum designers, and teachers. The objective of HSTP was to stimulate children's curiosity instead of simply providing information, to relate science to daily life rather than let it remain an abstraction. The project consisted of a package, including textbook design, teacher training, and continuous academic support. It meant discussing issues that teachers and children found problematic, irrelevant, or boring.

Kerala Shastra Sahitya Parishad (KSSP)

KSSP started in 1962 with the objective of establishing an egalitarian society through educational interventions, including an emphasis on the scientific approach and the development of a rational attitude toward social norms. People were organized and mobilized through cultural programs through which common people were imparted scientific temper. The emphasis has always been on using the mother tongue. KSSP has 40,000 members, and 2,000 units throughout Kerala.

KSSP envisaged education as means to lift the poor out of the trap of exploitation, and recognized the value of political links with the left parties. KSSP took part in the Total Literacy Campaign, and worked on health, women's development, and environmental issues. KSSP led the campaign to declare the

Silent Valley a protected area and was involved in micro-level planning exercises in development work.

KSSP focused on developing communication materials such as literacy magazines, etc. It published books, primarily based on KSSP's research and development activities, worth $257,000. KSSP has three education research units and environment centers. It has a huge mass base, from where it draws its strength and resources to run science education programs. KSSP does not accept foreign funds.

KSSP worked intensively to develop childcentered and child-friendly curriculums in cooperation with the District Primary Education Programme (DPEP) to inform it of intervention processes and, thus, make it more childcentered. Thus, KSSP and the program were involved in preparing school curriculums, which were ready for classes 1-7 and under process for class 8, when the government suddenly changed. It withdrew the KSSP curriculums and brought back the old syllabi. Only a few schools now use the KSSP curriculums.

KSSP sees a major impact of globalization on education. An example was the "black order" announced by the Kerala government withdrawing support for 2,644 government schools for being uneconomical, as they had less than 100 students. These schools are now being handed over to private institutions, which charge high fees. KSSP agitated against this order and is still struggling to force the government to recall it. The government, however, has turned a blind eye to these concerns and isadopting policies that prioritize the upper class and castes.

The Lokshala Experience

Lokshala, or people's center, is an alternative to patshala, or center of learning. The presentations about Lokshala involved two levels: broad policy issues and specific experiences. In 1991 the Bharatiya Gyan Vigyan Jatha (The National Knowledge and Science March) or BGVJ saw the coming together of groups working on education, environment, health, and technology under the leadership of Prof. Yashpal, with Prof. Anil Sadgopal as convener. This was closely connected with the All India People's Science Jatha, which involved 50,000 villages and several towns.

As a follow up, the National Brainstorming Conference, with over a thousand delegates, was organized in May 1994. This led to the initiation of the Lokshala process in 1995, with focus on developing an alternative vision of school education based on indigenous experiences. BGVJ organized a meeting of 6,000 persons, including educationists, academics and field activists. It adopted the perspective of working toward a synthesis between academics and activists, and working toward institutional transformation as part of a wider social change.

Several community development blocks were adopted as field laboratories. These included Jahanabad in Bihar, Dhubri in Assam, and blocks in Meghalaya, Nagaland, Mahrashtra, Orissa, Manipur, and Jehangirpuri (Delhi). Each field laboratory was unique and developed its own pace and style of functioning. People's perceptions were taken into consideration in identifying priorities, and this provided the basis for intervention. The emphasis was on decentralization and on learning from each other's experience.

Policy analysis is a complicated, constant process of inquiry and learning, involving, among other things, accurate translations of documents. It indicates, for instance, that emphasis on nonformal education actually aids and abets child labor. Policy analysis also shows that the government tends to use education and literacy as synonymous terms, which must be questioned.

This was apparent in the way in which the commitment to free and compulsory education for all children up to age 14, guaranteed in Article 45 of the Constitution, had been diluted. Although India accepted the Jomtien Declaration on Elementary Education as a right, this is now being diluted and projected as a commitment to nonformal education.

Perhaps more important were the long-term changes in attitudes and ideas that had been generated by these activities. Education is now recognized as a political issue in the area and has generated a lot of debate within the community. People now understand the difference between education and mere literacy, and can raise these issues with their political representatives, like Members of Parliament, and Members of Legislative Assembly. Social activists have developed a deeper understanding of the political context and have created a space for critical analysis of the existing situation. This process has opened up avenues to search for alternative educational strategies in a region, which is undergoing violent eruption.

IMPACT OF DPEP

The government introduced the District Primary Education Programme (DPEP) in early 1990 with a loan of US$434 million, of which 24% was spent on infrastructure alone. Another sizeable amount of money was allotted for teacher training, but no money was allocated for the appointment of teachers. As a result, there has been a dependence on untrained, poorly paid para-teachers, threatening the school structure. This was the national scenario.

Meanwhile, the Bihar Education Project and the DPEP in Bihar were supposed to provide alternative systems of comparable standards to the disadvantaged groups.It is worth noting that the loan under DPEP was only 4.5% of the total central government budget on education, yet this tiny contribution of foreign funds has harmed school education. The way DPEP was introduced was also significant. The three apex bodies supposed to discuss and determine education policies-CABE, Parliament, and NCERT-were not consulted. This major intervention in education was simply introduced as a project.

Even the District Institute for Educational Training and the State Council of Educational Research and Training were kept out of the scheme. Instead, the project was handed over to

Educational Consultants India Limited for management. Some academics, including university teachers, were co-opted into the project for teacher training and material development, leading to a further divide between those who participated and those who did not. In spite of all the hype, DPEP did not help increase the enrolment of children.

Constitutional Amendment

The introduction of the 93rd Amendment also came under scrutiny. The participants recalled that in 1993 the Unnikrishnan judgment (Supreme Court) declared education to be a fundamental right. However, the government decided to circumvent this through the 93rd Amendment, which ostensibly guaranteed the right to education but reduced the accountability of government to children. The government also ignored the requirements of children 0-6 years, who are within the purview of Article 45 of the Constitution. As in other sectors, the government abdicates its responsibility in education for this category of children.

Privatization

More and more government schools are being handed over systematically to private institutions. The government, as it does with "sick units" of the industry, declares government schools to be economically unviable and conveniently hands them over to private companies. Recently, 12 schools were shut down in Indore, Madhya Pradesh, and the children transferred to other schools. The land where the schools were was transferred to a commercial complex.

In Andhra Pradesh, schools are being closed down and the emphasis is shifting to nonformal education. In Delhi, elite private schools have been volunteering to run government schools, which hold classes for only 3 hours in the afternoon. Attempts are being made to shift the students from formal school to the open school stream.

INDEX